Psychological Support for Workers on the Move

This book examines the psychological pressures faced by workers who migrate for short periods, exploring what it means to work in high-stress environments, often on time-limited contracts and with low levels of support; and how best to protect this kind of key worker.

The text addresses three central questions. First, how we can think about the experiences of workers on the move? Second, what forms of support given by who, and when, provide the best staff care? Finally, how can appropriate and timely staff support by organisations influence the lives of workers on the move? The authors, all psychological therapists and many former international workers, offer recommendations for workers in humanitarian aid, the mission sector, international contracting and seafaring, among others, taking into account the changing world of work, and the impact on this of the Covid-19 pandemic.

Psychological Support for Workers on the Move provides essential guidance to organisations posting personnel internationally, to psychological and well-being therapists working with them, and to individual workers themselves.

Kate S. Thompson, PhD, is a counselling psychologist with long experience supporting highly mobile clients including refugees in the UK, humanitarian staff and serving military personnel/veterans, humanitarian staff and serving military personnel/veterans. Her key interests are in the impact of transition on identity, the social meaning of war and the use of community as a tool for healing.

"A crucial topic, a crucial book. Understanding and caring for the neglected often misunderstood but growing number of those travelling to improve our world. And critically for the organisations to whom they belong. This book is profound, readable and practical. We come to grips with the real issues through explanation, story and example. We learn about essential ways to bring focus on many diverse groups of people. A book not just for the bookshelf, but to read, consult and have with you in the office, clinic or place of work."

—**Dr Ted Lankester**, *Travel Health Specialist,*
Co-Founder of InterHealth and Thrive-Worldwide

"If you are a highly mobile, international worker, you will probably see your experiences and struggles reflected in this engaging, informative book. Whether you are an international aid worker, volunteer, contractor or seafarer, reading this book will help you realise you are not alone and that help is available. Written by mental health practitioners with a clear grasp of the common challenges faced by workers on the move—such as moral injury, the role of religious and spiritual faith, and relationships and family life—this book is full of insights, case studies and practical recommendations. An essential guide on mental health support for organisations, staff and service providers alike."

—**Gemma Houdney**, *Author of 'The Vulnerable Humanitarian:*
Ending Burnout Culture in the Aid Sector'

Psychological Support for Workers on the Move

Improving Global Staff Care

Edited by Kate S. Thompson

Routledge
Taylor & Francis Group

LONDON AND NEW YORK

Designed cover image: Photographs (clockwise from left) - Alan Stratford and Associates Ltd.;
Fleet Management Limited; Hendrik Oosterhuis; Getty Image

First published 2023
by Routledge
4 Park Square, Milton Park, Abingdon, Oxon OX14 4RN

and by Routledge
605 Third Avenue, New York, NY 10158

Routledge is an imprint of the Taylor & Francis Group, an informa business

British Library Cataloguing-in-Publication Data
A catalogue record for this book is available from the British Library

ISBN: 9781032200446 (hbk)
ISBN: 9781032200439 (pbk)
ISBN: 9781003261971 (ebk)

DOI: 10.4324/9781003261971

Typeset in Times New Roman
by Newgen Publishing UK

This book is dedicated to the international workers who, as clients, colleagues and friends have shared their stories of hurt and healing with us.

Contents

Contributors

Pennie Blackburn (MA Hons, D Clin Psych) is a consultant clinical psychologist, and proud daughter of a master-mariner. After specialising in trauma, torture and psychosocial support, Pennie was serendipitously invited to speak at a maritime industry conference in 2016. Pennie is the author of *Mentally Healthy Ships* and the International Seafarers Welfare and Assistance Network's series of *Good Mental Health Guides for Seafarers*.

Leslie Brownbridge (MA Couns Psychology FHEA) is a lecturer who works with humanitarian organisations including the Helen Bamber Foundation, Médecins du Monde, Freedom from Torture, Students for Global Health Migration (UCL), and the Centre for Business, Society and Global Challenges. Her key interests are in psychology and humanitarian and conflict response.

Graham Fawcett (Dip Clin Psy, AFBPsS) is a consultant clinical psychologist at Thrive Worldwide with over 20 years' experience in the international aid sector with Medair, Tear Fund, World Vision and YWAM, and 20 years' experience in the UK National Health Service (NHS). His particular focus is staff well-being in high-stress environments.

David Hawker (PhD, D Clin Psy) is a clinical psychologist who has worked in child and adolescent mental health services. He is based in England, but offers remote support to humanitarian/mission workers around the world and their families. He has worked in over ten countries.

Debbie Hawker (PhD, D Clin Psy) is a clinical psychologist. She is based in England, but offers remote support to humanitarian/mission workers around the world. She has worked in over 30 countries, is involved with research and has written nine books.

Beth Hill (DClin Psy, PG Dip.) is a clinical psychologist who has lived and served internationally before and after training. She has been working in Community Child and Adolescent Mental Health Services in City and

Hackney (UK) since 2006. Alongside this post, Beth worked at InterHealth Worldwide from 2011 to 2019.

Lynn Keane (MA, AdvDip) is a counsellor, psychotherapist and trainer based in London. She has a particular focus on critical incident response work with survivors of sexual trauma in the aid and development sectors.

Ben Porter (MA) is a staff care consultant and psychotherapist with Thrive Worldwide. Ben's work and writing are influenced by a decade of psychosocial programming in East Africa where he founded The Recreation Project, while also researching and supporting staff care in humanitarian organisations around the world.

Felicity Runchman (MBACP (Accred), MA Counselling & Psychotherapy) is an accredited psychotherapist specialising in working with international staff, particularly from the humanitarian sector. With a professional interest in stress, burnout and trauma in individuals in high-risk contexts/ remote settings, she is committed to providing a range of remote therapy options to clients, especially through text-based work.

Mark Snelling (MA Oxon, PGDip, MSc) is a psychotherapist in private practice with 15 years' experience supporting international frontline workers, including humanitarians, missionaries, journalists, diplomats and military personnel. Prior to training as a therapist, he worked as an International Red Cross delegate in Africa, South Asia and the Asia-Pacific Region.

Kate S. Thompson (PhD, QCoP) is a counselling psychologist with long experience supporting highly mobile clients including refugees in the UK, humanitarian staff and serving military personnel/veterans. Her key interests are in the impact of transition on identity, the social meaning of war and the use of community as a tool for healing.

Foreword

I am delighted to have been asked to write the foreword to this important and timely book. It covers a range of issues in an accessible, thoughtful and open manner, describing the challenges and opportunities of this work as well as making recommendations for upholding and improving good practice. The editor of this book has done an excellent job in bringing the chapters together into a cohesive and comprehensive book. Each chapter touches upon an important issue or range of issues and the book will be useful to a range of audiences. These will include policymakers, humanitarian agencies, national and international organisations, humanitarian workers, maritime institutions, contractors and people considering undertaking international work. It will also be of interest to those working elsewhere within the mental health field, as some of the issues discussed also have relevance to working in other contexts and have the potential to enrich therapeutic practice in other settings.

The reader does not need a specialist background to appreciate the book. The inclusion of contractors, missionaries or faith-based workers and seafarers brings an additional richness to this volume. As well as discussing all aspects of global staff care, the book also considers the potential effects on families and partners who may accompany workers or who may remain in their home country and whose needs are often forgotten or minimised as they are not the employee or contractor. Several of the chapters make excellent and helpful recommendations for practices at the individual and organisational levels and for therapists working with humanitarian workers. All the chapters are written by people with considerable experience in the humanitarian field and extensive backgrounds in psychology, psychotherapy or counselling. The book provides a range of helpful examples drawn from the authors' own experiences of working with international organisations.

Issues relating to humanitarian work are frequently more complex than is assumed and can be misunderstood or oversimplified. This book grapples with many of these complex dilemmas and the psychological impact of these in relation to staff care. Humanitarian interventions can make an enormous difference to people's situations and can provide much-needed resources and support during or after emergencies or in ongoing crises. They can provide much-needed materials, as well as expertise to communities, and may help local systems become re-established or developed. People undertake such work for a range of reasons including a desire to help, to share knowledge and because this work aligns with their personal value systems or faith. Motivations may also include the desire to travel, gain new experiences and learn about diverse countries and cultures.

That said, an individual's desire to help others and humanitarian organisational missions need always to account for issues of power, privilege and coloniality. The roles of giver and recipient contain a set of ascribed roles and expectations, which are often not adequately considered and deconstructed. Systemic or structural inequalities are ever present and often determine the way in which international work is framed and undertaken. There can be issues of the *white saviour complex* and these need active and constant attention at the individual and organisational level. Negotiating across culture and language is a complex arena for psychological therapists (Fernando, 2017; Tribe, 2014) and humanitarian workers as well as for those receiving assistance, and this needs to be foregrounded in training and professional development offered by humanitarian organisations, while also being actively and continuously considered by individual humanitarian workers. The best interventions are often those that are co-produced or agreed rather than imposed by an organisation or individual.

Geopolitics forms the backdrop to all international work, and it has been argued that mental health should become part of foreign policy (Persaud & Bhugra, 2022). We know that violence, poverty, war and living with threat are not conducive to good mental health, although they are often ignored as key negative contributory factors when considering difficulties with mental health and well-being. This interface is discussed further in the emerging discipline of geopsychiatry. Geopsychiatry examines the relationship between geography, geopolitics and psychiatry. In the case of humanitarian work, it is often suggested that this work should be neutral and unaffected by politics, but this is naive, as geopolitical factors are woven into its very essence, at its most basic level, and are ever present, even if hidden and unarticulated. Issues of racism, colonialism, power structures and the historical relationship between countries and people influence, albeit in covert ways, how international work takes place, including in some cases how it is financed.

Many organisations and agencies have moved a long way forward in considering these issues, and the underlying assumptions, power structures and historical factors involved. In the past, people from host countries were often employed as national staff on different (lower) wage bands with reduced benefits and little chance of career progression in comparison to international staff. This is now being reconsidered and reconfigured in many organisations with expansions to ensure that salary bandings are more equitable, that security arrangements are extended to cover national staff and that pathways from national to international staff member exist.

There can also be discrepancies between what the worker envisaged they would be doing and the reality on the ground, which can be chaotic, dangerous and contain personal and organisational dynamics which are challenging. In addition, workers may observe or experience events or incidents which are brutal, traumatic or not in line with their personal belief systems or codes of practice. Dissonance between what workers hoped to be able to achieve and what is possible given constraints from a variety of sources or just lack of personal power may affect workers' well-being and sense of purpose. The issue of moral injury is discussed well in this book, and a range of examples can be located throughout the chapters.

In summary, this rich and informative book discusses a range of issues relating to workers on the move and details the importance of a considered and well-resourced global staff care system if organisations are to offer the best environment and support to meet the needs of staff working in international settings. Numerous recommendations for therapists working with these workers are also made. Future work, building on this area, might wish to consider further issues of colonialism and power to ensure these are given the attention they merit. This book has the potential to make a real difference to policy, practice and the thinking around these issues. It makes a really helpful contribution to our knowledge within a fast-developing and important area. I highly recommend it.

Rachel Tribe, *University of East London and Queen Mary University of London*

Fernando, S. (2017). *Institutional racism in psychiatry and clinical psychology. Race matters in mental health.* New York and Basingstoke: Palgrave Macmillan.

Persaud, A., & Bhugra, D. (2022). Geopsychiatry – *"putting mental health into foreign policy"*. *International Review of Psychiatry, 34*(1), 3–5. https://doi.org/10.1080/09540261.2022.2032615

Tribe, R. (2014). Culture, politics and global mental health: Deconstructing the global mental health movement: Does one size fits all? *Disability and the Global South, 1*(2), 251–265.

Acknowledgements

Photographs for the front cover used with kind permission of Alan Stratford and Associates Ltd., Fleet Management Limited, and Hendrik Oosterhuis.

This book would not have been possible without the support and input of a number of key people. I would like to thank particularly Anna Motz, Dr Tirril Harris, Professor Rachel Tribe, Gemma Houdney, Dr Ted Lankaster, Sarah Davidson, and all those who have offered support, made suggestions, and been open to discuss our ideas along the way. Thanks also to the Routledge Editorial team whose help and direction have been invaluable.

Introduction

Kate S. Thompson

When the Covid-19 pandemic hit, I was in Sudan. We had been watching things develop, and we were trying to work out what it would mean for us, assuming that we could take some steps and keep on working. What happened was that we had 24 hours to decide whether we were going to stay or go home. I was so torn. I thought our work was so urgent that I should stay. I was also scared myself, what about me getting sick far from home and when the organisation I work for could not guarantee they could get me out or get me treatment. In the end I went back to my country, but I had nowhere to live as I had given up my place when I went abroad, and I was self- isolating in a hotel, trying to carry on working with my team, but the time zones were completely awry. I am so unsure if I made the right decision to come out, as some of my colleagues are still there working. I feel like a coward, and I am not sure whether I will be able to go back at all when things settle, but if I stay here, what am I going to do?

(An international staff member, April 2020)

Workers are on the move as never before. Migration overall is increasing: Since 1970, the number of people living outside their country of origin has tripled and there are now estimated to be 272 million international migrants, 3.5% of the world's population (Edmond, 2020). Although people move for reasons other than work, particularly to flee violence, conflict or climate pressures, there is now a global churn moving workers, both skilled and unskilled, between different locations. Some move permanently, but there is also an increase in those embracing a more nomadic lifestyle, moving from one work location to another. This book is about these workers and their "high-transition" lifestyles, about staff *on the move*.

In the past year, workers away from home were often caught as the Covid-19 pandemic swept around the world, severely restricting movement and creating huge new anxieties about personal safety, impossible choices and the well-being of families living far away. Some humanitarians and international workers stayed for long periods in locations in which staff would usually rotate or have set times for leave or cycles of rest and recuperation (known

DOI: 10.4324/9781003261971-1

as R & R). Some seafarers were caught at sea, unable to dock in port, and with no clear time frames to disembark and limited access to communications with families. For those working in emergency settings, the problems of negotiating lockdowns in urgent contexts exacerbated pressures, highlighting the particular strains of working internationally at a time of pandemic.

It will take time to evaluate the impact of Covid-19 on international staff, but in this book we will be looking at the psychological pressures faced by workers who migrate for short periods, offering speculations about the impact of the pandemic, and about what it means to work in high-stress environments, often on time-limited contracts, with low levels of support, as well as considering how best to protect this kind of key worker.

What is known from research is that moving for work can be stressful (Mckay, 2007). Research into expatriate workers (defined as: Anyone outside their country of birth for a temporary period of work) has largely focused on exploring the stressors and mitigating factors that prevent the recruitment and retention of staff in international postings (Bonache, Brewster, & Froese, 2020). In the case of humanitarians, international assignment has been linked to problems with mental health, as well as lower levels of life satisfaction and increased misuse of alcohol and drugs (Lopez Cardozo et al., 2012; De Jong, Martinmäki, Te Brake, Haagen, & Kleber, 2020; Connorton, Perry, Hemenway & Miller, 2012). Even business travellers, moving for very short periods, show an uptick in physical and mental health difficulties, linked particularly to the juggle of balancing work away and on return (Striker, Luippold, Nagy, Liese, Bigelow, & Mundt, 1999; Burkholder, Joines, Cunningham-Hill, & Xu, 2010).

Research into the experiences of other staff groups considered in the book is limited, but the experts writing in this volume will comment from practice-based evidence on the impact of working on the move for seafarers, international consultants, mission workers and grassroots activists. There are challenges in each setting and the pressures of the pandemic will have crisscrossed other demands: having to work in high-threat or conflict environments, teams under stress, the need for frequent or rapid transitions, insecure employment conditions.

This is, overall, a book of stories. It tells of what happens when individuals move pursuing diverse goals, dreams and adventures, and by what means they thrive or suffer in doing this. For aid workers, activists or mission staff, whose movement is often impelled by questions of principle, faith or a desire to help, there can be a mismatch when the messy reality of conflict or disaster situations, exhausted teams and political paralysis undermines the very moral centre of the person concerned. For contractors or seafarers whose choices are in part about capturing opportunities, the mismatch may be between what has been promised by employers, anticipated by employees and what they find in the international workplace. In all cases, the choice to leave also has costs and these can be felt in the families left behind, the relationships that fall fallow and a loss of the ongoing sense of what it means to be "at home" in any one place.

This is the backdrop for many of the workers considered in this book: The balance between the opportunities for psychological growth that moving for work can offer against the challenges to identity, values, relationships and well-being that a life in transition can bring. Layered on top of this may be the impact of traumatic experiences when staff face kidnap, hostage taking, piracy, threats or acts of violence; witness the suffering or death of others; and find themselves powerless to intervene. These events are another part of the story for workers on the move, and important to consider, but should not be the sole focus of enquiry when asking about well-being for these employees.

Who Moves Country to Work and Why

There is a question about who moves location to work and what might be the motivations behind this. Most migrant workers move from less wealthy countries to those with higher wealth, or to sectors of employment that offer additional opportunities. More than 40% of those working away from home countries are said to have been born in Asia (Edmond, 2020). The total number of expatriates is estimated at around 66.2 million worldwide and is increasing (Finaccord, 2019, as cited in Bonache et al., 2020).

The drivers that can motivate international migration for work do not operate without restriction. Immigration regulations in many wealthier nations make it difficult for workers to move freely, and those from less wealthy countries may find they are obliged to relocate permanently by systems of visa control or guest working that do not allow for moving between locations (Harris, 1995). For this reason, *expatriate* workers have traditionally been considered separately from migrant workers, no matter how similar the circumstances of each group's time spent working in another country. This emphasis of difference creates a literature in which it is hard to find commonalities, and its potentially discriminatory assumptions could benefit from challenge, given that migrant workers might well choose to move less permanently if their passports allowed (Al Ariss, 2012).

In this book, we consider the experience of workers who can move freely[1] and who have often chosen a transitory lifestyle outside their country of origin, moving frequently, completing short contracts and living in different settings, without a commitment to one employing organisation. In the past, most research focused on nationals of wealthier countries, employed by organisations based in the global north and west. Latterly, however, the world of international working has transformed and there is a sense in which a spell of international work is seen as an essential addition to a well-rounded CV for many in low- or middle-income countries (Bonache et al., 2020). In the humanitarian sector, progression from national staff member to international or expatriate staff member with the same or another organisation has become an accessible route to career advancement, meaning that those offering services in one conflict setting may have direct experience of providing humanitarian support or as beneficiaries of aid in their home country. This is undoubtedly a helpful change in this sector given its history of sometimes divisive and disempowering employment practice (Houldey, 2021).

The question of *why* people move to work often leads us to the most interesting areas of all. Motivations for pursuing international roles, particularly for those who make a free choice in this (rather than being compelled by political, economic or social circumstances), show great variability. In the HSBC Expat Explorer Survey (2017), financial gains were listed as the number one motivating factor for taking an international post. This included gains from both increased income – up by an average of 25% for these expatriates – and financial uplift (an increase in disposable income and thus in the ability to build savings). Despite this being the most commonly named motivating factor, however, respondents also listed a range of other drivers including the chance to gain additional work experience, new areas of professional development and the opportunity to alter the balance of work and home life.[2]

In the case of humanitarians, motivations given for choosing to work in the sector often begin with values-based statements about wanting to help drive changes in the world and improve the situations of those suffering poverty or those without resources like healthcare, sanitation or education. These are key drivers for working in the sector, but again it is the subheadings that can offer further important insight into the choices that workers make. Often, one will be told of a desire to be part of something bigger, or perhaps part of world events. As Heidi Postlewait puts it: "I've discovered what had been missing in my life and can never go back. My role in the success of the election is small, but I have been part of something huge" (Cain, Postlewait, & Thomson 2006, p. 85). This statement also includes another important motivator for humanitarians and other overseas workers: A sense of lacking something in life as it is lived in the home country. In the case of Alexander (2013), the writer is clear that her move into humanitarian work is in part driven by a need to get away after the premature death of her mother. In other accounts, a sense of creeping alienation with life as lived in developed economies often precedes the decision to work internationally. Finally, as discussed in chapter 9, choosing an international posting as a contractor can be a way to sidestep the transitions that ending military service or retirement in a profession like policing or construction would otherwise provoke.

Before leaving the interesting topic of motivations to engage in international working, I wanted to offer two further ideas from Alexander's (2013) account. One is the way in which international work seems to offer a life unbounded by the usual trappings of one country. In the humanitarian context, Alexander notes:

> We all knew someone who had worked with somebody somewhere [...]
> The illusion of this industry was that we worked in the whole wide world –
> that the seven continents were just one big office to us. The truth was, our
> world was tiny, and it got smaller with every job we took. (Alexander,
> 2013, p. 146).

Despite her recognition that the idea of "working the world" was illusory,
it certainly can exercise a seductive power on many international staff, not
just humanitarian workers. A further idea links motivation to a perception
detected in others that international work is impressive or cool. Alexander
writes: "By virtue of our chosen profession, aid workers are automatically
ascribed certain qualities: bravery, righteousness, badass-ness. We never had
to actually prove that we possessed these attributes – the job title spoke for
itself" (Alexander, 2013, p. 255).

Here we seem close to the old adage of *moving abroad for a life of adventure*. However, despite its somewhat hackneyed flavour, it would be foolish
to underestimate this as a potential motivating factor for international
working amongst those with freedom to choose, particularly when other
avenues for challenge or gain are not available. Although other motivating
factors were offered when seafarers responded to a recent study (including
increased earning power, career development, accession to family wishes,
desire to follow a family tradition), the "*adventurous nature of working at sea*"
was also invoked as a main reason to follow the occupation (Baum-Talmor,
2021). Appearing "bad-ass" to others and feeling adventurous to yourself
may be important areas of motivation, worth exploring with staff working
internationally.

Expatriates and Beyond

In the business research studies of old, the focus of exploration was on a particular type of expatriate worker now called the *traditional expat*: A man in
his 40s or 50s working at senior executive level and assigned to work in a subsidiary of his company by his employing organisation (often after service at
the company headquarters). This man (and it was always a man) would also
be accompanied by a non-working wife and children. Studies showed how
frequently such expatriate assignments failed and thus generated questions
about how to support these workers to stay the full course of their contracts
and work as productively and effectively as needed. However, these rather old-
fashioned conceptions of the world of international work, even in decades
past, limit the applicability of this research.

Above all, what is missing is the worker as an active agent. Past studies
seem to view international employees as simple, generic resources to be sent
around the globe by their employer. Those employees not fitting the mould
of a traditional expat, tended not to be considered at all. This excluded

migrant workers, as mentioned, as well as the *non-traditional expat* (anyone else given a job internationally by their employer, including women, younger or older professionals, professionals from non-Western backgrounds or those working at lower professional levels, and dual-career families). It also excluded a more recently defined category of *self-initiated expat* (Doherty, Richardson, & Thorn, 2013), further discussed below, not to mention self-employed consultants, those on short-term contracts (like academics, actors or musicians), international business travellers and international commuters who live in one country and travel to a neighbouring country to work (Bonache et al., 2020). This earlier narrowness in the field of study is often linked in recent literature to changes in the world of work since the 1990s. While the world of work has certainly changed, it could be argued that the idea of the *traditional expat* has always somewhat blinded the focus of enquiry, leaving out many more international employees than it included.

The staff considered in this book do not fit the mould of the traditional expatriate, instead representing a diversity of gender, age, ethnicity, nationality and motivation for the work they undertake. In some cases, they may be *non-traditional* expatriates when they work for an organisation based in many countries and follow cycles of assignment directed by their employer. In the main, however, they represent groups of *self-initiated* expatriates whose choice to work internationally predates any particular contract or location of posting. Sometimes, the life chosen is one of constant movement (in the case of seafarers), or of shorter- or longer-term postings (for contractors, humanitarians), or even of voluntary roles undertaken for reasons of faith or conviction (mission sector workers, grassroots activists). It is, however, a life chosen rather than given by an employer, making clear that it should be viewed as self-initiated.[3]

Adams and van der Vijver (2015) note the differences in position and opportunity that expatriate workers of all kinds experience when compared with both host populations and other groups of international arrivals (for example, settled migrant workers, international students or asylum seekers and refugees). As a group, they are often remunerated well, but even if this is not the case (for example, in the case of mission sector workers), their position in the receiving country may still allow them areas of power that are not open to other groups, so that the push to become acculturated in the host country is less pressing. If acculturation can be seen as increasing the power of some marginalised groups arriving in a new national home, this is not necessary for a group already relatively powerful by virtue of professional status, pay grade or national–racial privilege.

This power can certainly have a darker side. In 2018, revelations about sexual exploitation in the aid sector began to emerge. Reports concerned multiple well-known non-governmental organisations including Oxfam, Save the Children and UNAIDS, whose staff had abused their positions to exploit the very populations they were employed to serve. Even more damning were the failings of these organisations to investigate allegations and take action to protect whistle-blowers and prosecute perpetrators. This is a stark reminder of the powerful position often available to expatriate staff members, and the way in which this can provide a vehicle for criminals and predators to find new avenues in their abuse of others (see chapter 10, this volume). Sadly, despite efforts to address these issues in the aid sector, experts still report that problems are "widespread", and in many cases have been exacerbated by Covid-19 (Worley, 2020).

Overall, it is important to remain mindful that, although an increasing number of humanitarians and mission sector workers are drawn from the global south, most organisations with international reach are firmly located in richer countries and their organisational cultures and recruitment practices reflect this. Even amongst seafarers, a truly international workforce, the views of some staff are likely to be privileged over and above others. Questions of power are important when workers move, and also when a workforce has staff drawn from a range of countries and backgrounds. Power needs to be considered as much on board a vessel between different ranks of seafarers as it does when humanitarians engage with vulnerable communities at risk.

What Do We Already Know about Staff on the Move?

As stated, much of the earlier research on *traditional expatriates* is of limited applicability in considering the experience of those who choose a life on the move. The main focus of this work was to support the recruitment and retention of staff within a global organisational context, and so studies looked at the impact of different stressors on the worker with a view to mitigating these. A key area was thus on the concept of *adjustment,* looking at the process experienced by workers in adapting to new environments (see Lessle, Halsberger, & Brewster, 2020 for a clear discussion of the limitations of this research and the need for greater conceptual clarity). Much research explored the different characteristics likely to enhance adjustment including *cross cultural competence, cross cultural adaptability, emotional intelligence* (Liao, Wu, Dao, & Ngoc Luu, 2021) *extraversion, openness to experience, self-efficacy, positive affectivity, cultural flexibility* and *communication willingness* (as mentioned in Chiang, Van Esch, & Birtch, 2020), as well as characteristics of the environment (for example, the *cultural distance* between home and assignment location (Shenkar, 2012), or of the interface between worker and role (for example, Chen, 2019 explores *job involvement and enthusiasm for job-based identity*). In many cases, the concepts discussed in this research appear poorly differentiated and overlapping, making it hard to understand and generalise from the findings as presented.

One finding that does appear useful in the literature relates to the ways in which organisations can effectively support their international staff. Kraimer and Wayne (2004) described three dimensions of organisational support considered most relevant to expatriate success: (1) *adjustment support* (helping expatriates and their families adapt in their international assignment), (2) *career support* (offering career-related guidance and clarity of contracting arrangements), and (3) *financial support* (providing monetary incentives and assistance). Chen (2019) notes the particular negative impact on workers of uncertainty related to poorly defined job specifications, unclear timelines for start and return, and unspecified rotations, again arguing the key role of career support. This study further reports the need for adjustment support to mitigate pressures related to unknown environments, language barriers and cultural differences. As the anxieties generated by uncertainty at work and adjustment to environment are likely to be held at a family level, this suggests the need to involve all members of international families in a truly supportive managerial approach. This would certainly tally with the view of Hill and Hawker (see chapter 5) and would support the stance of writers like Bushong (2013) that international families are profoundly affected by the organisational systems of the employers involved with them.

The duty of care of an employing organisation to its workers is a theme that will return in a number of the chapters in this book. Although currently each organisation determines its own policies to support international staff and intervene if there is a crisis or critical incident, there is an argument for sharing of best practice, particularly in a more fluid workplace where better support benefits may determine the choices of self-initiated expatriates to leave one employer for another.

Returning to the vexed concept of "adjustment" in international postings, recent writers are clear that this cannot be measured in a static way as an unchanging characteristic of a staff member, but rather suggest seeing it as part of a dynamic dance between person and context, changing over time and engaging the staff member and their family in a variety of different ways (Lessle et al., 2020). In this book we argue that a more helpful concept may be that of "fit" between a staff member, their occupational role and the organisation they work for, as well as the cultural setting of their post (as developed further in chapter 1). In teams with regularly changing personnel, like those in the humanitarian sector, or in international consultancy, "adjustment" may be inappropriate. In this case, staff may be better served by developing what is described as a *cosmopolitan* expatriate identity, developing skills to negotiate a wide range of cultural settings while also maintaining a well-rounded sense of self. In the words of Adams and van der Vijver (2015), "cosmopolitan expatriates have developed the necessary interpersonal prowess needed to manage interpersonal interactions at different levels, across different cultures and contexts". For the workers discussed in this book, the development of a cosmopolitan expatriate identity may be an important coping mechanism for frequent changes of location, and psychological support should thus consider issues of belonging, and the dilemma of feeling "at home" while balancing being "in the field" or "on mission".

Overview of the Chapters in This Book

This book aims to explore three questions: Firstly, how to best think about the experiences of workers on the move and which ideas help us to do this; secondly, what forms of support given by who, and when, provide the best staff care; and thirdly, how does the wider context influence the lives of workers on the move for good or ill, offering suggestions to mitigate difficulties where possible.

The first area of the book is conceptual, addressing key ideas for understanding the experiences of workers on the move. In chapter 1, Felicity Runchman discusses the concept of "fit" between individual staff members in the aid sector and their employing organisations. Runchman argues that this is a key guiding idea in pre-assignment psychological assessment, but also should be used to measure the health of the relationship between employer and employee over the life of their contract. She points to the importance of exploring motivation for work, employee and employer identity, and the ways in which both parties manage anxiety, to build a clearer picture of "fit" in what is often a complex relationship.

Debbie Hawker and David Hawker explore the concept of resilience in chapter 2, a term ever more widely used to denote coping capacity at work. The authors present the SPECS model which helpfully separates out aspects of resilience in key areas: Spiritual, Physical, Emotional, Cognitive & creative, and Social & systemic. They then guide us through the ways in which fortitude can be supported in these different spheres and offer a broader view of what it means to be resilient. Rather than remaining focused solely on individual life choices or personal coping (described as a "neoliberal" approach to resilience by Houldey, 2021), an expanded model can include the impact of external and social power structures and the way that these are influenced by factors such as race, gender and class, as well as areas of privilege.

In chapter 3, Mark Snelling draws on his clinical experience to provide a compelling account of the relationship between attachment style and difficulties that can arise for humanitarians. His case material illustrates how the itinerant nature of aid work can prove a draw for people seeking to sidestep difficult relational experiences, as well as prevent effective coping through social support. It also highlights the interaction of attachment, compulsive caregiving and the risk of burnout, clarifying how this might be avoided. Snelling offers helpful recommendations that can be used as a resource for individuals working in the sector and experiencing relational challenge, as well as employing organisations and psychological practitioners involved in their support.

In the fourth chapter, I discuss the concept of moral injury, arguing that this expands our insight into the existential challenges of humanitarian work more than concepts like burnout or diagnostic categories like post-traumatic stress disorder. If we accept that the values-based choices that workers make to join the sector can be mirrored by the moral and existential challenges of the work, this has implications for their employers in terms of duty of care. It should also influence thinking about the kinds of psychological intervention appropriate to offer when staff experience potentially morally injurious events (PMIEs).

In the fifth and final chapter in this area, Beth Hill and David Hawker explore the concept of family to understand both the experiences of families on the move and individual workers. They use a wider sense of the concept to include not just nuclear and extended families, but also close friends and colleagues who can become surrogate family for international workers, especially those who are travelling alone. This chapter has recommendations throughout suggesting ways in which organisations can support couples, single workers, families and third culture kids (TCKs: Children living internationally and balancing their parents' home culture, the culture of their resident country and the culture drawn from these and other influences seen as a third culture).

The second area covered by this book deals with how best to provide psychological care for a range of different staff groups. In chapter 6, Leslie Brownbridge describes her research with staff attempting to develop support for grassroots activists, many of them volunteers, working in the refugee camps of northern France and Greece. This is a group for whom organisational support is often very limited, if it exists at all and Brownbridge's chapter reports on specific initiatives, also often by volunteers to offer both psychological support and solidarity.

In chapter 7, Graham Fawcett argues for offering psychological support that is mindful of faith, be this in supporting a staff member whose faith is a key motivation for their work, or when designing staff care strategies for organisations. His chapter underlines the way in which the faith sector and the humanitarian sector have operated differently with regard to staff well-being, and the opportunities for learning across these sectors. Fawcett points out the common pitfalls of offering support, including devaluing the faith of staff members, failing to recognise the psychologically supportive aspects of faith itself and failing to plan appropriately for staff care that is faith aware. His chapter offers some guidance for individual workers, employers and psychological therapists to maximise the benefits of drawing faith more fully into their thinking

Pennie Blackburn develops her ideas on how best to support the well-being of seafarers in chapter 8. Traditionally, this group of highly mobile workers has been overlooked in discussions about the psychological care of expatriate staff and Pennie explains why this might be, while illustrating the difficulties it creates for those working in this often-challenging context. The events of the Covid-19 pandemic over the last two years have had a disproportionate impact on shipping, affecting seafarers profoundly. Seafarers are also often in the front line of international conflict by virtue of their mobility, although this is rarely talked about, and Pennie refers to the impact of the contemporary war in Ukraine for seafarers based in the Black Sea. Her recommendations represent a call to action for employers in the maritime industry but are also a call to psychological professionals working with international staff, who are so rarely approached to offer support to seafarers.

In chapter 9, Mark Snelling, Lynn Keane, and I offer suggestions and thoughts to consider when providing psychological support to short-term contractors working in unstable or conflict settings. These workers are often excluded from staff care policies, particularly if working as consultants but can face the same pressures and difficulties as other staff in these contexts. In an echo of chapter 1, we argue that understanding employee motivations and expectations is key to offering effective support, and that the identity of the contractor is affected by their attachment to place and relationship, much as has been argued for other groups of staff.

In chapter 10, Lynn Keane reflects on the need for robust support and survivor-centred care for those involved in safeguarding investigations, building ideas about best practice for organisations alongside guidance for those psychological therapists offering staff support in this most fraught and difficult of situations. Lynn offers recommendations for individuals employed internationally to ensure their organisational support is grounded in good practice, a truly helpful primer for anyone considering such a role. Recommendations are also offered for organisations, both generally and in response to safeguarding incidents, as well as guidance for mental health and psychosocial support practitioners and other psychological staff.

In the eleventh chapter, and the final one in this part of the book, David Hawker and Beth Hill discuss psychological support for children and young people and their families in an international context, drawing on the well-developed literature of member care in the mission sector. They consider needs across the duration of a family's international posting from before they set off to their repatriation, arguing that organisational support should be flexible and nuanced, and recognise a wider definition of duty of care.

A final area of this book links the earlier chapters on key concepts and how best to offer psychological support, with some considerations about wider context. In chapter 12, Ben Porter reflects on the experience of a psychological practitioner in providing services to organisational clients from within a specialist organisation. This three-way relationship (therapist-client-employing organisation) requires some thinking about and can lead to complexities that require a reflective and boundary-focused approach. Porter offers a unique insight into the way that provision of occupational psychological health in such a setting can give important benefits if these complex relationships are harnessed effectively.

A last chapter, chapter 13, discusses the use of online therapy employing different media to support international staff. Felicity Runchman and I evaluate the evidence for the effectiveness of remote therapy with international staff and offer some recommendations for individuals, employing organisations, and psychological therapists to maximise the gains of this most flexible support option.

The concluding chapter after this offers a summary of key points discussed in this volume and some suggestions to organisations assigning personnel internationally, to psychological and well-being therapists working with them, and to individual workers themselves.

Notes

1   It is worth noting here that freedom to travel for work is always relative and reflects the political, social and economic realities of staff members. As noted by Houldey (2021), the concept of making a free choice in relation to work may be bounded by the needs to balance financial commitments to family or to navigate high unemployment that makes mobility a necessity.
2   This report is based on survey data for expatriates in contact with the international bank HSBC and includes those who have retired in another country. This sample is less heterogeneous than the group of staff on the move that we are considering, and its lower response rates from expatriates hailing from Africa, Latin America and Asia make this clear.
3   In this, I am following Cerdin and Selmer (2014), who argue for using four specific criteria to define someone as a self-initiated expatriate: (a) having initiated international relocation oneself; (b) being in or intending to be in regular employment; (c) intending on a temporary stay; (d) possessing skilled/professional qualifications. However, see Doherty et al. (2018) for further discussion on conceptual difficulties with the concept of self-initiated expatriate.

References

Adams, B.G., & van de Vijver, F.J.R. (2015). The many faces of expatriate identity. *International Journal of Intercultural Relations, 49*, 322–331. https://doi.org/10.1016/j.ijintrel.2015.05.009

Al Ariss, A. (2012). Ethnic minority migrants or self-initiated expatriates? Questioning assumptions in international management studies. In M. Andresen, A. Al Ariss, & M. Walther (Eds.), *Self-initiated expatriation: Individual, organizational, and national perspectives* (pp. 235–241). Abingdon: Routledge. https://doi.org/10.4324/9780203111505

Alexander, J. (2013). *Chasing chaos: My decade in and out of humanitarian aid.* New York: Crown.

Baum-Talmor, P. (2021). Careers at sea: Exploring seafarer motivations and aspirations. In V.O. Gekara & H. Sampson (Eds.), *The world of the seafarer*. WMU Studies in Maritime Affairs, vol. 9. Cham: Springer. https://doi.org/10.1007/978-3-030-49825-2_5

Bonache, J., Brewster, C., & Jintae Froese, F. (2020). Global mobility: Reasons, trends and strategies. In J. Bonache, C. Brewster, & F. Jintae Froese (Eds.), *Global mobility and the management of expatriates*. Cambridge Companions to Management. Cambridge: Cambridge University Press. https://doi.org/10.4324/9780203111505

Burkholder, J.D., Joines, R., Cunningham-Hill, M., & Xu, B. (2010). Health and well-being factors associated with international business travel. *Journal of Travel Medicine, 17*(5), 329–333. https://doi.org/10.1111/j.1708-8305.2010.00441.x

Bushong, L.J. (2013). *Belonging everywhere and nowhere: Insights into counselling the globally mobile.* Indianapolis: Mango Tree Intercultural Services.

Cain, K., Postlewait, H., & Thompson, A. (2006). *Emergency sex and other desperate measures: True stories from a war zone.* London: Ebury Press.

Cerdin, J.L., & Selmer, J. (2014). Who is a self-initiated expatriate? Towards conceptual clarity of a common notion. *The International Journal of Human Resource Management, 25*(9), 1281–1301, https://doi.org/10.1080/09585192.2013.863793

Chen, M. (2019). The impact of expatriates' cross-cultural adjustment on work stress and job involvement in the high-tech industry. *Frontiers in Psychology, 10*, 2228. https://doi.org/10.3389/fpsyg.2019.02228

Chiang, F.F., van Esch, E., & Birch, T.A. (2020). Repatriation and career development. In J. Bonache, C. Brewster, & F. Jintae Froese (Eds.), *Global mobility and the management of expatriates.* Cambridge Companions to Management. Cambridge: Cambridge University Press. https://doi.org/10.4324/9780203111505

Connorton, E., Perry, M.J., Hemenway, D., & Miller, M. (2012). Humanitarian relief workers and trauma-related mental illness. *Epidemiologic Reviews, 34*(1), 145–155. https://doi.org/10.1093/epirev/mxr026

De Jong, K., Martinmäki, S.E., Te Brake, H., Haagen, J.F.G., & Kleber, R.J. (2021) Mental and physical health of international humanitarian aid workers on short-term assignments: Findings from a prospective cohort study. *Social Science & Medicine, 285*, 114268. https://doi.org/10.1016/j.socscimed.2021.114268

Doherty, N., Richardson, J., & Thorn, K. (2013). Self-initiated expatriation and self-initiated expatriates: Clarification of the research stream. *Career Development International, 18*(1), 97–112. https://doi.org/10.1108/13620431311305971

Edmond, C. (2020, 10 January). Global migration by the numbers: Who migrates, where they go and why. *World Economic Forum.* Retrieved from www.weforum.org/agenda/2020/01/iom-global-migration-report-international-migrants-2020/

Harris, N. (1995). *The new untouchables: Immigration and the new world worker.* London: I.B. Tauris.

Houldey, G. (2021). *The vulnerable humanitarian: Ending burnout culture in the aid sector.* Abingdon, Oxon: Routledge.

HSBC (2017). *Expat explorer global report: Broadening perspectives. HSBC Holding PLC.* Retrieved from www.hsbc.com/news-and-media/media-releases/2017/hsbc-expat-explorer-2017.

Kraimer, M.L., & Wayne, S.J. (2004). An examination of perceived organizational support as a multidimensional construct in the context of an expatriate assignment. *Journal of Management, 30*(2), 209–237. https://doi.org/10.1016/j.jm.2003.01.001

Lessle, A., Haslberger, A., & Brewster, C. (2020). Expatriate adjustment. In J. Bonache, C. Brewster, & F. Froese (Eds.), *Global mobility and the management of expatriates.* Cambridge Companions to Management (pp. 57–79). Cambridge: Cambridge University Press. https://doi.org/10.4324/9780203111505

Liao, Y.K., Wu, W.Y., Dao, T.C., & Ngoc Luu, T.M. (2021). The influence of emotional intelligence and cultural adaptability on cross-cultural adjustment and performance with the mediating effect of cross-cultural competence: A study of expatriates in Taiwan. *Sustainability, 13*, 3374. https://doi.org/10.3390/su13063374

Lopes Cardozo, B., Gotway Crawford, C., Eriksson, C., Zhu, J., Sabin, M., Ager, A., Foy, D., Snider, L., Scholte, W., Kaiser, R., Olff, M., Rijnen, B., & Simon, W. (2012). Psychological distress, depression, anxiety, and burnout among international humanitarian aid workers: a longitudinal study. *PloS one, 7*(9), e44948. https://doi.org/10.1371/journal.pone.0044948

McKay, L. (2007). On the road again: Coping with travel and re-entry stress. *Headington Institute.* www.headington-institute.org/wp-content/uploads/2021/01/HI-Travel-Stress-Reading-Course-R25.pdf

Shenkar, O. (2012). Cultural distance revisited: Towards a more rigorous conceptualization and measurement of cultural differences. *Journal of International Business Studies, 43*, 1–11. https://doi.org/10.1057/jibs.2011.4

Striker, J., Luippold, R.S., Nagy, L., Liese, B., Bigelow, C., & Mundt, K.A. (1999). Risk factors for psychological stress among international business travellers. *Occupational and Environmental Medicine, 56*, 245–252. http://dx.doi.org/10.1136/oem.56.4.245

Worley, W. (2020, 28 April). DFID must remain "rigourous" on safeguarding amid pandemic. *DEVEX Inside Development.* www.devex.com/news/dfid-must-remain-rigorous-on-safeguarding-amid-pandemic-97123

Chapter I

"Good fit" and righting the relationship

An exploration of employee and organisational relationships in the international aid sector

Felicity Runchman

The question of whether an individual is a "good fit" for their organisation lies at the heart of the pre-posting psychological health consultation many aid workers are asked to undertake by their employers. Carrying out these consultations, generally known as "psychological clearances", whilst working as a psychotherapist within the international aid sector, I help staff prepare for what might lie ahead on their assignments, assisting them in making a final "inner check" that they are happy to proceed, and screening for any clear psychological risk factors. The stark simplicity but underlying trickiness of the central question, "how good a fit do you think you are for your organisation?" always stands out within this process. How well can someone know at the start of a new relationship with their employer (or the beginning of a phase represented by a new role or posting) how things will unfold and how well suited they will be?

There are many factors that might indicate the likely course of the trajectory – for example, an individual's prior work experience, evidence of their personal coping and relational styles, plus their hopes and motivations. Alongside this lies their perception of the organisation they are either joining or continuing to work for. What are the organisation's key aims and values? How are these upheld and reflected in day-to-day work, and, perhaps most importantly, how does this manifest in the way the organisation treats its staff?

Given that a "good fit" rests upon the idea of two inevitably changing variables – the individual and the organisation – my experience makes me doubt that gauging it at the start of a new assignment can ever be done with precision. I have also learned that the most telling points for measuring good fit often come further down the line, at times of crisis – be these personal (such as a staff member's bereavement or a mental health difficulty), organisational (such as a restructure or the need to issue redundancies), or external (such as the coronavirus pandemic, or a critical incident brought on by civil unrest or natural disaster). Such times can be testing and are often points when disorganisation, disenchantment and "acting out"[1] mean the concepts of fit and cohesion between an individual and their organisation seem at

DOI: 10.4324/9781003261971-2

their most tenuous. However, these are also times with powerful potential for learning and change, where the attachment-based concept of "rupture and repair" (Bowlby, 1988) can come to light in the relationship.

Using case examples and personal observations, my aim in this chapter is to explore the concept of "good fit" in more depth, looking at what both individuals and organisations typically contribute. I will highlight times when "good fit" between an employee and their organisation might be challenged – considering how such situations can be managed, and what learning gleaned from them.

It feels important to state at the outset, that most of my work has been with aid workers from the global north preparing for posting in the global south, and this is reflected in the case examples I have given. However, organisations are increasingly requesting clearance and other psychological health consultations for nationally assigned staff, or staff from the global south assigned there. This represents important and timely recognition of the distinct practical and psychological challenges they also face in their roles.

"Cultural/Organisational Fit" – Its Importance and Implications

The distinction between "job fit" and "cultural" or "organisational fit" has been recognised for some time within the fields of human resources (HR) and management studies (Bouten, 2015). To simplify, "job fit" (the question of whether a candidate meets the criteria on a job spec and demonstrates appropriate experience for the job in question) is different to "cultural" or "organisational fit", which is more concerned with whether a candidate's beliefs, values and expectations align with those of their employer.

Cultural or organisational fit is the concept of fit I shall be discussing in this chapter, as job fit is invariably established before offers of employment are made and psychological screenings take place. This type of fit is more nuanced and subjective than job fit, and, in the international aid sector, is often higher stakes. Aid workers tend to make significant life changes, what many would term "sacrifices", when undertaking their roles. They may relocate – usually abroad, and to culturally different and politically fragile contexts. They may also accept an increased risk to personal safety through their work,[2] accompanied by restriction of day-to-day freedoms, and regular exposure to distressing material in jobs that involve attending to other people's suffering.

The importance of feeling truly wedded to what an employing organisation stands for therefore takes on increased significance for aid workers. The disillusionment, regret and anger that can emerge at a mismatch between an organisation's professed values and the reality encountered by a staff member is often profound, as I have observed in many a critical incident or post-assignment debriefing session. The implications of this lack of "fit" can be far reaching. Describing burnout, Pigni (2016) writes:

(It) creeps in when meaning is lost, when you no longer feel what you do matters; when you experience a dissonance between your values, what you believe in, and what you are asked to do; and when there is a gap between what your organisation preaches and what it actually does. (p. 30).

She argues that staff in the international aid sector are more likely to suffer mental health difficulties due to burnout caused by loss of meaning in their work and exposure to a toxic work culture, than on account of post-traumatic stress disorder due to traumatic events. Serious burnout, which can prompt individuals to leave their employment, or to take a significant amount of time off sick, is not only damaging to the individual. It is also highly disruptive and costly to teams and organisations, fracturing working relationships, reducing morale and accruing costs linked to the "medical evacuation" of staff home and replacing them.

These factors make clear the importance of ensuring "good fit", but, as stated, measuring or predicting fit at the start of a contract or posting can be difficult. This is because determining the culture of a particular workplace is difficult until you're actually working in it. It is also impossible to foresee what factors – personal, political or otherwise – might affect staff members, teams and organisations, either individually or collectively, during any given period of time. Even in generally healthy work environments, unexpected challenges such as the sickness and absence of a key team member, or the more all-encompassing sweep of something like the Covid-19 pandemic, can upset the balance. Additionally, despite bold mission statements, and well-intentioned trainings and initiatives to promote supportive working environments, work culture within organisations rarely remains static. Nor is it uniform in a sector where teams and projects are in varying locations around the world, in diverse contexts and with similarly diverse staff.

Having pointed out these difficulties, there are three factors I have found worth exploring when considering the likelihood of a "good fit". These are "motivation", "identity" and "the management of anxiety". From my experience as a psychotherapist working with individuals, I usually look at these from the perspective of the staff member. However, I would propose organisations examine their own stance in relation to these themes as well.

Motivation

Questioning an employee's motivation to undertake or continue work in the international aid sector is a key part of the psychological clearance process, and with good reason. Exploration of motivation uncovers information about an individual's values which, as stated, must remain aligned to those of their organisation and their work if the risk of burnout is to be mitigated.

A desire to address injustice, tackle inequality and alleviate suffering are motivations that are typically reported – particularly by aid workers from the global north, whose perception of their own relative privilege may be a driving force behind their decision to undertake humanitarian work. Such responses often shine a light on deeply rooted and laudable personal values. However, they demand further unpacking. A passion to undertake personally meaningful work is positive, but it's also appropriate to ask how a person foresees fulfilling this through their role, as a means of "reality checking". How, for example, might an employee feel if something like restricted access to resources, staff restructures or a major security issue prevents them from accomplishing their value-based wishes as initially envisaged?

Some forethought and flexibility on this feels like an important marker of maturity in candidates. Peter, an early-career aid worker I spoke to recently exemplified this:

> I think we expect the meaningful moments to be the ones where we have direct contact with beneficiaries, and actually see food being distributed, schools being built, and medical facilities improved etc. However, that sort of thing doesn't happen overnight, and often things don't go according to plan. Of course, I want to use my privilege to make a difference, but I can do that just as well by being a supportive colleague and by doing stuff behind the scenes rather than always being at the forefront of projects.

This open outlook bodes well for a person's ability to fit into an organisation, which, due to the context in which it operates, may not always be able to provide predictable and stable working conditions and outcomes.

It also feels pertinent to ask employees how value-based motivations, such as a wish to help others, or to promote human rights, are met in other areas of their lives, outside work – particularly if work might present blocks and frustrations to the fulfilment of such wishes. Sir Thomas Browne's famous statement from *Religio Medici* (1643/2016), *"charity begins at home"* comes to mind here. I generally ask how individuals uphold values like justice or compassion in their day-to-day lives with families, friends and home communities rather than when they are in the field or focusing on work-related campaigns. Channelling all one's hopes to make a positive difference into work suggests a narrow outlook of what it means to be an agent of change. It can also point to a splitting of identity in which the "virtuous" image of aid worker is used to facilitate, conceal or excuse less prosocial, even harmful, behaviour in other areas of a person's life – something we are perhaps more aware of since the recent scandals regarding sexual abuse in the sector (McKenzie, 2018; McVeigh, 2021).

For these reasons, I'm often refreshed and encouraged by those who name a range of motivations – some practical or based on personal interests – for seeking to work in international aid, rather than purely value-based or altruistic reasons. This suggests someone is in touch with their own needs and wishes, seeing these as valid. It stands in contrast to someone striving to fit the image of what Houldey (2021) deconstructs as "the perfect humanitarian" – someone divorced from their own needs and personal responsibilities (for example, to their families and loved ones) because their focus is purely on helping others deemed to be less fortunate. Whilst they may refer to value-based motivations, I find it is often national or regional staff who are more honestly able to name career progression and economic advantage as key reasons for entering or staying within the field of international aid.

As a psychotherapist, considering people's unconscious, as well as consciously named, reasons for wanting to work in the sector is also vital. It can be hard to bring such sensitive subjects to light in a single psychological clearance session, particularly when meeting an individual for the first time.[3] In research based on interviews with seasoned aid workers, Snelling (2018, and also chapter 3 in this volume) suggests that their choice of vocation may demonstrate an unconscious desire to avoid or control certain relational processes (such as dealing with intimacy or negotiating boundaries) due to difficult early attachment experiences. Aid work typically presents those seeking to establish stable monogamous relationships and conventionally "settled" family lives with challenges in which these processes are enacted. From my own observations, another similar unconscious draw towards a career in aid work – particularly in conflict or emergency settings – is experiencing a childhood or personal history with a high degree of conflict or chaos, perhaps through domestic violence, parental substance misuse or mental health issues within the family. Many individuals who grew up in such contexts quite literally come to feel "at home" in war or disaster zones. This was an insight reached by Charlie, a young British aid worker I saw for counselling back in the UK shortly after she had completed gruelling consecutive assignments in Yemen and South Sudan. Growing up with a mother who had bipolar affective disorder meant Charlie was accustomed to outbreaks of hostility within the family home and had become attuned to the "peaks and troughs" of her mother's moods and levels of activity. Whilst it could be draining and distressing, just like her mother, Charlie found the peaks of crisis, action and drama that she encountered in the field more comfortable than the troughs of loneliness and passivity that she associated with being back home or working in more stable environments.

People often feel self-conscious or reluctant to reveal such personal information in psychological clearance consultations in case it leads to them being seen as a "poor fit" for their organisation, or as someone with a propensity to be antisocial or unstable. This is unfortunate and not necessarily true. The phrase "awareness is all" may sound like a cliché, but the wisdom and self-knowledge that contribute to personal resilience in such a challenging sector (knowing why one is *really* drawn to working within it, and checking to see if buried needs can be met in any other way) is far more helpful than a psychological blind spot. With a clearer understanding of the sense of fit she felt with her vocation, Charlie continued her career in international aid. However, she made a conscious effort to build in appropriate breaks between high-intensity assignments, and to find ways of seeking stimulation and fulfilment in her life away from the field.

Identity

An organisation's identity informs how it sees itself and, consequently, how it operates. This goes on to influence how it is viewed by others and their expectations. Many organisations within the international aid sector are household names. People may have grown up learning about the work they do through television campaigns and newspaper articles, seeing charity collection tins being shaken in town centres, or when receiving fundraising sponsorship requests from friends. Such organisations easily acquire familiarity and prestige in the minds of the public, who may elevate them to a "pedestal position" and idealise what it might be like to work for them.[4]

This aspect of an organisation's identity often creates a powerful pull for prospective employees, buttressing fantasies that working for such an organisation will bring respect, fulfilment and meaning to their lives. As with any type of idealisation, this can lead to employees overlooking disappointments and difficulties, perhaps leading to overwork, failures to seek support or improper practices. Many clients I have encountered have described their employment within a particular aid organisation as feeling like an "honour" or a "lifelong dream come true". This attitude can contribute to an unhelpful splitting off or denial of frustration or constructive criticism towards their employers, which, at a later stage, "blows up" in terms of anger, acting out and absenteeism. In its early stages this may present as employees feeling they just have to put up with any difficulties at work to balance out or pay off what feels like a privilege. This was the case with Jenna, an aid worker I supported who regularly had to "double-hat" and assume the duties of other absent staff members on top of her own:

> Getting a job with an organisation like this felt like such an achievement for me, I had to pinch myself to believe it was true. It feels hard to tell my friends and family what it's really like, though, let alone challenge my manager about the endless frustrations I experience at work and the unrealistic expectations she has of me. It would feel like crushing my dream and damaging the organisation's image.

The tendency to idealise might have its roots in an individual employee's early relational history and can be understood generally through the lens of object-relations theory. Put simply, in the early stages of infancy, we all tend to "split" – idealising the mother/caregiver who is present, attentive and responsive to our needs, but denigrating and raging against the same mother/caregiver when they are absent. It is only later in our development that we are usually able to accept, perhaps with some disappointment, that this mother/ caregiver is, in fact, one and the same person – someone who is hopefully present and responsive enough to our needs, but also humanly fallible and not always able to perfectly meet them. Klein (1946), the key proponent of object-relations theory, refers to this as the depressive position which, despite any immediate implications the term "depressive" may hold, is generally considered to be a healthy developmental milestone.

Not all individuals are able to reach or sustain this more nuanced way of thinking, though, and many regress temporarily to the "black and white" realms of splitting people, situations and, indeed, organisations, into "good" and "bad". This is particularly common during or immediately after prolonged periods of stress or trauma which, of course, are not uncommon in the international aid sector. During such times, we can mentally adopt a survival position, becoming more reactive and emotionally charged in our responses to the world around us. Put simply, we lose the ability to "see the bigger picture".

If organisational or cultural fit is to be understood as a flexible and changing construct, then long-term adherence to this split style of thinking – lofty idealisation or hostile denigration of current, prospective or former employers – may be a cause for concern amongst employees at clearance stage, or a reason for friction further into their employment. More optimistic indicators of fit are to be found in an individual's ability to move away from the pedestal position or, equally, from a wholly demonising position, when describing their current or previous workplaces. This also needs to be reflected in how employees see themselves, for example having the capacity to see themselves as "fallible", and with self-compassion and understanding, to see where some of their stronger feelings and reactions might come from.

This came to mind when I conducted counselling sessions with Shen, a long-term client who is an experienced aid worker. Whilst completing an assignment in a highly volatile location recently, he had to be evacuated at short notice and under stressful circumstances, saying goodbye to nationally based colleagues, unsure of their future safety. Leaving them and other locals with whom he had formed connections brought up uncomfortable feelings for Shen as he travelled to the airport, knowing they didn't share his fortune in having a secure exit. For several sessions his anger about the perceived bureaucracy of his well-known and highly regarded organisation was palpable. He spoke in very critical terms about the way in which his HR department had upheld rules around annual leave and relocation expenses in a manner he viewed as heartless and pedantic given the suffering and chaos he'd recently witnessed. Over the course of a few weeks, though, as the likely impact of a trauma reaction ebbed, Shen's outlook similarly softened:

> Actually, I can see now that these people are just trying to do their jobs, and that they have structures and procedures to follow. They ask us to let

them know if we have any questions and, to be fair, they try to answer. I can't say I agree with it all, but I'm not as angry as I was.

This is not to say that an employee's anger towards their organisation should always be viewed as a "passing phase" born out of a stress or trauma reaction. However, the ability to look at a situation from different perspectives, and to appreciate the part different players take within it, is important. Having had the privilege of working with Shen for several years, I now see he has developed capacities to reference and make sense of reactions which he has in the workplace that are strongly linked to his personal history. These include a resistance to authority born of having a very "regimented" and expectant father, and a strong identification with those perceived to be from marginalised communities due to his sexual identity as a gay man. He has developed away from broad generalising perspectives about his organisation and its beneficiaries (largely determined by past conflicts) to revise his view in light of current circumstances.

Whilst long-term therapy is not something all staff working in the international aid sector will wish to access, it can have benefits for those who make thoughtful use of it. Regardless of whether a person has undergone therapy, though, evidence that they have done some work on examining how they see themselves and others – the fundamentals of identity – is important when considering fit and how well their relationship with their employer is likely to pan out. However, organisations and senior staff within them also need to take their own identities into account. It builds trust with staff when they can be honest about their shortcomings, growing edges and problematic pasts as well as focusing on their strengths and future ambitions. This is, thankfully, something we are beginning to see more of as the commissioning of the *KonTerra Report* by Amnesty International (Avula, McKay, & Galland, 2019)[5] exemplifies. However, as *Sunday Times* journalist Matthew Syed (2021) suggests, many high-profile organisations set up for the public good still unfortunately display traces of "organisational narcissism", viewing themselves as being above the checks, balances and "rules" that govern organisations with less immediately worthy aims.

Management of Anxiety

In a sector where a degree of tension, danger and unpredictability will inevitably be present on a macro level (due to the conflicts or urgent situations an organisation is responding to), and likely also on a micro level (due to individual staff members' personal issues and concerns), a key question regarding fit is how both employees and organisations manage anxiety. Here I am referring to anxiety less as a clinical or diagnostic construct, but more as a way of describing generic worry and uncertainty, with a curiosity as to how this is held or contained.

Few people seek work in the international aid and humanitarian sector expecting a predictable and stable working life. Indeed, many are attracted by the buzz and excitement of the sector's inherent riskiness and volatility. It is thus uncommon at clearance stage to encounter individuals whom one might conventionally understand as anxious. Conversely, many will present a love of adventure, a high tolerance for change and sometimes a clear rejection of the routine and mundane as reasons for taking on their roles. This suggests a commendable "hardiness" – although it can also raise concerns. This is because the reality is that, even in the most unstable of contexts, most aid workers will likely have to endure long spells of monotony and boredom on their assignments, particularly if living on compounds or in similarly restrictive environments.

When an employee presents a very cool and unphased outlook, it's important for me to ask whether they are splitting off their experience of anxiety – an all-too-human and often very functional phenomenon – by disowning or disallowing it. The danger in this kind of mindset is that anxiety supressed can flare up at a later stage. Perhaps this will be in the form of panic attacks, or feelings of anxious malaise that prompt an individual to "self-medicate" with alcohol or other unhealthy behaviours. More worryingly, it might point to an individual being so desensitised to anxiety that they unconsciously or consciously court risk, compromising their own safety and that of others.

Whilst recognising that extreme or clinical anxiety can be an unhappy and life-limiting condition for those who experience it, fundamentally, a certain degree of anxiety is normal and often helpful. It might give us the jolt that prompts us to prepare for danger, or signal to us that we're in a situation that sits uneasily with our values or principles. For this reason, my line of questioning with individuals is always around *how* they deal with stress and anxiety as opposed to *whether* they experience it. Good awareness of early stress indicators, and the ability to name healthy ways of responding to these (for example, seeking clarification and support in the workplace, engaging in self-care practices and making time for friends, family and leisure activities outside of work) suggest far better outcomes in terms of an individual's ongoing resilience than an attitude of "*I don't get stressed or anxious*". That said, it is important to hold in mind that understandings of stress and anxiety used in psychological health assessments tend to be drawn from a Western framework – focusing, for example, on heavy workload and multiple demands made of a person. Aid workers from other cultures may have a different appreciation of, and different thresholds of tolerance for stress and anxiety – particularly if they have grown up in contexts where very tangible stressors such as poverty or conflict have been present.

On the other side, particularly where the matter of fit is concerned, lies the question of how organisations manage anxiety. Organisations, particularly those involved in supporting people in life and death situations, can find it especially hard to manage anxiety. This is a subject explored in depth by renowned psychoanalyst and social scientist Isabel Menzies Lyth in a paper she wrote in 1959, based on observations of the training and supervision of nurses in a large hospital. Menzies Lyth describes how, in an attempt to alleviate individual nurses from the intense anxiety and primitive feelings that caring for dying patients entails, the hospital, as a system, put structures and rules in place (for example, regularly moving nurses from patient to patient to avoid close relationships being formed, "depersonalising" patients and staff, and encouraging ritualistic as opposed to responsive performance of tasks) as a means of containing this anxiety. Whilst in many respects this served a protective purpose, in terms of keeping the worries that might destabilise young and inexperienced nurses at bay, Menzies Lyth's central argument seems to be that it prevented the nurses from growing and developing personally through connecting with anxiety and learning how to manage it in their own way.

Can the same kind of tendencies be seen within the international aid sector? Do organisations adopt a similarly benevolent yet paternalistic approach – placing staff into situations where high levels of anxiety, even trauma, will likely be evoked, yet seeking to defensively "manage" the strong reactions that result? It would be crass for me to generalise here, given that I have worked with staff from numerous organisations, working on diverse projects and in differently managed teams. Much of how staff members are supported in dealing with anxiety at work can, I believe, be put down to the personalities and temperaments of their immediate managers and teammates. However, these will be influenced by organisational culture, and I frequently sense a fear of anxiety within organisations, which can lead to unhelpful practices and attitudes. In a training on The Many Faces of Trauma run in 2021, Fiona Dunkley described a typical response to traumatic events within organisations as being to "*deny, distort, avoid*". The same can be said be said for how many organisations respond to uncertain or anxiety-provoking situations, such as some of those which I will go on to describe.

Staff mental health issues, or reactions to critical incidents, tend to cause a lot of anxiety for employers within the sector. This may be fuelled by concern about claims of discrimination or legal redress if they are deemed to "get it wrong" in responding, or by guilt around having put staff in challenging and dangerous situations in the first place. Whilst these concerns are understandable, they often generate a sense of panic and the immediate urge to "hand over to the experts" by calling in mental health professionals. A willingness to provide specialised psychological support for staff can, in many respects, be seen as the hallmark of a responsible, forward-thinking and well-intentioned organisation. However, this depends on how it is managed. Fretful and perhaps uncertain of their own ability to respond appropriately, managers often refer directly to counsellors or hastily arrange debriefs with external professionals when a staff member shows signs of distress at work or has a concerning response to a critical incident. This can be done without taking time to "lean in" and acknowledge the difficulty themselves, offering, in the first instance, the most basic human level of recognition and support to the staff member concerned. When this happens, it can leave a sour taste in the mouths of employees, as well as feelings of rejection and mistrust. This was the case with Sophie, an aid worker recently referred to me for a trauma consultation after an incident of civil unrest threatened her safety, and that of her colleagues, in their place of work:

> It felt like the organisation didn't want to acknowledge what had happened and wanted to brush it under the carpet – perhaps because we'd raised concerns in advance that they didn't really respond to. I'm not expecting them to be mental health experts, or to provide counselling, but it would have been nice for them to have had more of a conversation with us about how we were affected.

Psychological first aid (PFA) training is something managers can undertake to build skills in initiating these types of conversations. Increasingly used within organisations, PFA enhances staff members' confidence and ability to respond, in the first instance, to those affected by critical incidents or mental health issues at work. It also incorporates guidance on when to refer to other professionals, hence minimising the likelihood of this kind of anxious "reactivity".

It would be helpful for organisations to hold in mind that providing staff members with access to psychological support can sit alongside other interventions that they may want or, indeed, need to make. Very often I am asked to conduct psychological consultations for staff members for whom capability issues and absence at work have become significant problems over a long period. Whilst mental health difficulties may be contributing to the situation, and counselling or other forms of psychosocial support may be appropriate, it can be frustrating to learn that managers have done little or nothing to confront the situation themselves, either through performance management strategies or, in the earliest stages, by having a caring but frank conversation with the staff member about what is going on. Hastily passing the problem on to mental health professionals can indicate precisely the sort of avoidance Dunkley refers to when speaking of "deny, distort, avoid".

Whilst starting conversations around mental health might be daunting for managers and HR professionals, my experience suggests staff members value being asked about their situations before external support is brought in. During the Covid-19 pandemic this was particularly so. Throughout this period of unprecedented, enforced change to people's lives, I conducted counselling for staff members, and ran several organisational workshops on stress management within the international aid sector. A key recommendation for managers within the workshops was to familiarise themselves with the personal circumstances of their individual staff members (for example, are they homeschooling young children, living in a busy house-share, or potentially isolated due to living alone?) so that these might be born in mind and reasonable adjustments to working life granted where necessary. Much of the stress I observed in individual staff members during the pandemic felt like it could have been eased if this had taken place. For example, I worked with several staff members like Lucy, who had to leave her project during the pandemic to return to her home country, which was several time zones away. The expectation that she would join online meetings in what, for her, was often the middle of the night, prevailed, as the reality of her relocation seemed to pass her colleagues by. Much of my work with Lucy involved helping her feel able to challenge the expectation that she would work outside what might be deemed reasonable working hours, and to propose alternatives. The onus seemed somewhat unfairly to be on her, though, causing her opinion of her organisation to falter.

Conclusion

Having explored various aspects of the relationship between staff members and their employing organisations within the international aid sector, there are several key points I would like to stress in my conclusion. Firstly, the relationship is a relationship like so many others – generally forged in a spirit of goodwill, in the hope of a long-standing, harmonious and productive union. However, as with any type of burgeoning relationship, there will be characteristics and attributes each party wishes to foreground at the start of the relationship, and others they wish to hide or may not even be aware of. Staff members will often, for example, present enthusiasm, value-driven motivations, admiration for their organisations and a sense of being composed or unperturbed by fear. They may hide more personal agendas (both conscious and unconscious), and the propensity towards emotional states such as anger and anxiety (though these, in themselves, are not always problematic if attention is paid to when they arise and how they are dealt with). Organisations, on the other hand, will likely present the best of their past achievements and future aims through positive mission statements and carefully curated publicity, alongside assurance of being able to contain and manage staff concerns at times of crisis and uncertainty. What they might hide will be the shadow of their fallibility, the inevitability that they will sometimes "get it wrong", and the impossibility of their ability to allay or avoid all staff worries. In essence, both sides may hide their vulnerabilities in ways that become limiting and problematic.

In pointing this out, I am not suggesting either party necessarily "lays themselves bare" and reveals all that they might be seeking to conceal at the start of the relationship. However, as the relationship continues, challenges are likely to arise that will bring some of these things to light. Therefore, an openness on both sides to engage in self-reflection and development is important. This also needs to be an ongoing process rather than one that is solely considered at the start of a staff member's new posting. Seeking to gauge fit at this point is a worthwhile enterprise but of limited long-term use. The term "fit" implies durability over time, flexibility in the face of change and the periodic need for remeasurement, adjustment and repair.

What might this look like? As indicated earlier in this chapter, alongside initial "clearance" consultations, regular opportunities for staff members to have confidential psychosocial "check-in" appointments (pre-, mid- and post-assignment, plus opportunities after critical incidents) with a named external mental health practitioner is recommended. These appointments could provide an opportunity for the question of fit to be reviewed regularly in a context perceived by the staff member to be safe. However, I would not want to suggest that managers and organisations shy away from posing the question to staff themselves, bringing any lapses in fit to light, and providing the chance for these to be addressed and learned from. This might be through tailored staff training (such as training on PFA, or mental health issues common to the sector, like vicarious trauma), the revising of policies or, most simply and often most effectively, conversations where difficult issues are acknowledged, and constructive solutions mutually sought.

Notes

1   By this, I mean acting inappropriately to relieve stress, frustration or conflict outside a person's awareness
2   Although Houldey (2021) makes the relevant point that international aid workers from the global north are typically afforded higher levels of comfort and security, living in secure compounds, and driving in armoured vehicles, than their national or regional counterparts.
3   For this reason, Dunkley (2019), and others providing psychosocial support within the international aid sector, recommend an established "pathway" of support for employees, encompassing several consultations (pre-, mid-, and post-assignment), ideally with the same practitioner.
4   Although recent scandals regarding misappropriation of publicly donated funds and sexual impropriety (McKenzie, 2018; McVeigh, 2021) within the sector have countered this and perhaps equally fostered cynicism.
5   This comprehensive review of staff well-being was commissioned by Amnesty International in the wake of the suicides of two staff members, Gaëtan Mootoo and Rosalind McGregor, in 2018. Making for challenging reading, it identifies significant problems in organisational culture (such as a culture of secrecy, bullying and abuse of power) and management failings as key causes of staff well-being issues. The report was responded to upon its publication in January 2019 by incoming Secretary General Kumi Naidoo with a commitment "to address the challenges with a genuine desire for restoration, reconnection and renewal for employees across the organization".

References

Amnesty International. (2019, January). *The KonTerra (wellbeing) review: Response by Kumi Naidoo.* www.amnesty.org/en/wp-content/uploads/2021/05/ORG6097642019ENGLISH.pdf

Avula, K., McKay, L., & Galland, S. (2019, January). *The KonTerra Group: Amnesty International Staff Wellbeing Review.* www.amnesty.org/en/wp-content/uploads/2021/05/ORG6097632019ENGLISH.pdf

Bouten, K. (2015, 17 July). Recruiting for cultural fit. *Harvard Business Review.* https://hbr.org/2015/07/recruiting-for-cultural-fit

Bowlby, J. (1988). *A secure base: Parent-child attachment and healthy human development.* New York: Basic Books.

Browne, T. (2016). *Religio Medici.* Scotts Valley, CA: CreateSpace Independent Publishing Platform. (original work published c. 1643)

Dunkley, F. (2019). *Psychosocial support for humanitarian aid workers: A roadmap of trauma and critical incident care.* Routledge Focus on Mental Health. Abingdon, Oxon: Routledge.

Houldey, G. (2021). *The vulnerable humanitarian: Ending burnout culture in the aid sector.* Routledge Humanitarian Studies. Abingdon, Oxon: Routledge.

Klein, M. (1946). Notes on some schizoid mechanisms. *International Journal of Psycho-Analysis, 27*(3–4), 99–110. PMID: 20261821.

McKenzie, S.C. (2018, July 31). Sexual abuse "endemic" in international aid sector, report finds. CNN. https://edition.cnn.com/2018/07/30/uk/sexual-abuse-aid-sector-uk-report-intl/index.html

McVeigh, K. (2021, January 15). *Aid sector is "last safe haven" for abusers, UK investigation warns. The Guardian.* www.theguardian.com/global-development/2021/jan/14/aid-sector-is-last-safe-haven-for-abusers-uk-investigation-warns

Menzies Lyth, I. (1959). A case-study in the functioning of social systems as a defence against anxiety: A report on the study of the nursing service of a general hospital. *Human Relations, 13*(2), 95–121. https://doi.org/10.1177%2F001872676001300201

Pigni, A., & Slim, H. (2016). *The idealist's survival kit: 75 simple ways to avoid burnout.* Berkeley, CA: Parallax Press.

Snelling, M. (2018). The impact of emergency aid work on personal relationships: A psychodynamic study. *Journal of International Humanitarian Action, 3*(1). https://doi.org/10.1186/s41018-018-0042-7

Syed, M. (2021, May 22). *The BBC, the NHS and Oxfam have a bad case of institutional narcissism.* Comment | *The Sunday Times.* www.thetimes.co.uk/article/the-bbc-the-nhs-and-oxfam-have-a-bad-case-of-institutional-narcissism-93vnhz8pn

Chapter 2

Building resilience among staff working internationally

Debbie Hawker and David Hawker

When assessing candidates for international assignments, employers seek staff who are resilient. Back in 1970, in an article entitled "What It Takes to Work Abroad", Oates described rather humorously the resilience sought in someone going to work outside their own culture:

> he should have the stamina of an Olympic runner, the mental agility of an Einstein, the conversational skill of a professor of languages, the detachment of a judge, the tact of a diplomat, and the perseverance of an Egyptian pyramid builder ... he should also have a feeling for his culture; his moral judgment should not be too rigid; he should be able to merge with the local environment with a chameleon-like ease; and he should show no signs of prejudice. (Oates, 1970, p. 24)

In 1970, most corporate expatriate workers were men on high incomes, sometimes accompanied by their families. Nowadays, a much more diverse group of people work internationally.

Given that it is absurd to expect all the qualities described by Oates, what sort of resilience should we seek? More importantly, as resilience is not static, how can resilience be built among staff working internationally?

Resilience has been defined as "the capacity to deal well with pressure" (Barrett & Martin, 2014, p. 165). People who work internationally are required to deal with pressures related to working in a different culture (and possibly language and climate), away from their usual support network, often in challenging circumstances. When there is a risk of insecurity, violence or natural disasters, resilience is especially vital.

Psychological research indicates that different factors contribute to resilience. We will discuss the SPECS model of resilience developed by Horsfall and Hawker (2019). SPECS is an acronym for the Spiritual, Physical, Emotional, Cognitive & creative, and Social & systemic aspects of resilience. Individuals may be more resilient in some of these aspects than others (and consider some more important than others). Their overall level of resilience will be a combination of these different factors.

DOI: 10.4324/9781003261971-3

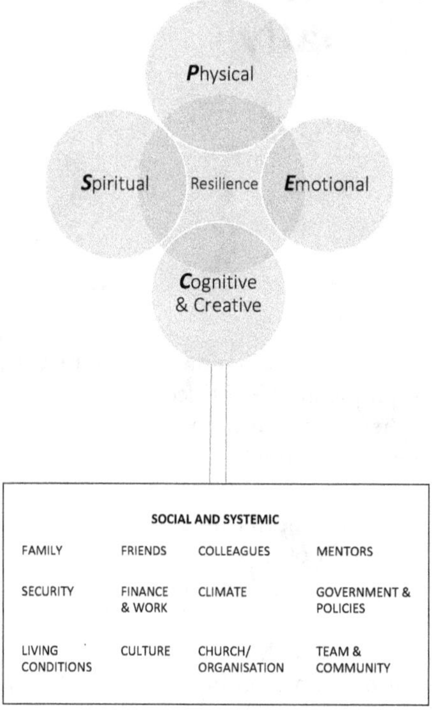

Figure 2.1 The SPECS model of resilience.

Figure 2.1 illustrates this model. The personal aspects of resilience (contained within an individual) are shown as petals on a flower. The social and systemic aspects are shown as the soil (or conditions) in which the flower grows. Just as a plant needs air, water, light and nutrients to be healthy, so humans need certain conditions around them in order to thrive.

We will discuss how to help international staff build resilience in each of these domains.

Building Spiritual Resilience

Spiritual aspects of resilience do not need to reflect a religious faith, although many international workers do have a faith (see chapter 7). Spiritual aspects of resilience include having a sense of meaning, hope and optimism, and gratitude. People are more able to endure hardship if they have a sense of meaning or think that they are doing something worthwhile (see Frankl, 2004). Humanitarian workers keep going during difficult times if they believe their efforts are worthwhile (Lovell, 1997). If they feel their efforts are pointless, they are likely to become disillusioned, cynical or burnt out. Teams can help maintain a sense of meaning by talking about the bigger picture, and sharing reports and outcomes of their work, especially to those who do not see the results themselves (e.g. staff working in offices in the background).

Not all international workers feel that their work is as fulfilling as that of humanitarian workers. However, many people who work internationally feel a sense of psychological richness due to the new experiences, unexpectedness, interest and change of perspective. This sense of psychological richness is associated with well-being and therefore with resilience (Young, 2021).

Another feature of resilience is having a sense of hope, or realistic optimism (Gillespie, Chaboyer, Wallis & Grimbeek, 2007). Hope can protect against anxiety (Bressan, Iacoponi, de Assis & Shergill, 2017). Optimism can lift mood and protect against depression. Team leaders can try to generate a sense of optimism during team meetings, reminding people of positive aspects of their situation instead of just focusing on the negatives. Being part of a community who share similar values or beliefs also helps build resilience, and so working in teams and communities, rather than alone, can be important.

Research indicates that people who practice gratitude regularly tend to be happier, healthier and more optimistic than those who do not. They also have more energy, better sleep and better relationships. In other words, practising gratitude enhances resilience (Emmons, 2007). Employers and team leaders can model gratitude to their teams.

> Jacob[1] attended a routine debriefing appointment at the end of a term of working overseas. He said he had a sense of vocation from an early age around being a doctor in a place where there were few medical facilities. As a student, he described it as a sense of "calling". He went with a charity to work in a hospital in central Africa. While he was there, there was a pandemic and a coup. Despite all the challenges (including oppressive heat and a shortage of staff and equipment), Jacob felt content. He believed that he was where he was meant to be and that he was making a positive difference. His sense of vocation helped him to keep going during difficult times. He also had a sense of optimism, that things would improve. He frequently wrote a list of things that he was grateful for and chose to focus on those rather the difficulties.

Building Physical Resilience

It is hard to be resilient when we feel tired, hungry, weak, ill, in pain or short of breath. In a disaster such as a fire, flood, an earthquake or a terrorist attack, physically resilient people have the strength and energy to survive for longer and can sometimes help themselves and others escape.

Behaviours which promote physical resilience include taking sufficient rest; exercising regularly; eating a healthy diet and practising good food hygiene;

drinking sufficient water; using sun protection; and avoiding excessive alcohol, nicotine or caffeine or harmful drugs (which may be low cost and easily available in the new location).

Many international workers are well educated and know the basic facts. In pre-departure briefings, workers can be given location-specific information about disease prevention (e.g. guidelines to reduce the risk of malaria, or food hygiene and water purification techniques).

In a book entitled *Emergency Sex (and Other Desperate Measures)*, three United Nations and Red Cross personnel wrote of their field experiences, noting it was not uncommon for disaster workers to have unprotected or otherwise risky sexual encounters which might be out of character and in response to stress, trauma or to cope with feeling low or lonely (Cain Postlewait & Thomson, 2006). This could have put them at risk of HIV infection. The term "sex-patriates" has been adopted to describe a small minority of expatriates who have numerous sexual partners while working internationally. In recent years, information has come to light about sexual behaviours of some development workers which go beyond risky into criminal behaviour, such as the abuse of children or taking advantage of vulnerable beneficiaries (see chapter 10, although there is reference to recent shocking cases in many of the chapters in this volume).

Education alone is rarely sufficient. High-risk behaviours (whether in terms of risky sex, excessive alcohol intake, drug use or not following security guidelines) are sometimes the result of high stress, and sometimes related to boredom. Employers should help build physical resilience by facilitating the practice of healthy behaviours, including strategies to reduce stress. For example, non-governmental organisation (NGO) workers in high-security settings are often entitled to leave the country every eight to ten weeks for a week of "rest and recuperation" (R & R) as described in the introduction to this volume. This is in addition to regular holidays. R & R provides time for stress levels to reduce in a context where the worker does not need to be on high alert. NGOs should have policies in place to ensure that R & R occurs and provide sufficient time and funds for travel. In addition, the workload should be reasonable, to allow for days off every week, and sufficient rest and sleep. There should be consideration of what the worker can do in free time.

> Sara attended an individual resilience briefing before being deployed to Darfur as a humanitarian worker. She asked for guidance on how to stay healthy while based in Darfur, where she would not have opportunities to exercise outdoors. Sara was helped to consider exercise opportunities which would be available in the restricted environment (e.g. using an aerobics DVD indoors; weight training using cans of food as weights; skipping with a rope). She also asked her NGO whether they might help to provide some gym equipment on the compound.

Table 2.1 Tips for good sleep

- Take some exercise during the day, as this is associated with better sleep at night.
- Avoid caffeine after early afternoon, including coffee, tea, caffeinated drinks and chocolate (as caffeine is a stimulant).
- Avoid looking at screens (such as phone screens, television and computer) for the hour before going to bed.
- Have a "wind down" routine before going to bed. This might include a relaxing bath or reading a novel, or some peaceful music.
- Some people find that the smell of lavender aids sleep. Others find that certain foods or drinks such as bananas, kiwi fruit, warm milk or camomile tea in the evening are helpful.
- Share any worries with someone or write them down, so that they don't keep going round and round in your head. Keep a pen and paper beside your bed so that you can write down anything you want to remember, without getting up.
- Try to concentrate on slow breathing, to relax yourself. Breathe in through your nose for four seconds, hold your breath for seven seconds, then exhale through your mouth for eight seconds. Repeat this until you fall asleep.
- If you cannot sleep because your brain is too active, try a mental activity such as counting down from 5,000 in threes. Do this while lying in bed with your eyes closed. Activities which are mentally tiring, dull and distract you from other thoughts should help you sleep.
- Do not check the time if you wake in the night as that is likely to wake you up more fully.

During the resilience briefing, Sara was encouraged to avoid overwork, and to ensure that she took at least one day off work each week to help reduce the risk of burnout. Her NGO offered a health check every six months and she was encouraged to take this up. When asked about any health problems, Sara disclosed that she struggled with sleep when she was anxious, as her mind tended to be buzzing. She was given techniques to help combat this (see Table 2.1).

When Sara was followed up two months after arriving in Darfur, she reported that she had been exercising regularly indoors as well as walking round and round the compound. She felt this was helping reduce her stress level. The counting technique was helping her get enough sleep. She was generally feeling well and was looking forward to an R & R break.

Building Emotional Resilience

Resilience does not mean never crying or feeling angry or upset. Resilient people can acknowledge their emotions and find healthy ways to deal with them. This might include talking to someone; writing about their experiences; exercising to reduce their sense of stress or anger; playing or listening to music which resonates with their feelings; using mindfulness or meditation; or finding other outlets. Resilient people may also seek opportunities to enhance positive emotions – allowing time for enjoyment, relaxation and laughter.

A resilience briefing prior to departure can help workers consider how they will stay emotionally healthy while working internationally. For example, what equipment should they take with them to ensure that they can use their coping resources (e.g. their musical instrument; an e-book reader to download books; games; craft materials). How will they achieve a healthy work–life balance?

During the resilience briefing, workers can be given the message that they are welcome to ask for help (or time off) when they need it. This is a sign of strength and resilience, not weakness.

Employers can help by encouraging an atmosphere where it is OK to ask for help, and by funding counselling or therapy when required, as well as noticing differences between individual staff with regard to help seeking (see also chapter 3):

> Kevin and Katie were two single colleagues who were both caught up in a violent robbery. Afterwards, they both had symptoms of trauma, including nightmares, being hypervigilant (very alert to potential danger), and wanting to avoid reminders of the incident.
>
> Kevin felt ashamed of his reaction, and told himself that he should be coping better, as he was a man and a humanitarian worker. He worried that he was overreacting and "going mad". He withdrew from other people as he did not want anyone to know what he was experiencing, and his symptoms got worse. He turned to alcohol to help him forget about his problems.
>
> Katie, on the other hand, asked for a debriefing. During this, the debriefer explained that her reactions were understandable given her experience and were likely to get better over time. The debriefer encouraged Katie to talk to people and seek support. Katie took some time off work to do things which helped her relax, including walking with friends. Within a couple of weeks, she felt much better and returned to work. Having talked with other people who had been robbed, she realised that robberies were common in this culture and foreigners were targeted, but that if she handed over her money, she was very unlikely to be hurt. She no longer felt anxious about being robbed. She took old credit cards and very little money with her, so that she had a purse she could hand over if she was robbed again. She felt stronger than ever, telling herself, "I coped with that experience, so I can probably cope with anything life throws at me here!"

Building Cognitive and Creative Resilience

Cognitive Resilience

The word "cognitive" refers to anything connected with thinking or conscious mental processes. One cognitive aspect of resilience is problem-solving. Good problem solvers think about possible solutions and evaluate the pros and cons of each action. They show flexibility in their thinking, being willing to consider different options. Poor problem solvers may feel trapped and that there is no way out of difficult circumstances. Poor problem-solving skills are associated with angry outbursts, feelings of hopelessness and suicide attempts (Cuijpers, Van Straten & Warmerdam, 2007).

Problem-solving can be learned as a structured process, involving the following steps: 1) define the problem, including who it is a problem for and what feelings it evokes; 2) brainstorm possible solutions, not ruling out any at this stage, even the most outlandish; 3) consider the pros and cons of each solution in turn; 4) make a shortlist of the best solutions; 5) try them out; 6) evaluate the outcome.

Staff working internationally can be helped by having people who go through the problem-solving process with them. This is especially useful when working in a foreign culture where the options may be unclear or unknown, and staff may be unfamiliar with culturally appropriate ways to deal with the problem. A cultural mentor might be able to help when thinking through the likely implications of different options.

Another way to help build cognitive resilience is to provide time and resources for continual professional development. Providing resources and time for courses, language study and individual reading is beneficial.

If a worker is struggling with depression, anxiety or other mental health issues, cognitive behavioural therapy (CBT) or another form of therapy might help build their coping strategies. CBT can help people challenge unhelpful thoughts.

Creativity

Being creative can also help international workers be resilient. Creative hobbies can help people relax and enjoy themselves and switch off from work – whether by baking, drawing, playing music, making crafts, doing DIY, writing, taking photographs, gardening or some other creative outlet.

Using the imagination can also boost our resilience (Lahad, Shacham & Ayalon, 2012). Daydreaming about a special event or holiday might help us feel better, even if it never happens.

Camilla Carr and Jon James were held hostage in Chechnya for 14 months (Carr & James, 2008). While in captivity, they problem-solved whether to try and escape. They decided it would be too risky. So, they problem-solved how to spend their time when they were kept in a small space with little to do. They decorated their room with dried orange peel, and they made games with whatever they could find. They also meditated and had an exercise routine. They refused to give up hope. This all helped them to cope well with the trauma. Since their release, they have helped train other workers in how to cope with abduction.

Building Social and Systemic Resilience

Our resilience is affected by our environment, including our support network, and the systems we are in (e.g. family, team, colleagues, organisation, community). Our environment may help protect us, or it may be a risk factor.

Social Support

A wide body of research indicates that support from friends and family members reduces the risk of developing mental health problems such as depression and post-traumatic stress disorder (Hobfoll et al., 2007; Brewin, Andrews & Valentine, 2000; Haglund, Nestadt, Cooper, Southwick & Charney, 2007). When international workers move to another country, they move away from a lot of that support. There can be a sense of loss and isolation. This is compounded by the fact that international workers often say goodbye to colleagues and friends in their new community, as expatriates move frequently. Resilience can be increased by helping people maintain some close relationships with supportive people, even if they can only speak remotely by internet or phone. However, individuals differ in their need for support. Some, especially those from more individualistic cultures, may be more concerned about having opportunities for time and space alone (for example, by not sharing a house) than having help with social contact.

Couples and families who move together may be able to create a sense of stability and security (although marriages can come under strain due to travel, and relationship therapy is sometimes needed).

Organisational Resilience

Companies which send workers to a new culture have a duty of care to look after them, including carrying out appropriate risk assessment and contingency planning (e.g. evacuation plans). Resilience can be increased by having good procedures for selection; matching the right people to the right posts (and building healthy teams with appropriate leadership); preparing and training workers for their role and location; providing a cultural mentor to help the worker integrate into the new culture; enabling work–life balance; offering support if there is a crisis or difficulties; and preparing for relocation (see Brooks et al., 2015). Organisations can help build resilience through having supportive policies.

Other Environmental Factors

Environmental factors which impact resilience include security; finance; climate; living conditions; cultural patterns; policies and government. It is usually not possible to change these, but it is important to consider them when selecting someone for an international post, and then to prepare the worker for these. Workers who come prepared practically (with the right equipment) and mentally (expecting the conditions) are likely to be a better "fit" for their role (see chapter 1) and be better able to cope with the stress of a new location.

> Keren went to Thailand to work with trafficked women. Keren had been sexually abused as a child, and had developed an eating disorder, which she had recovered from some years before going to Thailand. Listening to the stories of the trafficked women upset her as it reminded her of her own experiences. However, she found people in her new community very hospitable. In order to fit in and not feel lonely, she accepted meal invitations even though she struggled with fried food. When a Thai colleague told her, as a compliment, "You have gained weight", Keren relapsed into her eating disorder behaviours. She restricted what she ate and made herself sick after meals. She rapidly lost weight. When her manager noticed that she had been self-harming, she was sent back to her home country for treatment.

This situation might have been avoided if Keren had had a psychological resilience assessment before being accepted to work in Thailand. Many companies and charities now include such assessments, which include investigating any previous history of mental health problems. A history of mental health problems does not rule someone out of working internationally. However, if someone has such a history, it is helpful to consider whether there is a risk that they might relapse, and how to reduce that risk and manage any symptoms. Frank discussion with the employer/company about any reasonable adjustments or support that they might need is important, just as it is if someone has a physical illness or disability (Barrett, Hawker, Liu, Murphy & Prestage, 2018). If someone is taking regular medication, they should check in advance how they will be able to access this in their new location (and what its local name is). They should carry a supply in their hand luggage in case their checked luggage gets delayed or lost.

Keren might have been fine if she had been matched to a less emotionally demanding type of work and offered a mentor to help her think and talk about her experiences in the new culture.

Conclusion

Working far away from friends and family members, in an unfamiliar culture and often with unfamiliar equipment, bureaucracy and ways of working, requires psychological strength. Depending on their location, international workers may be at increased risk of accidents, robbery, violence, insecurity, natural disasters or other traumatic events. Resilience is needed if they are to stay and to thrive in their new location. This chapter has discussed different aspects of resilience and how they can be built.

Companies with good policies of recruitment, training, orientation and support help improve the systemic resilience of their employees.

A resilience briefing prior to departure is a good opportunity for workers to consider how they can build coping strategies when they are working internationally. We recommend that international workers complete a resilience plan (see Table 2.2) and review it regularly. This can include planning for regular times of R & R and holidays.

Resilience Plan

Table 2.2 Template for a resilience plan

Physical **Looking after my body**	1. 2. 3.
Emotional **Coping strategies to reduce stress**	1. 2. 3.
Cognitive and creative **Problem-solving, and creative activities**	1. 2. 3.
Social and systemic **Supportive relationships, and a healthy environment**	1. 2. 3.
Spiritual **Building meaning, hope, optimism and gratitude**	1. 2. 3.

Note

1   Names and details in the case studies have been changed to protect confidentiality.

References

Barrett, E., Hawker, D., Liu. P., Murphy, J., & Prestage, P. (2018). *International Citizen Service (ICS) and mental health: Exploring the relationship between international youth volunteering and mental health.* Retrieved from www.volunteerics.org/sites/defa ult/files/inline-files/18146_a4_ICS%20mental%20health%20summary_AW3.pdf

Barrett, R., & Martin, P. (2014). *Extreme: Why some people thrive at the limits.* Oxford: Oxford University Press.

Bressan, R.A., Iacoponi, E., Candido de Assis, J., & Shergill, S.S. (2017). Hope is a therapeutic tool. *British Medical Journal, 359,* j5469. https://doi.org/10.1136/ bmj.j5469

Brewin, C.R., Andrews, B., & Valentine, J.D. (2000). Meta analysis of risk factors for posttraumatic stress disorder in trauma exposed adults. *Journal of Consulting and Clinical Psychology, 68,* 748–766. https://doi.org/10.1037//0022-006x.68.5.748

Brooks, S.K., Dunn, R., Sage, C.A.M., Amlôt, R., Greenberg, N., & Rubin, G.J. (2015). Risk and resilience factors affecting the psychological wellbeing of individuals deployed in humanitarian relief roles after a disaster. *Journal of Mental Health, 24*(6), 385–413. https://doi.org/10.3109/09638237.2015.1057334

Cain, K., Postlewait, H., & Thomson, A. (2006). *Emergency sex (and other desperate measures).* London: Ebury Press.

Carr, C., & James, J. (2008). *The sky is always there.* Norwich: Canterbury Press.

Cuijpers,P., Van Straten, A., & Warmerdam, L. (2007). Problem solving therapies for depression: A meta-analysis. *European Psychiatry, 22,* 9–15. https://doi.org/10.1016/ j.eurpsy.2006.11.001

Emmons, R.A. (2007). *Thanks! How practicing gratitude can make you happier.* New York: Houghton Mifflin.

Frankl, V. (2004). *Man's search for meaning.* London: Rider.

Gillespie, B.M., Chaboyer, M., Wallis, M., & Grimbeek, P. (2007). Resilience in the operating room: Developing and testing of a resilience model. *Journal of Advanced Nursing, 59,* 427–438. https://doi.org/10.1111/j.1365-2648.2007.04340.x

Haglund, M.E.M., Nestadt, P.S., Cooper, N.S., Southwick S.M., & Charney, D.S. (2007). Psychobiological mechanisms of resilience: Relevance to prevention and treatment of stress-related psychopathology. *Development and Psychopathology, 19,* 889–920. https://doi.org/10.1017/s0954579407000430

Hobfoll, S.E., Watson, P., Bell, C.C., Bryant, R.A., Brymer, M.J., Friedman, M.J., Friedman, M., Gersons, B.P., de Jong, J.T., Layne, C.M., Maguen, S., Neria, Y., Norwood, A.E., Pynoos, R.S., Reissman, D., Ruzek, J.I., Shalev, A.Y., Solomon, Z., Steinberg, A.M., & Ursano, R.J. (2007). Five essential elements of immediate and mid-term mass trauma intervention: Empirical evidence. *Psychiatry, 70,* 283–315. https://doi.org/10.1521/psyc.2007.70.4.283

Horsfall, T., & Hawker, D. (2019). *Resilience in life and faith.* Abingdon, Oxon: BRF.

Lahad, M., Shacham, M., & Ayalon, O. (eds.) (2012). *The "BASIC PH" model of coping and resiliency.* London: Jessica Kingsley.

Lovell, D.M. (1997). *Psychological adjustment among returned overseas aid workers* [Unpublished doctoral thesis]. University of Wales, Bangor.

Oates, D. (1970). What it takes to work abroad. *International Management, 10,* 24–27.

Young, E. (2021). It's a good life: The role of "psychological richness". *The Psychologist*, November 2021, 22–23. https://digest.bps.org.uk/2021/09/14/weve-neglected-the-role-of-psychological-richness-when-considering-what-makes-a-good-life-study-argues/

Chapter 3

Searching for security

An attachment perspective on aid worker relationships

Mark Snelling

Ask any humanitarian aid worker what they find most challenging about the job and you will get a range of answers. Some will talk about the traumatic events that they have either witnessed or been involved in. Amidst this chronic exposure to suffering, you will also hear about the challenge of remaining motivated and compassionate in the face of overwhelming needs. A depressing truth is that many will not talk about humanitarian work at all, but point to struggles with management and the pressures of organisational politics and inter-agency competition (Brooks et al., 2015). You will also almost certainly hear many describe the impact of chronically long work hours and the ever looming menace of burnout.

After many hundreds of hours of counselling humanitarians, however, I feel that I can safely assert that a majority will, sooner or later, start talking about relationships. Whatever the issue that initially prompts them to seek therapy, including involvement in traumatic incidents, as has struck me again and again, aid workers will eventually want to explore relationship challenges. This was certainly the case for me in the personal therapy that I undertook after my own early career in the sector and I have seen it borne out in my own subsequent research (Snelling, 2018). And while some of these challenges have arisen as a consequence of working in aid, it cannot be overestimated how often people talk about patterns of relating that were put in place long before they entered the sector.

This chapter will therefore explore a phenomenon that I believe is widely recognised by those who work in the sector but is given little formal attention when it comes to recruitment, induction, training and support programmes. Put simply, while the itinerant, disruptive nature of international humanitarian work can certainly *cause* challenges for people wanting to maintain consistent, reliable relationships, it can also – on a much more unconscious level – seem to offer an almost uniquely powerful *solution* to personal relationship insecurities, which often have their roots in difficult early childhood experiences.

DOI: 10.4324/9781003261971-4

In order to explore this process, this chapter will be guided by *attachment theory*, a body of research and clinical practice aimed at understanding the dynamics of relationships pioneered by the British psychologist John Bowlby (1969, 1988) and his American-Canadian colleague Mary Ainsworth. Their monumental study of human development from birth to old age demonstrated conclusively that when we feel stressed, threatened or afraid, our first instinct is to seek physical and emotional closeness to a trusted other. Despite the value that Western culture continues to place on rugged independence, reinforced for aid workers by the distinctly *tough-guy macho culture* (Cockcroft-McKay & Eiroa-Orosa, 2021) of the sector, attachment theory shows us that meaningful and reliable contact with others represents our most fundamental strategy for both surviving and thriving in life. We are, first and foremost, a "social, relational and bonding species" (Johnson, 2019, p. 5). Bowlby and Ainsworth were also the first to systematically map the ways that the reliable presence of sensitive, available caregivers early in life sets up an enduring capacity to both manage one's own emotions internally, and establish and maintain secure relationships externally. Crucially, they showed that this security facilitates our capacity to go out into the world with a genuine sense of curiosity and exploration (Holmes, 2001), and, of obvious relevance for the humanitarian sector, that this openness to experience paves the way to offer meaningful care and support to others, without becoming distracted and sidelined by one's own unmet needs.

Where caregiving has been inconsistent, inadequate or absent, they found that people have an abiding sense of insecurity about how to manage their feelings and deal with the challenges of relating to others. The insecurely attached often carry a firm belief – borne of bitter and repeated experience – that it is risky, painful and fruitless to seek support from others. This struggle to cope with what can feel like a frightening and unpredictable world leaves people vulnerable to both depression and anxiety. It can also set up a lifelong quest to look for external sources of security that are perceived as more reliable than other people (Flores, 2012; Maté, 2018).

There is, of course, much about working in aid that can build a positive personal sense of doing worthwhile and beneficial work. However, when it comes to insecure attachment and the range of potential psychological challenges it presents, humanitarian work can offer powerful – and potentially much more problematic – solutions. It does this with a heady mix of constant novelty and stimulus, frequent travel, risky and exciting environments, a focus away from personal pain towards the needs of others, a sense of belonging to an exclusive and widely admired club, all accompanied by intense but often short-lived relationships.

This powerful combination of factors then exerts an addictive pull on workers, giving them a temporary sense of power and meaning whilst protecting them from potentially uncomfortable encounters with personal vulnerability and the risks of real intimacy. As such, humanitarian work can easily begin to manifest the three key defining aspects of any addiction (Miller et al., 2011). It is done regularly, repeatedly and habitually (in the form of constant and repeated postings). There is a compulsive quality that can appear beyond people's control; many aid workers speak of wanting to stop but find that they keep accepting missions, and it persists despite adverse consequences, including increasingly impoverished support structures when they get back to their home country.

As careers progress, this repeating cycle can become ever more avoidant and self-defeating, making it increasingly difficult to establish a sense of security and belonging. This, again like all addictions, traps people into repetitive and escalating attempts to meet unmet needs whilst almost guaranteeing that that goal of relational security remains out of reach (Flores, 2012). While this process will often lead to no more than personal unhappiness, it can take a far darker turn when the recipients of the aid cease to be viewed as whole people in need of understanding, empathy and meaningful help, but are turned into mere objects to be used in the continuing quest for personal gratification and fulfilment.

This does not, of course, mean that many people do not come to the sector with authentic and values-driven motivations to make the world a better place (Tassell & Flett, 2013; Eriksson et al., 2009). Nor does it ignore the reality that altruistic motives to help others will inevitably include elements of self-interest (Mikulincer Shaver, Gillath, & Nitzberg, 2005; Cialdini et al., 1987).

Attachment theory offers us a framework for understanding that anyone entering the sector carries their own particular way of relating to themselves and others, which will have significant implications for how well they cope with the many demands of the job. As such, it offers us a road map to assess which of two particular pathways we may be headed down: a *resilience pathway* (Bifulco & Thomas, 2012) that enables the person to find the support they need to cope with the stresses of the job (so that they can then offer meaningful support to the recipients of their aid); or a *risk pathway* (ibid.) with the capacity to draw them into repetitive and self-defeating ways of coping which could harm both themselves and those they are serving.

The good news from attachment theory is that insecure attachment styles are by no means set in stone. With the right kind of consistent support, insecure attachments can be transformed into healthier ways of relating, a process that has been dubbed *earned security* (Main, 1989, as cited in Hesse, 2016; Pearson Cohn, Cowan, & Cowan, 1994). Unfortunately, however, in my experience as a clinician, aid workers do not try to seek formal help until things have started to go wrong. Furthermore, despite the abundance of literature and the availability of therapists, aid workers often simply do not know where to look for support (Cockcroft-McKay & Eiroa-Orosa, 2021). As such, I would argue that if the sector were geared to proactively helping humanitarians ask important questions about their own relational patterns from recruitment onwards, they could build higher levels of personal resilience and an enhanced capacity to assess and respond to the needs of others, independently of their own desires and vulnerabilities. A focus on prevention rather than cure would also have significant implications for overall organisational resilience and effectiveness.

This chapter will aim to do the following: First I will consider the basics of attachment theory and how it can help us understand what a humanitarian on the resilience pathway might look like. That will be followed by an exploration of what the risk pathway looks like in the humanitarian field, particularly in the form of addictive and compulsive behaviours and the catastrophic results that can ensue. Finally, I would like to take the concept of *earned security* to look at the ways that humanitarians can be supported to maintain and enhance their capacity for secure relationships, altruistic empathy and levels of ongoing resilience. I will finish with some recommendations for the sector, including a call for greater supervisory support.

It is important to state at the outset that this chapter focuses on the experience of Western expatriate aid workers working in emergency settings and as such does not necessarily reflect the relational experiences of nationally hired staff, who work in their home countries, or the increasing numbers of non-Western expatriates who now deploy around the world. There is no doubt that the mental health of non-Western staff demands significantly more attention than it receives (Ager et al., 2012; Porter & Emmens, 2009). At the same time, it is safe to say that Western expatriates are often the source of many problems, especially in the way that they use or misuse the power that they wield over their non-Western colleagues and beneficiaries (Houldey, 2021). My focus here on Western expatriates is in no way intended to minimise or overlook the experience of other staff, but seeks to shed some much-needed light on how they might more effectively address the negative and harmful patterns of relating to which they may be prone.

To bring these arguments alive, I will describe three "composite" humanitarians to illustrate different attachment styles, whose stories I have based on sessions with clients, conversations with colleagues, interviews with research participants and my own personal experience. Details have been changed and new names assigned, but the content represents authentic voices and views from the frontlines of humanitarian work.

The Secure Humanitarian

Sally, as we'll call her, is an example of a securely attached humanitarian. She grew up with a sensitive and attentive mother and as a result internalised a core belief that she was valuable and lovable in her own right. Her parents' marriage was not perfect; indeed, she told me that they argued quite often, but they had a capacity to resolve disagreements with respectful and honest communication. They were also available and attentive whenever Sally was anxious, which enabled her to develop a capacity to acknowledge, validate and express a full range of her own emotions. This gave her a foundational sense of security that facilitated the development of a genuine sense of curiosity about the outside world as well as optimistic beliefs regarding her own capacity to go out into that world and explore. That wish to explore gave her an openness to new ideas and experiences, which eventually turned into a lifelong love of travel and she spoke of her travels with a deep sense of interest and engagement.

I met Sally when she sought trauma counselling after a particularly terrifying armed robbery, during which she was convinced that she was going to die. She felt understandably overwhelmed by the experience, but had not hesitated to reach out to close friends and to bolster that social support with professional help. This ability to express her needs and evoke responsiveness meant that she could draw on a reliable support network, populated by people whom she experienced as "accessible, responsive and engaged" (Johnson, 2019).

Over the course of our conversations, it was clear to me how Sally's essentially secure attachment style had instilled in her a conviction that obstacles can be overcome and that distress is something that can be managed (Mikulincer, Shaver, & Pereg, 2003). As she navigated this horrific experience, she showed a clear *expectation* that others would treat her with acceptance and positivity (Ainsworth, Blehar, Waters, & Wall, 1978). This enabled her to manage emotions by confidently seeking contact with trustworthy figures capable of supporting her (Mikulincer & Shaver, 2016).

Her sessions with me, combined with conversations with close friends and family, helped her process the initial shock and the accompanying powerful emotions. She spoke about her life in a linguistically coherent way, talking about both recent and childhood experiences with clarity and consistency, both indicators of attachment security (Holmes, 2001). As she stabilised, she was able to re-engage with her capacity for practical problem-solving (Mikulincer et al., 2003) working out how best to return to work and support her colleagues.

Sally worked as a hospital administrator and spoke movingly of her colleagues and the patients they served, even as she processed her own trauma. I got the sense that she was valued and appreciated by those around her, which did not surprise me given the level of attention and understanding she appeared able to offer them. Her openness to others here provided a particularly vivid example of Bowlby's observation that the stable psychological foundation of secure attachment also facilitates the development of an ability to empathetically focus on the needs of others without being overwhelmed by their suffering (Mikulincer et al., 2005). Securely attached people are able to access a genuine sense of altruism.

Noteworthy here is the fact that Sally's own traumatic experience had not obliterated an awareness of the needs of others. At the same time, however, she knew she had to devote some time to focus on her recovery and did not use the requirements of her job as a way of sidestepping the personal and painful work she needed to do with me. In reflecting on her life, it seemed to me that humanitarian work represented an excellent "fit" for her, combining as it did her love of exploration with her deeply held altruistic impulses. Sally showed a high degree of resilience, even in the face of trauma, and was eventually able to get back to her work in a way that was beneficial to herself and genuinely helpful to other people.

The Risk Pathway

Having looked at what secure attachment can look like on the humanitarian field, let's turn our attention to the insecure styles of relating and the difficulties that these can set up for aid workers.

Perhaps the single most significant contributor to insecure attachment is disruption of early interactions between mother and infant (Bowlby, 1951). This can happen in extreme ways, for instance by death, displacement, abuse or complete abandonment. However, the research has also shown that much subtler disruptions can also have significant impacts. Ainsworth and her colleagues observed that children respond to these disruptions in different ways. If the mother is very inconsistent, sometimes available sometimes not, children can develop what she called an *anxious* attachment style (1978), characterised primarily by clinging to the caregiver in a bid to minimise the frightening sense of unpredictability (Holmes, 2001). A second category is what Ainsworth called *avoidant attachment* (Ainsworth, Blehar, Waters, & Wall, 1978), which is likely to develop when the caregiver is more consistently absent, rejecting or preoccupied for whatever reason (e.g. their own stress, depression, obsession with work). Mothers of avoidant children can often be very loving in their manner, but consistently fail to fully "get" what is going on for the child. In response, avoidant children achieve a sense of safety by essentially deactivating their needs in a bid to avoid the continual disappointment and exposure to what feels like rejection.

In adult life, those with an anxious style respond to stress by clinging to others and making sure they are not left alone. They can present as jealous and angry, but also passive and fearful (Holmes, 2001). Avoidant people tend to minimise their need for other people, maximise self-reliance and can be dismissive of relationships and blaming of others (Shrivastava & Burianova, 2014). It is important to note, however, that avoidant children and adults only *look* calm and can in fact be experiencing high levels of attachment distress, but on more suppressed or even unconscious levels (Johnson, 2019).[1]

The Avoidant Humanitarian

Having met our secure humanitarian, Sally, let me introduce you to Tim, who presents with many of the hallmarks of avoidant attachment, and Jane, who is by her own admission highly anxious.

Tim contacted me for therapy whilst still on mission in a central African country. When I asked him what he was wanting to address in our sessions, it was immediately clear that he did not seem completely sure, a marked contrast with Sally's clarity and coherence. Speaking in a flat and distant voice, he told me that he felt lost, but couldn't expand on that idea. When I asked him who he usually turned to for support, he told me he had a girlfriend and parents back in the UK, but often found that he "couldn't be bothered" to speak to them. He knew he wanted to be independent and autonomous but could also see that on some level he wanted to be in a relationship. He just couldn't see how to put these two impulses together. Again, the contrast is clear with Sally's secure attachment, which enabled her to exercise autonomy when exploring whilst also able to return to dependable relationships when needed. Tim, on the other hand, worried that investing in the relationship he longed for would, by definition, erode and compromise the independence that he felt he needed. In our early sessions, he spoke with horror of the thought of having to "settle down", which he feared could bore him quite literally to death.

It was challenging to explore his early life because he said he didn't have many memories of growing up, which can in itself be a sign that conscious awareness of difficult memories has been suppressed. As we explored his childhood, a picture emerged of a mother who was overwhelmed by the demands of work and family life and quite unequipped to attend to the emotional needs of her children. On the occasions that he remembers needing her, such as when he was badly bullied at school, he recalls her responding with irritation at his interruptions. He was frequently physically unwell, but again could offer no recollection of being cared for and comforted. Over time then, experience taught him that comfort and consolation were not available, so he progressively shut down his own needs and feelings.

He remembered that his life changed during his year off between school and university when he began travelling, and it is here that we began to see how the humanitarian life became an effective solution to the emotional challenges of a bleak and lonely childhood. Although he was not able to identify anything particular that he enjoyed about the countries he visited, he did seem to find considerable relief in the experience of moving from one place to another. He even talked about having a competition with a friend to see who had visited more countries and to this day kept a running tally every time he went somewhere new. Having started with gap year travels, Tim quickly found his way to a career that enabled this high-transition lifestyle and never looked back.

Where Sally's openness to exploration paved the way for a sense of interest and curiosity, Tim seemed to crave the stimulus of constant novelty, but almost for its own sake. And while Sally spoke of her travels as enriching and rewarding, Tim told me that no matter how many times he moved, he still couldn't quite shake off feelings of apathy and isolation. This, I felt, offered a clear example of Ainsworth's startling conclusion about avoidant babies

(1978), namely that in order to protect themselves from the pain of separation, they appeared entirely to sacrifice connection in favour of distraction. Put differently, she observed that they would keep looking for new toys to play with, not as a creative act of exploration but as a way of avoiding contact with a mother whom they assumed was going to be unreliable and rejecting.

Tim certainly had some awareness of his compulsive need for frequent relocation and, over time, we began to understand his wanderlust as something that operated very much like an addiction. In fact, we identified a variety of addictive tendencies. Alongside the compulsion to keep moving geographically, he also described traits which many aid workers would recognise as those of an *adrenaline junkie*.[2] He was honest with me about the excitement he felt in areas of intense armed conflict, even talking about the relief he felt sometimes when arriving back from leave and first seeing armed military patrols.

Alongside the brain's dopamine systems, there is another system involving what are known as endogenous opioids, the most commonly known of which are endorphins. When the body is filled with adrenaline, it releases endorphins that act as powerful natural painkillers. Ainsworth, Blehar, Waters, and Wall (1978) have demonstrated that repeated exposure to trauma releases endogenous opioids in the human body that provide soothing relief from anxiety. Although the term "junkie" is obviously unfair and pejorative, Naparstek (as cited by Thomas, 2016) has argued that individuals can indeed become hooked on their own biochemical responses to trauma, setting up patterns of behaviour that act like any other addiction.

Yet another behaviour that Tim found regrettable but in his view almost unavoidable, was his tendency towards sexual promiscuity. Even though he expressed contentment with his girlfriend back in the UK, he often ended up spending the night with women. He told me that he did not do this because he found the sexual experience particularly exciting. He did, however, speak of a need for contact. As we are seeing, a basic premise of addiction is that it is an attempt to compensate for attachment deficits. As such, the goal is often comfort and contact, not pleasure (Khantzian, 2014).[3]

Tim had found a variety of ways to manage the attachment wounds that he carried. By essentially medicating himself, he had learned to manufacture a sense of self-sufficiency that helped him feel powerful and special, whilst anaesthetising the pain of everyday life. However, as with all addictive processes, the rewards had diminished over time. The novelty was wearing off; the "hit" of dopamine and adrenalin were wearing off more quickly, and Tim was finding himself sinking into what felt like isolation and depression. Although he was still functioning at work, the sense of "gnawing emptiness" (Flores, 2012, p. 11) was beginning to make him seriously question how much longer he would be able to sustain this lifestyle before having some kind of breakdown.

Something that often felt disturbing in Tim's narrative was his marked difficulty in accessing feelings of empathy, either in the form of compassion for his own plight or in relation to the emotional hurt he was inflicting on his girlfriend and other abandoned partners. He also often talked in quite cynical and disparaging terms about the people who were receiving the aid his organisation was distributing. Early research into altruism (Batson, 1991) has shown that the self-focused worry of personal distress interferes significantly with a capacity for effective helping. Subsequent work supports this idea that attachment insecurity significantly limits people's inner resources to attend empathetically to others. This loss of empathy can, of course, also take a much darker turn.

Although unfortunate and self-defeating, I never detected any behaviour on Tim's part that I would describe as abusive. But it is important not to overlook the ugly fact that some aid workers have engaged in long-standing patterns of sexual exploitation and abuse (Alexander & Stoddard, 2021), including recent scandals in Haiti (Dodds, 2017; O'Neill, 2018). It of course goes without saying that not everyone with attachment difficulties becomes an abuser, and abuse cannot be exclusively explained away by attachment difficulties. But it is definitely worth saying that unsatisfactory early attachments lead to chronic loneliness, which the evidence clearly shows can set the stage for aggression, self-serving behaviours and an inability to empathise with other people's distress, all of which are consistently observed features of sex offending (Marshall, 1993). It is not difficult to see how putting people with disturbed and unresolved interpersonal issues into powerful and often unmonitored positions of power with vulnerable people becomes a disaster waiting to happen.

The Anxious Humanitarian

Having considered the experiences of an avoidantly attached aid worker, we now turn our attention to what can happen when someone with an anxious attachment style chooses to work in the sector.

Jane presented for counselling with what she described as severe burnout. She was still posted overseas and was working in a Middle Eastern country as an emergency response coordinator. She reported several textbook symptoms of burnout, including emotional and physical exhaustion and a sense of failure (Maslach & Leiter, 2016). She was most concerned about her deep feelings of cynicism about the whole humanitarian project, and most distressing of all, she realised that she had almost completely lost any sense of empathy for the suffering of the people she was supposedly there to help.

Unlike Tim, who spoke about everything with a tone of ironic detachment, Jane was visibly much more distressed and spoke in much more emotionally laden language. Her father had been a diplomat and she had grown up in several different countries, moving between the UK and his overseas postings. She spoke with some pride of her identity as a so-called Third Culture Kid (see chapter 5 and 11), a term first coined in the 1950s to describe the children of expatriate workers, including diplomats, missionaries, engineers and military personnel. While there are documented benefits to being a TCK, including an expanded world view and a high degree of adaptability, studies have also shown developmental challenges caused by repeated separations and multiple losses (Useem & Downie, 1976). Despite clinging to the TCK identity, Jane often spoke of feeling unsure about "who she was" and certainly could not say with certainty where "home" was for her. In attachment terms, she lacked a secure base both in terms of a literal place and of an internal sense of stability. Compounding her attachment challenges, her mother had been an unstable and unpredictable presence, veering between expressions of tenderness one moment and explosive outbursts of criticising anger the next.

As many anxiously attached children do, Jane coped with this precarious environment by clinging to her mother to feel less at the mercy of her inconsistency (Holmes, 2001). She also worked hard to please in any way she could in a bid to pre-empt her mother's frequent attacks. This extended to school, where she studied extremely hard and frequently scored top marks. She did less well at university, where her studies were somewhat compromised by her full embrace of a party lifestyle. Her relationship history was patchy because, as she explained, she felt she "scared off" potential partners with her intense need for attention and reassurance.

Interested as she was in international matters, but reluctant to follow in her father's footsteps, Jane did a master's degree in international development and found her way onto the employment roster of a major aid agency. She described her first mission overseas in glowing terms, telling me that she felt she had found her "true tribe". Many humanitarians speak of the rapid formation of what feel like strong, deep relationships under the often adverse conditions of field life, frequently fuelled by a distinctly gallows humour, to say nothing of copious amounts of alcohol. Looking back, Jane could see that the experience felt very much like a secure base after years of feeling alone and anxious. But she could also see how effective those early career years were in quashing anything that looked like uncomfortable emotions. "Feeling lonely? Grab a drink, grab a man", was one of her more memorable sayings, echoing the same compulsive tendency reported by Tim.

Where Tim reported an absence of empathy for those around him, including beneficiaries, Jane on the other hand reported intense and preoccupying thoughts and feelings about the struggles of those her organisation was seeking to help. She spoke passionately about global inequities and social justice, yet regularly struggled to articulate her own fears and needs. Whenever I attempted to engage her in reflection on her own emotional wounds, she would quickly reference the sufferings of the beneficiaries as clearly worse than anything she was going through. Viewed from the perspective of material deprivation, we noted that that was certainly true. But we also explored what a powerful protection that argument had become against any real encounter with her own difficulties.

So where Sally was able to engage with the needs of beneficiaries motivated by a sense of authentic care, Jane seemed vulnerable to something that Bowlby (1979) termed *compulsive caregiving*, always focusing on the welfare of others as a way of minimising and avoiding overwhelming personal feelings and needs (Tolmacz, 2010). Barbanell (2006) has gone so far as to name a whole new diagnosis that he calls *caretaker personality disorder*. This, he suggests, is driven by a compulsive need to be needed which conceals profound fears of abandonment and loneliness. Sufferers, he says, are relentlessly over-responsible, frequently taking on more than they can handle. At the same time, they repress their own needs for joy, pleasure and intimacy and are left with emotional exhaustion, emptiness and loneliness. At its worst, this can begin to look like a subtle form of masochistic self-harm, where some form of stability and sense of control is established by essentially annihilating one's own needs (Holtzman & Kulish, 2012).

Just as Tim began to experience significantly diminishing rewards over time, Jane reported feeling increasingly exhausted and burned out as the years went by. Although intense, she said that the relationships forged in the field had begun to feel increasingly shallow. Realising that she had effectively put her "personal life on hold" for much of her adult life, she said that friends advised her to put down roots somewhere in order to try and meet someone. Although she longed for that stability, she also saw this as a terrifying, high-stakes gamble in which she might potentially give up the – albeit fading – benefits of her current lifestyle but then end up not meeting anyone.

As noted, her symptoms of burnout were also accompanied by an increasing loss of empathy for those she had poured so much into helping. This sense of *compassion fatigue* (Figley, 1995) came to a head on a visit to a refugee camp where she remembered interviewing a man who had been separated from his family, did not know where they were, and was suffering from HIV without access to the drugs he desperately needed. Jane recalled vividly thinking that she simply could not find anything within herself to care about this man's desperate plight. She had nothing left to give. In attachment terms, burnout and compassion fatigue are overlapping concepts, but both have been associated with poor social support (Adams, Boscarino, & Figley, 2006) and Jane just did not have the relational resources to sustain her any further.

Finding Security ... and Keeping It

Having read thus far, you might be tempted towards a certain pessimism about the prospects for Tim and Jane, and if you recognise any of your own story in their experiences, you might be feeling some of that about what the future holds for you. Sally, our secure humanitarian, might seem to have it all sewn up, we might say, but what hope is there for the rest of us? Attachment theory has indeed been criticised for its perceived determinism (Diamond & Kotov, 2003, as cited in Cortazar & Herreros, 2010), telling us that once our patterns have been established by our early environment, we are effectively condemned to act them out over and over again for the rest of our lives.

Bowlby himself, however, thought otherwise (1988) and insisted that relationships with important people throughout life can significantly update insecure attachment models. In the years since, attachment research has shown clearly that our models are much more fluid than was initially believed, especially as a result of new experiences (Johnson, 2019), and as mentioned above, the concept of *earned security* reflects that some people who start life in very adverse insecure circumstances, characterised by separation and loss, are able to find consistent and reliable relationships later in life. For some, this can be through individual therapy. Indeed, the research evidence from thousands of studies on the effectiveness of psychotherapy is now pretty much unanimous that it is the quality and depth of the therapeutic relationship that is the most important predictor of significant change (Mearns & Cooper, 2005).

The evidence is also clear that it is not just therapy and marriage that can provide the protected space needed to establish and grow a sense of security. Secure relationships of pretty much any kind offer a safe haven in which this work can be done (Pearson et al., 1994). Put simply, "trusting relationships and communication have the ability to heal the mind" (Guina, 2016, p. 235). This includes trusted friendship circles, peer support groups and faith communities. With reference to the latter, regular participation in religious services has been widely demonstrated to promote social cohesion (Haidt, 2012; Houldey, 2021). Building on the spiritual dimensions of attachment, researchers have even looked at the relationship with God himself as a foundational element of security and resilience for many people (Birkett, 2015; Johnson & Sanderfer, 2016; Leman et al., 2018 and further discussed in chapter 7, this volume).

Back in the world of work, many helping professions such as counselling, nursing and social work build secure structures for their practitioners with the use of individual and group supervision, regarded universally in those professions as essential to good practice. Regularly meeting with someone to discuss work-related challenges provides an opportunity to reflect on motives, unmet needs and personal and professional dilemmas (Hawkins & Shohet, 2012). Strangely, this practice is missing in humanitarian aid (Fechter, 2012), leaving many aid workers with the sense that they have to work it all out for themselves (Snelling, 2018).

In finding a way forwards, therefore, all three of our humanitarians realised in different ways that access to consistent and ongoing contact with a known support figure was going to be key. Sally had been fortunate to experience what has been called *continuous-security* (Pearson et al., 1994) in her life, but she had enough awareness to understand that this was something that needed to be intentionally maintained. Once we had completed our processing of her traumatic experience, she contracted with me that we would speak twice a year so that she could evaluate how she was doing. She was particularly keen on making sure that she would be able to know when she had reached her limits in terms of life on the front lines. After another couple of years, she realised that she was beginning to feel increasingly weary and isolated, and we talked through a timetable for her return to the UK. She was able to secure a job working at her organisation's headquarters, which she felt excited about. After her return, we talked a couple more times as she reconnected with old friends and adjusted to the so-called *reverse culture shock* of life in the UK after so many years away.

For Tim and Jane, the road to earned security was somewhat more challenging and in their different ways the challenge continues, though both made a good start. Tim had first contacted me knowing that he felt unhappy with life but not at all sure why. Over the course of our sessions, he was able to use the space with me to begin to identify the reasons behind his need to shut down his feelings. This then enabled him to make contact with the previously suppressed feelings of loneliness and longing and to take the risk of acknowledging his very real needs for connection and contact. Over the months that we met, he reported increasing feelings of tenderness and affection towards his girlfriend, which culminated in a decision to relocate to the city where she lived and begin to build a life together. Instead of speaking about her as no more than a threat to his perceived freedom and independence, he began to speak very movingly about the sense of security that he felt with her and the hope that he had for their future life together. In terms of his attachment style, there was no doubt that he still evidenced some insecurity. He was, for instance, still very anxious about the prospect of having children. But he showed all the signs of having moved from a very avoidant style to something more mildly withdrawn, which some researchers have shown can actually be adaptive and beneficial to levels of coping (Bifulco & Thomas, 2012).

Jane was also able to use the regular structure of our sessions to consider how driven she had been to use her career to try and construct a solid sense of identity and self-worth. Although it was sad to acknowledge, she was able to see how many of the relationships she had formed in the field were based on intensity far more than by enduring commitment. Having said that, she was able to see which of her friends in the field had shown themselves to be reliable and trustworthy, and was able to devote her energies to investing in them. She was also able to face up to the deep grief that she felt in relation to the many losses and missed opportunities that she had experienced in her life. But allowing herself to experience and mourn these losses in a safe space eventually freed her up to look ahead to the life ahead of her.

She made the decision to relocate to her home country, where she bought a flat and started to put down roots. She continued to work in the humanitarian space, but found a job that required a couple of field trips every year as opposed to constant travel, which she found interesting and rewarding. Fascinatingly, she also reported a significant shift in how she felt about beneficiaries on these trips. Having previously felt overwhelmed and burned out by the limitless needs of the populations around her, she told me that she had started feeling much more connected to the individuals that she met, and felt motivated by a genuine concern for their welfare rather than a more self-interested need to be needed. In terms of intimate relationships, she cautiously began dating again, but told me that she was much quicker to spot people who she could see were not going to be good to her. She also noted that she felt much less cynical about the overall humanitarian project and felt able to celebrate "amazing people doing amazing things". What had once been an *obsessive passion* (Tassell & Flett, 2013), driven by a compulsive need for social acceptance and self-esteem, had become a *harmonious* one (ibid.), representing a freely chosen desire to work in synchrony with her own personal values. As our therapeutic work came to an end, she found an older colleague whom she asked to mentor her, further bolstering her sense of relational stability and a reliable secure base where legitimate needs could be heard and understood.

Conclusion

Attachment theory has been described, quite accurately, as a "theory of threat management" (Rheem, 2017). When we are faced with something that is unusual, threatening or frightening, what do we then do? Do we detach and shut down? Do we fall into panic and anxiety? Or are we able to recognise our in-built need for support and comfort, which then enables us to access the relational resources that we need to successfully navigate the challenge before us?

Aid workers live their lives in high-transition, high-pressure and high-risk environments, so if anyone would need to be able to draw on the latter strategy, it would surely be them. As such, we can therefore confidently view attachment as a theory of resilience. The more we are able to resource ourselves securely, the more we are able to deal with adversity, the more effective and efficient we become in handling hostile environments.

What I also hope to have demonstrated is that attachment is also profoundly a theory of motivation. If I feel constantly insecure, afraid or angry on the inside (even if I am not fully aware of it), I am likely to make decisions that are geared towards protecting myself from potentially unbearable and overwhelming feelings. If on the other hand, I feel secure and adequately supported, confident that I can get the help I need when difficulties arise, I am then able to go out into the world genuinely freed to engage in understanding and supporting other people.

Anyone who has been in the humanitarian world for any length of time will know that aid work is powerful stuff. They will know that it can be a force for enormous and life-saving good, but they will also be painfully aware of how much damage ends up getting done both to the people who work in it and to the people who are supposedly getting helped. I trust that I have shown that an enhanced focus on the attachment fears, needs and longings of aid workers could have a significant impact on addressing this massive but often unaddressed problem.

Recommendations

For Individual Humanitarians:

- Take some time to reflect on your attachment history. Helpful questions include:
  - Who did I turn to as a child when I felt sad or afraid?
  - Was I able to express what I was feeling and did I feel understood?
  - What message did I learn from my family about emotions and vulnerability? What about conflict and disagreement at home?
  - Did I feel valued simply for who I was, or did I feel that I had to earn approval?
  - If no one felt safe or available, how did I comfort myself?
- Take some time to reflect on your relational patterns in the present. Helpful questions include:
  - When I feel anxious or afraid, do I feel that others are available and interested in me OR do I isolate and pull away from others OR do I work hard to maintain constant contact?
  - Do I feel that people close to me are reliable and trustworthy?
  - Do I allow myself to rely on others, or do I need to feel that I am solving problems on my own?
  - Do I find it hard to get close to people and, if so, what blocks me from doing so?
  - Are there any particular experiences in relationships that I feel I have over and over again (e.g. feeling left out, rejected, criticised)?
  - Do I use any substance (e.g. drugs, alcohol, medication) or behaviour (e.g. sex, travel, exercise, helping others) to manage my emotions?
- Ask a close friend or relative to talk to you about when they feel close to you and when they feel distant from you. What is your contribution at those times?
- As a result of your reflections, if you feel that you are carrying unresolved hurt from your childhood, be proactive about talking through this with a friend, relative or a therapist. (In cases of severe trauma, it can be wise to seek professional support.)
- Carefully consider whom you want to maintain contact with before, during and after missions and be proactive about maintaining those relationships.
- Consider finding a therapist whom you can check in with on a regular basis to assess levels of resilience and psychological health.

For Organisations, the Following Practical Recommendations for the Sector Are Offered (Snelling, 2018):

- Greater emphasis during recruitment on the exploration of applicants' motives for entering/continuing in the sector, with particular attention paid to coherence and consistency of internally generated values, motives and meaning.
- More detailed psychological assessment following recruitment, paying particular attention to attachment styles including early relational trauma, so that targeted recommendations can be made for those presenting with patterns of relating likely to interfere with resilience.
- Structured psycho-education at induction on the relationship between attachment and resilience, as well as careful consideration of the relational costs of aid work.
- Continuity of contact, so that the same therapist who undertook initial assessments is available for ongoing supportive counselling sessions or critical incident support.
- Annual psychological assessments designed to review levels of resilience and coping, again with the same therapist who conducted the pre-assignment assessment where possible.
- Regular individual or group supervision/staff support groups facilitated by external consultants or trained senior colleagues.
- Assessment with senior management of employment rosters to allow workers enough time out of the field to build a secure home base.
- Regular facilitated workshops/retreats both at headquarters and in the field, where workers can reflect in a secure and protected space on the impact of the work, share relational dilemmas, explore possible ways forward and create robust peer support networks.
- Seminars for senior management teams, explaining and exploring the impact of individual anxiety on wider organisational dynamics in order to make the case for more robust staff care structures.

For Psychological Therapists Working with Humanitarians:

- Take a full attachment history, paying close attention to presence or lack of significant attachment figures in childhood (see questions above) as well as previous and current relationships.
- Help clients locate and describe core negative beliefs about themselves (e.g. I am unlovable) along with their key representations of others (e.g. preoccupied, uncaring, rejecting) (Lemma, Target, & Fonagy, 2011).
- Track and collaboratively name the patterns of relational interaction both within your client and in their relationships with others (Johnson & Campbell, 2022).
- Assess the cost of negative patterns (Lemma, Target, & Fonagy, 2011)

- Support clients to slow down and access previously disavowed emotions and parts of self (Johnson & Campbell, 2022).
- Having recognised repetitive and unproductive relational patterns, help clients reflect on taking the risk of finding new and creative ways of meeting attachment needs.

Notes

1 A small percentage of people, mainly those who have suffered traumatic childhoods, will display what is known as *disorganised attachment*, which leaves them unable to choose any particular strategy for dealing with relational difficulties. This in turn drives them into sending out confusing and chaotic signals involving both clinging and rejecting behaviours (Fear, 2017).
2 While this term has become widely used slang, it is actually clinically quite accurate.
3 Recent studies have indicated physiological differences suggesting that sexually compulsive people are not able to fully regulate levels of the "love hormone" oxytocin (Bostrom et al., 2020).

References

Adams, R.E., Boscarino, J.A., & Figley, C.R. (2006). Compassion fatigue and psychological distress among social workers: A validation study. *American Journal of Orthopsychiatry, 76*(1), 103–108. https://doi.org/10.1037/0002-9432.76.1.103

Ager, A., Pasha, E., Yu, G., Duke, T., Eriksson, C., & Cardozo, B.L. (2012) Stress, mental health, and burnout in national humanitarian aid workers in Gulu, northern Uganda. *Journal of Traumatic Stress, 25*(6), 713–20. https://doi.org/10.1002/jts.21764

Ainsworth, M.D., Blehar, M.C., Waters, E., & Wall, S. (1978). *Patterns of attachment: A psychological study of the strange situation*. Hillsdale, NJ: Erlbaum.

Alexander, J., & Stoddard, H. (2021). Then and now: 25 years of sexual exploitation and abuse. *The New Humanitarian*. www.thenewhumanitarian.org/feature/2021/2/11/25-years-of-sexual-exploitation-and-abuse

Barbanell, L. (2006). *Removing the mask of kindness: Diagnosis and treatment of the caretaker personality disorder*. Plymouth, UK: Jason Aronson.

Batson, C.D., Batson, J.G., Slingsby, J.K., Harrell, K.L., Peekna, H.M., & Todd, R.M. (1991). Empathic joy and the empathy-altruism hypothesis. *Journal of Personality and Social Psychology, 61*(3), 413–426. https://doi.org/10.1037/0022-3514.61.3.413

Bifulco, A., & Thomas, G. (2012) *Understanding adult attachment in family relationships: Research, assessment and intervention*. London: Routledge.

Birkett, K. (2015). *Resilience: A spiritual project*. Oxford: The Latimer Trust.

Bostrom, A., Chatzittofis, A., Ciuculete, D., Flanagan, J., Krattinger, R., Bandstein, M., Mwinyi, J., Kullak-Ublick, G., Oberg, K., Arver, S., Schioth, H., & Jokinen, J. (2020). Hypermethylation-associated downregulation of microRNA-4456 in hypersexual disorder with putative influence on oxytocin signalling: A DNA methylation analysis of miRNA genes. *Epigenetics, 15*(1–2), 145–160. https://doi.org/10.1080/15592294.2019.1656157

Bowlby, J. (1951). Maternal care and mental health. *Bulletin of the World Health Organization, 3*, 355–533.

Bowlby, J. (1969). *Attachment and loss* (Vol. 1: *Attachment*). London: Hogarth Press.

Bowlby, J. (1979). *The making and breaking of affectional bonds*. Abingdon, Oxon: Tavistock/Routledge.

Bowlby, J. (1988). *A secure base: Clinical applications of attachment theory*. Abingdon, Oxon: Routledge.

Brooks, S.K., Dunn, R., Sage, C.A.M., Amlôt, R., Greenberg, N., & Rubin, G.J. (2015). Risk and resilience factors affecting the psychological wellbeing of individuals deployed in humanitarian relief roles after a disaster. *Journal of Mental Health, 24*(6), 385–413. https://doi.org/10.3109/09638237.2015.1057334

Cialdini, R.B., Schaller, M., Houlihan, D., Arps, K., Fultz, J., & Beaman, A.L. (1987). Empathy-based helping: Is it selflessly or selfishly motivated? *Journal of Personality and Social Psychology, 52*(4), 749–758. https://doi.org/10.1037//0022-3514.52.4.749

Cockcroft-McKay, C., & Eiroa-Orosa, F.J. (2021). Barriers to accessing psychosocial support for humanitarian aid workers: a mixed methods inquiry. *Disasters, 45*, 762–796. https://doi.org/10.1111/disa.12449

Cortazar, A., & Herreros, F. (2010). Early attachment relationships and the early childhood curriculum. *Contemporary Issues in Early Childhood, 11*(2), 192–202. https://doi.org/10.2304%2Fciec.2010.11.2.192

Diamond, D., & Kotov, K.M. (2003) The representational world of the mother in attachment and psychoanalytic theory: a review and critique, in D. Mendell & P. Turrini (Eds.), *The inner world of the mother* (pp. 117–147). Madison: Psychosocial Press.

Dodds, P. (2017, April 14). UN peacekeepers in Haiti implicated in child sex ring. www.independent.co.uk/news/world/americas/un-haiti-peacekeepers-child-sex-ring-sri-lankan-underage-girls-boys-teenage-a7681966.html

Eriksson, C.B., Bjorck, J.P., Larson, L.C., Walling, S.M., Trice, G.A., Fawcett, J., Abernethy, A. D., & Foy, D.W. (2009). (2009). Social support, organisational support, and religious support in relation to burnout in expatriate humanitarian aid workers. *Mental Health, Religion and Culture, 12*, 671–686.

Fear, R. (2017). *Attachment theory: Working towards learned security*. Abingdon, Oxon: Routledge.

Fechter, A.M. (2012). The personal and the professional: Aid workers' relationships and values in the development process. *Third World Quarterly, 33*(8), 1387–1404. https://doi.org/10.1080/01436597.2012.698104

Figley, C. (1995). Compassion fatigue as secondary traumatic stress disorder: An overview. In C. Figley (Ed.) *Compassion fatigue: Coping with secondary traumatic stress disorder in those who treat the traumatized* (pp. 1–20). New York: Brunner-Routledge.

Flores, P.J. (2012). *Addiction as an attachment disorder*. Plymouth: Jason Aronson.

Guina, J. (2016). The talking cure of avoidant personality disorder: Remission through earned-secure attachment. *American Journal of Psychotherapy, 70*(3), 233–250. https://doi.org/10.1176/appi.psychotherapy.2016.70.3.233

Haidt, J. (2012). *The righteous mind: Why good people are divided by politics and religion*. London: Allen Lane.

Hawkins, P., & Shohet, R. (2012). *Supervision in the helping professions* (4th ed.). Maidenhead: Open University Press.

Hesse, E. (2016). The adult attachment interview: Protocol, method of analysis, and selected empirical studies: 1985–2015. In J. Cassidy & P. Shaver, P. (Eds.) (pp. 553–597). *Handbook of attachment: Theory, research and clinical applications.* New York: Guilford Press.

Holmes, J (2001). *The search for the secure base: Attachment theory and psychotherapy.* London: Brunner/Routledge.

Holtzman, D., & Kulish, N. (2012). *The clinical problem of masochism.* Lanham, MD: Jason Aronson.

Houldey, G. (2021). *The vulnerable humanitarian: Ending burnout culture in the aid sector.* Abingdon, Oxon: Routledge.

Johnson, S. (2019). *Attachment theory in practice: Emotionally Focused Therapy (EFT) with individuals, couples and families.* New York: Guilford Press.

Johnson, S., & Campbell, T.L., (2022). *A primer for emotionally focused individual therapy (EFIT).* New York: Routledge.

Johnson, S., & Sanderfer, K. (2016). *Created for connection: The "Hold Me Tight" guide for Christian couples.* New York: Little, Brown Spark.

Leman, J., Hunter, W., Fergus, T., & Rowatt, W. (2018). Secure attachment to God uniquely linked to psychological health in a national, random sample of American adults. *International Journal for the Psychology of Religion, 28*(3), 162–173. https://psycnet.apa.org/doi/10.1080/10508619.2018.1477401

Lemma, A., Target, M., & Fonagy, P. (2011). *Brief dynamic interpersonal therapy: A clinician's guide.* Oxford: Oxford University Press.

Marshall, W.L. (1993). The role of attachments, intimacy, and loneliness in the etiology and maintenance of sexual offending. *Sexual and Marital Therapy, 8*(2), 109–121.

Maslach, C., & Leiter, M.P. (2016). Understanding the burnout experience: Recent research and its implications for psychiatry. *World Psychiatry: Official Journal of the World Psychiatric Association (WPA), 15*(2), 103–111. https://doi.org/10.1002/wps.20311

Maté, G. (2018). *In the realm of hungry ghosts: Close encounters with addiction.* London: Vermilion.

Mearns, D., & Cooper, M. (2005). *Working at relational depth in counselling and psychotherapy.* London: SAGE.

Mikulincer, M., Shaver, P., Gillath, O., & Nitzberg, R. (2005). *Attachment, caregiving and Altruism: boosting attachment security increases compassion and helping.* https://greatergood.berkeley.edu/images/uploads/367.pdf

Mikulincer, M., Shaver, P., & Pereg, D. (2003). *Attachment theory and affect regulation: The dynamics, development, and cognitive consequences of attachment-related strategies.* https://citeseerx.ist.psu.edu/viewdoc/download?doi=10.1.1.131.142&rep=rep1&type=pdf

Mikulincer, M., & Shaver, P.R. (2016). *Attachment in adulthood: Structure, dynamics, and change* (2nd ed.). New York: Guilford Press.

Miller, W.R., Forcehimes, A., & Zweben, A. (2011). *Treating addiction: A guide for professionals.* New York: Guilford Press.

O'Neill, S. (2018, February 9). Top Oxfam staff paid Haiti survivors for sex. *The Times,* pp. 1, 6.

Pearson, J.L., Cohn, D.A., Cowan, P.A., & Cowan, C.P. (1994). Earned- and continuous-security in adult attachment: Relation to depressive symptomatology and parenting style. *Development and Psychopathology*, 6(2), 359–373. https://doi.org/10.1017/s0954579400004636.

Rheem, K. (2017, 12 November). *Working with withdrawers in Emotionally Focussed Therapy (EFT)*. [Video]. YouTube. www.youtube.com/watch?v=_52r2wozHoI

Shrivastava, A., & Burianova, A. (2014). Attachment styles, physical proximity, and relational satisfaction: A study of working professionals. *Aviation Psychology and Applied Human Factors, 4*(2), 106–112. https://psycnet.apa.org/doi/10.1027/2192-0923/a000062

Snelling, M. (2018). The impact of emergency aid work on personal relationships: A psychodynamic study. *Journal of International Humanitarian Action, 3*(1), 1–15. https://doi.org/10.1186/s41018-018-0042-7

Tassell, N., & Flett, R. (2013). *Motivation in humanitarian health workers: A self-determination theory perspective. Development in Practice, 21*(7), 959–973. https://doi.org/10.1080/09614524.2011.590889

Thomas, R. (2016). *Psychological stress: Aid workers in complex humanitarian emergencies*. Saarbruken: Lambert Academic Publishing.

Tolmacz, R. (2010). Forms of concern: A psychoanalytic perspective. In M. Mikulincer & P. Shaver (Eds.), *Prosocial motives, emotions and behaviour: The better angels of our nature* (pp. 93–107). Washington, DC: APA.

Useem, R.H., & Downie, R.D. (1976). Third-culture kids. *Today's Education, 65*(3), 103.

Chapter 4

A sticking plaster on a gaping wound

"Moral injury", stress and burnout in humanitarian aid workers

Kate S. Thompson

> "When I think about the work we were doing with the team in Rwanda it just seems so little, so inadequate a response. Like trying to put a sticking plaster onto a gaping wound [...] there's no way for us to do anything that would make enough of a change. You've got to ask yourself, what's the point of it then?" (Email from a friend, an aid worker formerly based in Kigali, who "retired" from humanitarian work after a stint in Rwanda, 1996)

In the past, most distress in the humanitarian sector has been seen through the lens of either *burnout* (particularly when it comes on gradually and in contexts of overwork) or *post-traumatic stress disorder* (when it follows a critical incident and there are at least some of the symptoms associated with clinical diagnosis). Although both concepts can be useful, they limit focus, leaving out the person concerned, the meaning they assign their experience and the wider context. In this chapter, I consider whether the concept of *moral injury* helps our understanding of the experiences of humanitarian aid workers and takes us further than diagnostic concepts like *post-traumatic stress disorder* (PTSD) or the catch-all category of *burnout*.

As a psychologist working with trauma for many years, I have long felt that there was something missing in our understanding of the human reaction to traumatic events. While reactions like anxiety, horror, high arousal and intrusions (nightmares, flashbacks) are accounted for by models of fear, threat system activation and memory processing, these do not seem to capture another side of human reaction to traumatic events: The way in which these events impact on a person's *moral self*.[1] If the moral self is injured, the person's sense of goodness (virtue), agency and worth can be fundamentally altered (Papanikolaou, 2020).

I am not alone in seeking a way to discuss this aspect of the human reaction to traumatic events. Many writers and researchers have tried to grasp changes in personal meaning and values after devastating events with ideas like *shattered assumptions about a benevolent world* (Janoff-Bulman, 1992), *survivor guilt* or even the more global *enduring personality change after*

DOI: 10.4324/9781003261971-5

catastrophic experience (EPCACE) (Beltran, Llewellyn, & Silove, 2008).[2] In 1993, Turner and Gorst-Unsworth, exploring psychological reactions to the experience of torture, referred to *existential dilemmas* as a frequent post-torture phenomenon, noting, "The existential dilemma may be the most important and enduring of the psychological reactions to torture, although the most difficult to conceptualise in medical terms". It is this difficulty, that of finding a way to capture the subjective impact of traumatic experience, that is often lost in approaches centred on medical or psychiatric generalisation. In fact, Papadopoulos (2020) argues that using a psychiatric or mental health framework to understand the "distressing perplexity" of such existential challenges creates a problematic pathologising of human suffering.

Moral Injury to Explain the Existential Impact of Events

The concept of *moral injury* provides a way to explore this aspect of reaction to trauma. First developed by Shay (1991) to explain reactions of military personnel, moral injury is defined as "distress over having transgressed or violated core moral boundaries, accompanied by feelings of guilt, shame, self-condemnation, loss of trust, loss of meaning, and spiritual struggles (Koenig, Youssef, & Pearce, 2019). This perceived transgression may be by the person themselves through an act of commission (an act done with specific consequences) or omission (an act *not* done, thereby leading to consequences), or may be what Shay describes as an "act of betrayal", something done to that person or others by a third party, usually someone in power, leading to a conflict with fundamental values and accompanying guilt, shame, anger and self-judgement. The struggle to accommodate these *potentially morally injurious events* (PMIEs)[3] may prove impossible, particularly in the case that individuals withdraw from affirming relationships and lose their sense of being a good moral self (Lidz et al., 2009).

To date, there have been almost no research studies looking at the impact of PMIEs on humanitarian aid workers (see Truman & Berdondini, in press, for one exception). However, they are a professional group at high risk of experiencing such events. Their work often brings them into areas of conflict and natural disaster, and their roles in working with groups and communities directly affected by such situations, can lead to stark moral choices and areas of difficult responsibility. In addition to this, many humanitarians are clearly values-led individuals; they make a choice to work in the aid sector based on their values, suggesting that they may have a greater investment in moral reward from work. In this case, they are likely to suffer more when faced with complex moral choices and failures in the forge of real-world experience. Of course, there are many different types of humanitarians, and as Houldey (2021) notes, it is important to be mindful of the diversity of those working in the sector, who have a variety of motivations and backgrounds driving their choices at work.[4] Still, this from Andrew Thompson following his evacuation from Haiti to the Dominican Republic in 1993 shows the way in which moral language and thinking shapes the situations aid workers face:

> "The UN yanked us out against our will into this catatonic tropical suburbia, this retirement home for failed humanitarians, leaving us sidelined with no way back in. I am nauseated by the oiled-up tourists, defeat, and guilt [...] I need a ticket out to another mission. Give me Mozambique or Angola, Bosnia or Liberia. Or a package deal with a month of each. I don't need a salary or a job title; I'll even pay you to take me there. Just get me off the sidelines and let me redeem myself." (Cain, Postlewait, & Thompson, 2006, p. 187)

Burnout and PTSD in Humanitarian Workers

1. Burnout

The term "burnout", first coined in 1975 by Freudenberger, is now part of the lexicon of everyday: a problem or (sometimes) an *illness* that is referred to widely, but often imprecisely. Maslach and colleagues, developers of the Maslach Burnout Inventory (Maslach & Jackson, 1981), describe burnout as involving three elements: emotional exhaustion (feeling overextended and exhausted by one's work), depersonalisation (a sense that "the job is making me hard emotionally" or noticing increased cynicism), and reduced personal accomplishment (feeling ineffective at work and having difficulty to connect with past and present work accomplishments). Research has often separated out the three components for study or has focused on one element particularly. It is easy to see the way in which the second component – depersonalisation – could interact with the domain of a person's moral self, particularly in someone who values their ability to resist cynicism or prizes their altruism. In fact, some studies have conceptualised risk to humanitarians in terms of a disruption to an altruistic identity (see the work of McCormack and colleagues referred to below).

In Pigni's book *The Idealists Survival Kit* (2016), she notes in her section titled "Recipe for Burnout" that organisational factors (lack of control over the work, lack of participation in decision-making, insufficient or unfair reward systems, problems with team dynamics and poor management) alongside conflicts with personal values, create a burnout-inducing situation. She adds, "Do-gooders, you play your part too", suggesting that staff bring along

> perfectionism in abundance, personal values derived from how much you get done, fear of showing personal needs and emotions, total availability of your days, nights and weekends and an incapacity to say no and set

healthy boundaries plus high expectations and a romanticized view of the non-profit sector. (pp. 31–32)

Again, one is struck by the use of a language of values here: lack of respect, lack of fairness, personal perfectionism, overcommitment and misguided or unrewarded altruism. The meshing between situational factors, systemic pressures and individual values sets the scene for burnout.

In terms of prevalence, some studies have suggested that burnout may affect up to 40% of humanitarian aid workers at some point in their career (Eriksson et al., 2009; De Jong, Martinmäki, Te Brake, Haagen, & Kleber, 2021), although as noted by De Jong and colleagues, the suffering, exhaustion and moral challenges reported may reflect transient distress rather than the presence of a clinical pathology (as studies rarely assess with standardised measures). Eriksson et al.'s study indicated a strong relationship between feelings of depersonalisation in humanitarians and lower support from an employing organisation. Although the direction of causation is unclear, this does suggest that low support and its potential devaluing of the staff member may be a driver for the cynicism and loss of value at work manifesting as this element of burnout. A case from my own practice illustrates this:

Olivia was the only female staff member in a leadership team of five managers working in country for an international NGO. She noted that she was regularly given duties related to staff care (for example organising well-being activities or feeding back to management about the impact of changes). Her role was then expanded to include the psychological support of the beneficiaries in a new project. The team she worked in was characterised by some difficulties between staff and management, but the other managers always looked to her to sort out the problems and seemed to use her engagement in this as a way to sidestep their own responsibilities. Olivia tried to address this directly with her own line manager (also on the leadership team) and with the country director but found she was often silenced and shut down. She reflected in counselling that the vision of organisation and its commitment to the rights of women and children was in stark contrast to the attitude of her colleagues. The impact of this on Olivia was to make her feel quite low in mood and filled with self-doubt so that she began to question her achievements in the post. Despite a high commitment to the work of the team, she found herself increasingly alienated and, when asked to manage a restructuring process that left her a key point of contact for delivering bad news about redundancies, she began to look for another job. She was aware of the gendered nature of the actions of the team but found little comfort in this. When she gained another post, she moved on, promising that she would provide feedback about her experience to the HQ.

In Olivia's case, feelings of low mood, tiredness and alienation were directly driven by a disconnect between her moral values and the reality of her work on the ground. Her workload was certainly heavy, but this was not the key problem for her. The values she felt were being overlooked by her seniors in the team were just those professed in the vision statement of her employing organisation, and she described the lip service paid to such values by the very seniors who appeared to be working against them in their treatment of staff, beneficiaries and of Olivia herself. This created a serious gap between what she lived day-to-day and what she believed *should* be happening, generating growing estrangement, which she was unable to bridge by discussing it with her managers, who were quick to dismiss her concerns and to slough off any suggestions of sexism or stereotyping. In such a context, psychological therapy was useful in part to recognise the reality of this disconnect and to work against what appeared to be a total devaluation of her perspective by her team leaders. Crucially, seeing the problem as Olivia's individual difficulties with work–life balance would have been to miss the point by sidestepping the way power was being used in her team, and the moral impact of this on her.

2. PTSD

Much other research has explored the presence and prevalence rates of mental health difficulties in humanitarian aid workers including depression (Lopes Cardoso et al., 2012; Brooks et al., 2015), anxiety (Connorton, Perry, Hemenway, & Miller, 2012), and PTSD (Ager et al., 2012[5]). In a study by the *Guardian* newspaper (Young, 2015), drawn from a self-selected online survey, 79% of humanitarian professionals who responded had had one or more mental health problems, including anxiety in more than half; depression in 44%; and PTSD and panic attacks in a fifth. This self-report data is somewhat problematic, however, as it may reflect a tendency to couch distress in terms of well-known diagnostic categories rather than teasing out the role of exhaustion, depersonalisation, moral distress or existential issues. It also leaves out the potentially transient nature of distress at different career points (De Jong et al., 2021).

In fact, the concept of PTSD has a specific and limited view of what constitutes traumatic experience. Diagnosis requires a specific "criterion A" event, involving exposure to actual or threatened death, serious injury or sexual violence directly experienced by the person, witnessed occurring to others, learnt about in relation to a close friend or family member, or experienced by repeated or extreme exposure to details (for example, for first responders) (American Psychiatric Association, 2013). Although humanitarians work in unstable situations and conflict zones, and may well be witnesses to violence, the events that give rise to distress do not always (or even mainly) reflect this kind of critical incident or criterion A event. Frequently humanitarians report a gradual disillusionment with their work coupled with specific flashpoints in which a sense of moral distress becomes foregrounded, often related to organisational failings, poor management or refusals to share responsibility, as well as the recognition of injustices in the humanitarian system. It is this that happened to Olivia, described above, in relation to the team restructuring process she was coerced to manage. Interestingly, military research has shown that in the context of tight well-managed teams, critical incidents are less likely to lead to PTSD (Han et al., 2014), suggesting that even when criterion A events are present, context is crucial to understanding both the impact on staff and protective factors that may prevent trauma reactions.

Taking a wider lens means that a focus on diagnosing disorders like PTSD at an individual level may be misleading unless we decide that every difficult event should be viewed as a trauma trigger. In Dunkley's otherwise helpful book (2018), I would take issue with her remark that "trauma can just as easily be the result of cumulative stress, for example from harassment and poor management from organisations" (p. 3), and instead insert a more neutral word (distress, pain or injury) to maintain a wider perspective. As noted by several researchers, traumatic experience in the sense of clear provoking traumatic events (PTSD) is often not the key source of difficulty reported by aid workers (Curling & Simmons, 2010; De Jong et al., 2021), and more minor day-to-day stressors may be of greater relevance (Jatchens, Houdmont, & Thomas, 2018). Understanding the moral implications of these day-to-day stressors and their interaction with critical incidents is a task long overdue.

From PTSD/Burnout to Considering Potentially Morally Injurious Events (PMIEs)

A colleague spoke to me about her experiences during the Rwandan genocide when we were both working later in a neighbouring country. At the time of the start of events in 1994, she was filling in for the country director while this person was on leave. Interahamwe militias were roaming the streets of the capital Kigali, murdering those they believed were from the Tutsi ethnic group, or those whose more moderate views made them a threat. My colleague was asked by neighbours whether they could shelter with her in the house of the international NGO for whom she worked, believing that this would give them greater protection from the militias. This placed her in an impossible position as the team contained other staff members whose physical appearance might also have led to their being at risk if attention was drawn to the staff house, and she had to refuse. From an upstairs window, she saw her neighbours murdered by the Interahamwe, including several children. Once the militia left, she and a colleague went to the house to look for any survivors but had to carefully disguise that they had been there in case the militia returned. When

I met her some months later, she was haunted by the fact that she had refused their request and held herself responsible for their deaths. She had regular nightmares in which she saw again the family murdered and found on waking that she had clawed at her eyes and scratched her cheeks. It was impossible for her to see her actions as acceptable or justified, even though the situation was so unstable and she was making very difficult judgements after only a short time in country. The team evacuated from Rwanda almost immediately afterwards while the country went through the full turmoil of genocide.

This story is that of a young woman caught in an impossible situation, and her distress relates to an act of omission (not acting in the way that her moral values urged her to do) in a rapidly changing situation in which judging the outcome of any action was impossible. These morally injurious events left a deep scar on her, and although she received organisational support for PTSD at the time, she experienced this support as profoundly destabilising and unhelpful. As a was a common intervention at the time, she was pressed to speak about the events in Rwanda in a group setting. This intervention, aimed at fear processing, failed to recognise the deep impact of shame and grief on her, and the damage to her moral self. Her choice in coping was to return to the field, taking a post in a neighbouring country where she was working with elements of the same population, now displaced. Amongst those in the refugee camp in which she was working were individuals who had taken an active part in the genocide, creating a situation of great moral complexity for all the humanitarians involved. Learning from this and considering the potential for injury in such morally intricate situations both extends our understanding of the interaction of person and context, and allows us to better tailor support.

Research suggests that those who have lived through PMIEs are functionally affected beyond what would be explained by diagnoses of PTSD and depression, even when these are present (Maguen et al., 2020), and that treatment for PTSD or other disorders can be hampered by a history of having undergone PMIEs (Williamson, Stevelink, & Greenberg, 2018). There is also evidence of distinct neurobiology related to the impact of morally injurious events (Barnes, Hurley, & Taber 2019). Much of the research to date has focused on the impact of PMIEs on serving military personnel and veterans and has mainly studied US-based samples (see Williamson et al., 2018 for a helpful review). Recent evidence from the UK has shown that moral injury reactions are increased amongst military personnel with greater exposure to childhood adversity and amongst those with experiences of emotional or physical abuse during military service (Williamson, Greenberg, & Murphy, 2021).

Although much of this work is with populations diagnosed with PTSD or other disorders, it is recognised that moral injury can occur without PTSD, and that it might in fact be another way to view some manifestations of distress formerly seen as burnout. For example, in a survey of 80 journalists from nine news organisations covering stories related to refugee camps in Europe, reactions suggestive of moral injury were common, but there were few cases fitting a diagnosis of PTSD. In this population, such reactions were associated with working alone, a recent increase in workload, a belief that organisational support was lacking and limited control over the resources needed to report the story (Feinstein, Pavisian, & Storm, 2018). These indicators are strongly suggestive of factors linked with burnout reactions including overwork, low support from employers and lack of control. There was also a strong association between guilt and moral injury reactions, with stronger feelings of guilt in respondents who reported stepping outside their journalistic neutrality to assist migrants (suggesting a possible sense of responsibility towards the population reported upon).

The idea of moral injury is now being used to explore the experiences of other professional groups including police (Tapson, Doyle, Karagiannopoulos, & Lee, 2021), social workers (Fenton & Kelly, 2017), teachers (Sugrue, 2020), and increasingly to understand the reactions of healthcare staff to their work (Rodney, 2017).

Moral "Distress" in Healthcare Workers before and after the Pandemic

Work to explore the impact of *moral distress* on healthcare workers has a pedigree of some four decades (Jameton, 1993), starting well before our current pandemic era. There are overlaps with both omission and betrayal aspects of moral injury in the definition of moral distress. Studies of moral distress have expanded from nursing to include physicians, pharmacists, medical students and psychologists (see Lamiani, Borghi, & Argentero, 2017 for a comprehensive review). Links in the literature point to increases in distress when staff perceive a negative ethical climate in their care settings, when they are obliged to offer "futile care" or care not in the best interests of patients, and when they are challenged in inappropriate ways by patients or family members (Oh & Gastman, 2015). Further evidence suggests poor nurse–physician collaboration and lack of support from colleagues fuel higher distress (Lamiani et al., 2017). In terms of outcomes, moral distress has also been associated with staff attrition, deterioration of morale and teamwork and decreases in the quality of care and patient safety (Rodney, 2017), something that is suggestive of a cumulative effect of moral distress on staff. Rodney (2017) also suggests that a shift may occur when staff internalise external constraints on their work to such a point that their own moral values begin to shift, causing them to disengage morally, compromise their integrity and possibly engage in harmful practice. Again, the overlaps with the depersonalisation element of burnout are clear.

The Covid-19 pandemic has shone an additional spotlight on the experiences of healthcare workers in terms of moral injury (Williamson,

Murphy, & Greenberg, 2020), and writers like Wendy Dean argue for the vital importance of viewing staff reactions in context. For these writers, if health workers have moral injury rather than burnout or depression, they are reflecting broken healthcare systems and impossible competing demands rather than individual psychological difficulties (Talbot & Dean, 2018). To quote the medical commentator Dr Zubin Damania:

> So many of us in healthcare feel overwhelmed, demoralized, exhausted, cynical, afraid, and alone. It has to be our fault, right? We're not resilient enough, we don't work hard enough, we're not efficient enough, we're not good enough people to be taking care of others [...] What if we're all wrong? What if it's not us, it's them? A broken system destroying ideal-istic, good people. (ZDOGGMD, 2019)

There is a clear difficulty with any narrative that divides into "us" and "them" (as in the statement above). However, as with PTSD, there is a sense that "diagnosing" burnout (or "moral injury" if this is decontextualised) creates narratives that ignore context and associated power structures. If it is burnout, then nurses, doctors and psychologists need to do yoga and take regular breaks. If it is a reaction to morally injurious contexts, then health systems must look at how they allocate resources and prioritise patients as well as enshrine self-care practices (yoga, breaks) for all their staff.

One of the key aspects of the concept of moral distress is the way in which it intersects with power and hierarchy in health settings, taking us into deeply political questions about the allocation of resources and the way in which systems of power can crush both those they aim to serve and those who work with them to deliver services. Jones (1998) argues cogently that the creation of individualised disorders that can be treated with therapies may offer a way to sidestep "the complexities of political and social causation" (p. 243), a debate that has long been current in discussions related to the use of PTSD across cultures (Bracken, 1998). In the moral domain, where questions of injustice and forgiveness (of self or others) are carefully balanced in the delivery of help or care. this may be particularly pertinent.

> Fran worked as a volunteer in a refugee camp in northern France. On first arriving, she had been convinced that the outside world must not know how awful the conditions were for those living in the makeshift camp and under daily pressure to try and cross to the UK by train or lorry. She worked hard to invite journalists, politicians and media figures to the camp in which she and other volunteers were running all support ser-vices in the absence of any response by the French state. This raised the profile of the camps, but increasingly Fran realised that it did not matter. There was no political will to change the situation or to make sure that the asylum seekers arriving each day were treated fairly and with care.

Fran was often staying in the camp, working very long hours, becoming increasingly aware of the dangerous role of smugglers in controlling the population and its potential to pose a danger to her too. She became more and more affected by her experiences, and by the lack of justice for those staying in the camps even as she watched individuals risk, and sometimes lose their lives, as they attempted to reach the UK.

In Fran's case, moral injury arose again from a disconnect, in this case between the values she believed she shared with her own government (and perhaps the government of France) and what she observed happening to people whose vulnerability was clear to her. A creeping realisation that political structures were ranged against anything resembling positive change brought with it a despair into which she pushed her own considerable personal resources, working ever harder to stretch across the chasm between the needs she could see around her and the limited support available. At a certain point, Fran was unable to continue her work after reaching a breaking point, and the distress this caused her took some years to negotiate. Psychological therapy helped her recognise the intense moral dilemmas she had faced and her huge efforts to negotiate these dilemmas in ways consistent with her values and despite unyielding forces of power.

Humanitarians and Moral Injury

I have argued above that humanitarian aid workers are a population that one might expect to be affected by the moral dimensions of their work and to experience the disconnect keenly between their values and the work they can do. There is evidence that this is true. Frequently, studies make mention of "existential dilemmas" (De Jong et al., 2021), self-doubt and a sense of "failing" victims (Brooks et al., 2015) or "altruistic identity disruption" (McCormack, Douglas, & Joseph, 2021) in seeking to capture the way in which the moral sense of the person may be challenged by their relief work. Studies of health workers posted internationally as humanitarians also note the impact of ethical challenges and moral distress on participants (Hunt, 2008; Schwartz et al., 2010).

This highlights that there may be a different "flavour" to the way in which PMIEs are internalised by aid workers as opposed to military personnel. If morally injurious events in military staff are often connected with acts of commission (or active omission), leaving the person distressed at what *they* did or did not do, for humanitarians, PMIEs may be more linked to acts of omission or betrayal (failure to act, helplessness and confrontation with the limits of what is possible). Put another way, if those who have served in military contexts can be left feeling they are "monsters" (Papanikolaou, 2020), humanitarians may rather be hit with their own insufficiency, powerlessness and the impossibility of being good enough. It is this also that health staff frequently report when asked about moral distress, again making clear the commonalities between the existential challenges of humanitarians and health workers. As in the case of Fran above, this is perhaps most clear in the case of volunteers who have assembled in the European refugee camps in northern France, Italy and Greece whose narratives are often filled with dissonance between their initial expectations that they would be able to offer significant help to refugees and the reality of the situation once there (Truman & Berdondini, in press, and see also chapter 6, this volume).

There are factors which can aid humanitarians in coping with the moral challenges inherent in the work. Most often mentioned is social support, particularly within humanitarian teams, but also in some studies from friends and family based in other locations (Brooks et al., 2015; Eriksson et al., 2012). Again, of key importance is support from managers and an open two-way relationship with employing organisations. Lennon (quoted in Cornish, 2017) notes the complicated relationship her participants had with their organisations, which remained "passionate but also filled with anger and other emotions". The moral investment made to work in the sector brings with it reciprocal expectations of care and valuing that employing organisations may fail to understand or share.

This is to arrive at another place of intersection with the moral domain: Questions about a fair balance between what workers give through their labour and how they are rewarded, which is in keeping with the *Effort-Reward Imbalance* model of occupational stress.[6] This is an area that could stand further work to explore whether the presence of PMIEs changes the balance between perceptions of effort and reward at work. The narrative of having "given too much" and having been treated unfairly by employers is one frequently encountered when talking with aid workers and also those formerly employed in health services and the military.

Addressing moral challenges and injuries for aid workers could, then, require organisational change. It returns us to the original work by Shay on moral injury in the military, in which the vital importance of leaders owning their failures and recognising the impact of these failures on staff is highlighted. Shay (2014)notes succinctly: "All people watch the trustworthiness of those who wield power over them – all the time" (p. 186). Enhancing trust between managers and staff has also been highlighted as protective for humanitarians (Jatchens et al., 2018).

There has been a theme throughout this chapter, and more widely through this book, that real leadership requires listening to your staff, asking them what would really make a difference to their working lives and acknowledging non-defensively what is and is not possible within the urgent work being completed. This may mean considering the moral and spiritual needs of staff (Houldey, 2021), or equally may mean asking individuals directly about whether they are in distress and, if so, whether this distress is transitory or indicative of mental health difficulty (De Jong et al., 2021).

Above all it means acknowledgement of the impact of events on staff so that this can be held in safe managerial relationships with permission for staff to admit vulnerabilities and ask for help, alongside remaining resilient. Pigni (2016) tells the dispiriting story of S, an aid worker evacuated from Syria into Turkey after unwittingly being caught in a firefight in Aleppo. After a hurried journey by night, across the border she was met in Gaziantep by her Head of Mission and offered a generous glass of whiskey, "'I don't drink', she told me. 'He didn't ask if I wanted it. I think that was all he could do to take care of someone in shock. Then I went to bed. The matter was never addressed again'" (p. 46).

Houldey (2021) argues that the difficulty to allow for staff vulnerability permeates the humanitarian sector, pressing employees to measure themselves against an archetype of the "perfect humanitarian", "someone whose commitment and value is measured by how easily they can travel, their availability for the next mission or assignment and their ability to remain unflappable when confronted by risk or insecurity" (p. 28), and perhaps by PMIEs. The presence of this "ideal" in the background creates pressure to perform at work in ways that are not natural or easy, and intersect with issues of class, race and gender. A further pressure results from the assumption that the needs of others (in this case communities in need of aid) are paramount and that for the aid worker to focus on their own needs or difficulties is "selfish" or "self-indulgent". Other chapters in this volume explore the way in which this aspect of the work can attract individuals seeking to sidestep their own needs and find value in *compulsive caregiving* (see chapter 3 and chapter 12, this volume).

In Lennon's study, she noted that participants had taken many years to make sense of their experience as humanitarians, and for some people this was avoided altogether. She writes that rather than "coming to terms with their experiences, aid workers have a tendency to simply redeploy", jumping into the next mission with alacrity. Organisations can often collude with this as they seek to fill posts with experienced staff. Her conclusion that "self-care often came second to the organisation's response and needs" was echoed when individual staff members referred to a lack of organisational support and a failure to recognise the impact of the work on them, characterising the organisational stance as one of "harshness, disrespect and aggression" (Lennon, quoted in Cornish, 2017).

Limiting Moral Injury in Humanitarians Exposed to PMIEs – Recommendations

This chapter has argued that moral injury is a useful concept for understanding work-related distress in humanitarian aid workers, and that it takes us further than PTSD or burnout in understanding the relationship between context and individual, and the role of meaning-making in aid worker distress.

The literature has a range of suggestions for building checks and balances into the systems of care around international humanitarian staff and these are helpfully summed up in the article by Brooks et al. (2015, see p. 393). In addition to these recommendations, I would add:

For Humanitarians:

- Be aware of your values and the way in which these intersect with your motivations for humanitarian work. Check in regularly to make sure you are not carrying areas of potential injury related to the moral impact of the work you do.
- Keep a close eye on your relationship with your employing organisations, your immediate line managers and colleagues. When trust is strained, or you experience an imbalance in the rewards of your work against your efforts and commitment, take some action to prevent additional stress. Seek out support from managers or your headquarters if you feel you can do this safely and with honesty.
- Hughes, Burck, and Roncin (2019) speak of the key role of acts of solidarity and community activism they observed amongst volunteers and refugees in the European refugee camps. Depending on your professional situation, opportunities to use your privilege and raise your voice whether in-country or after your posting, particularly in concert with others, are likely to protect your moral self.
- Recognise areas of vulnerability in yourself and others, and work to challenge pressures to be perfect and to work ever longer and harder. Emergencies are often intractable, so question the tendency to keep on working very long hours as if this will make *all* the difference.

For Organisations:

- Check in with your staff and ask them regularly about what might be of use to them to manage work-related stress and PMIEs. Give control back to staff after critical incidents so they can determine what support feels helpful (but do gently question those who use working hard to manage anxiety or distress). Support should be optional and recognise that staff members may differ in coping style, and a variety of help may be needed. Support to create a culture of normalcy alongside watchful waiting may be important to avoid inflating the presence of clinical mental health issues (De Jong, 2021; Brooks et al., 2015).
- Take steps to actively monitor staff workloads and initiate dialogues to offer safety in discussions with line managers, country managers and the wider organisation so that narratives of moral distress, dissatisfaction with leadership and imbalance in the effort–reward of work can be discussed openly. In some cases, there may be a worry about

acknowledging grievance in a staff member, but not to acknowledge this and to press on with work regardless is no solution. Grievance should always be made explicit and discussed in a safe managerial relationship.

- Ensure access to the internet/telephone for staff to seek social support and consider ways to actively build social support in teams (Eriksson et al., 2013). Some activities could focus on the moral impact of the work done so that this is a shared conversation, and staff could be encouraged to raise their concerns about ethical challenges and organisational failures more directly and openly with leaders to keep questions of power and responsibility firmly in view.
- Houldey (2021) mentions that the increasing professionalisation of the sector, alongside and driving a heightened focus on staff security staff has led to increased separation of aid workers from the communities they serve. While this certainly limits harm to humanitarian bodies, it might be argued that this increasing sense of a worker "us" and population served "them" creates a disconnect that is potentially morally injurious.[7] As Andrew Thompson puts it, "for me, with each successive mission, individuals got lost; they became Haitians, Rwandans, Bosnians – populations not people" (Cain, Postlewait, & Thompson, 2006, p. 297). Discussions in relation to this, and the option to question practices may be an important counterbalance to the moral impact of this distancing.
- Access to more tailored psychological support is often valued by staff and a regular schedule of this can be helpful. Key points to offer this might be pre-departure, during assignment at set intervals, and post-assignment. Cockcroft McKay, and Eiroa Orosa (2020) argue that this support should be standardised and "opt-in rather than opt-out" to normalise regular psychological "check-ups" and encourage staff with more mixed feelings to access this support as a matter of course.
- Organisations might need to hesitate, however, before rushing to "bring in the psychologists", particularly after a critical incident or emergency situation (as outlined in chapter 1). It is important that managers offer direct support to their staff and that senior leaders in an organisation acknowledge the impact of PMIEs and critical incidents before delegating support roles to outsiders (UNHCR, 2001).

For Psychological Therapists:

- Be alert to the motivations for work of your humanitarian clients and explore these to understand better the way in which moral choices and PMIEs may have had an impact on them. Actively contextualise distress and recognise the reality of injustice in client narratives. Hughes et al. (2019) argue for taking a position of solidarity alongside humanitarian clients, so that therapeutic intervention recognises the shared challenges of managing injustice.

- Be mindful of the treatment recommendations for moral injury with a focus on building trust, exploring self-compassion and attending to the emotional impact of PMIEs. Clients may be reticent to speak about events that evoke shame or guilt, and approaching this with respect and humility may be important.
- Many of those working in the field of moral injury have argued for the inclusion of spiritual exploration as part of any intervention, be this linked to established religious practices and forms of support like chaplaincy/pastoral care, or broader spiritual approaches, perhaps incorporating religious rituals for purification or transition that involve the person more actively with their community (Nakashima Brock, 2020).

In summary, the response to managing the impact of PMIEs requires actions at both an individual and organisational level. While staff members may need to focus on self-care and boundaries at work, this is impossible in the absence of permission-giving by their employing organisations, particularly within line management relationships. Highly conscientious staff members may continue to work despite increasing demoralisation and despair, and when managers are unable to identify this form of presenteeism, opportunities for action will be missed.

Notes

1 I am following the definition of moral self of Jennings, Mitchell and Hannah (2014): "*a complex system of self-defining moral attributes*" (p. 3) including beliefs, dispositions and cognitive-affective drivers for behaviour integral to an individual's self-concept
2 Criteria proposed for EPCACE include "*pervasive hostility and mistrust, social withdrawal, feelings of emptiness and hopelessness, being chronically on edge and estrangement*". Later research added "enduring guilt" to this list, underlining the link between withdrawal from sustaining social relationships, guilt, shame and moral distress.
3 Despite some writing that treats moral injury as a disorder in its own right, in the main it is viewed as a powerful accompanying reaction to both traumatic events and ongoing life stressors. Many current researchers use measures of *potentially morally injurious events* (PMIEs) rather than measuring moral injury itself.
4 In terms of financial motivations, humanitarians can comprise people working in a semi-voluntary capacity or those who work for national rates of pay (which are often markedly lower than international wage rates) alongside highly paid expatriates working for the UN or international non-governmental organisations. The extent to which humanitarian working is a values-driven choice is thus highly variable.
5 This study is notable in its focus on national staff members posted in their home country and highlights the dangers for non-expatriate staff of working in the sector.

6   The Effort-Reward Imbalance model of occupational stress (Siegrist, 1996) is discussed more fully in chapter 9 in relation to the motivations of international consultants. It has been shown to be a factor exacerbating the risks of post-traumatic stress in response to work-related traumatic events in humanitarian aid workers (Jatchens, 2018).
7   The UNHCR staff well-being survey suggests that those who work with populations of concern may be more at risk of emotional exhaustion, while those not directly working with beneficiaries may be at risk of depersonalisation and a diminished sense of personal accomplishment, these last two burnout categories overlapping very much with moral injury (UNHCR, 2016).

References

Ager, A., Pasha, E., Yu, G., Duke, T., Eriksson, C., & Cardozo, B.L. (2012). Stress, mental health, and burnout in national humanitarian aid workers in Gulu, northern Uganda. *Journal of Traumatic Stress, 25*(6), 713–720. https://doi.org/10.1002/jts.21764

American Psychiatric Association. (2013). Trauma – and stressor – related disorders. In *Diagnostic and statistical manual of mental disorders* (5th ed.). https://doi.org/10.1176/appi.books.9780890425596.dsm07

Barnes, H., Hurley, R., & Taber, K. (2019). Moral injury and PTSD: Often co-occurring yet mechanistically different. *Journal of Neuropsychiatry and Clinical Neurosciences, 31*(2), A4–103. https://doi.org/10.1176/appi.neuropsych.19020036

Beltran, R.O., Llewellyn, G. M., & Silove, D. (2008). Clinicians' understanding of international statistical classification of diseases and related health problems, 10th revision diagnostic criteria: F62.0 enduring personality change after catastrophic experience. *Comprehensive Psychiatry*, *49*, 593–602. https://doi.org/10.1016/j.comppsych.2008.04.006

Bracken, P. (1998). Hidden agendas: Deconstructing post-traumatic stress disorder. In P.J. Bracken & C. Petty (Eds). *Rethinking the trauma of war* (pp. 38–59). London: Free Association Books.

Brock, R. Nakashima. (2020). Moral conscience, moral injury, and rituals for recovery. In R. Papadopoulos (Ed.), *Moral injury and beyond: Understanding human anguish and healing traumatic wounds* (pp. 37–52). Abingdon, Oxon: Routledge.

Brooks, S.K., Dunn, R., Sage, C.A.M., Amlôt, R., Greenberg, N., & Rubin, J.G. (2015). Risk and resilience factors affecting the psychological wellbeing of individuals deployed in humanitarian relief roles after a disaster. *Journal of Mental Health, 24*(6), 385–413. https://doi.org/10.3109/09638237.2015.1057334

Cain, K., Postlewait, H., & Thompson, A. (2006). *Emergency sex and other desperate measures: True stories from a war zone.* London: Ebury Press.

Cockcroft-McKay C., & Eiroa-Orosa, F.J. (2020). Barriers to accessing psychosocial support for humanitarian aid workers: a mixed methods inquiry. *Disasters, 45*(4), 762–796. https://doi.org/10.1111/disa.12449

Connorton, E., Perry, M.J., Hemenway, D., & Miller, M. (2012). Humanitarian relief workers and trauma-related mental illness. *Epidemiologic Reviews, 34*(1), 145–155. https://doi.org/10.1093/epirev/mxr026

Cornish, L. (2017, 9 May). Aid workers witnessing: What are the impacts on aid workers? *Devex News*. www.devex.com/news/aid-workers-witnessing-what-are-the-impacts-on-aid-workers-90193

Curling, P., & Simmons, K.B. (2010). Stress and staff support strategies for international aid work. *Intervention: International Journal of Mental Health, Psychosocial Work & Counselling in Areas of Armed Conflict, 8*(2), 93–105. https://doi.org/10.1097/WTF.0b013e32833c1e8f

De Jong, K., Martinmäki, S.E., Te Brake, H., Haagen, J.F.G., & Kleber, R.J. (2021). Mental and physical health of international humanitarian aid workers on short-term assignments: Findings from a prospective cohort study. *Social Science & Medicine, 285*, 114268. https://doi.org/10.1016/j.socscimed.2021.114268

Dunkley, F. (2018). *Psychosocial support for humanitarian aid workers: A roadmap of trauma and critical incident care*. Abingdon, Oxon: Routledge.

Eriksson, C.B., Bjorck, J.P., Larson, L.C., Walling, S.M., Trice, G.A., Fawcett, J., Abernethy, A.D., & Foy, D.W. (2009). Social support, organisational support, and religious support in relation to burnout in expatriate humanitarian aid workers. *Mental Health, Religion & Culture, 12*(7), 671–686. https://psycnet.apa.org/doi/10.1080/13674670903029146

Eriksson, C.B., Lopes Cardozo, B., Foy, D.W., Sabin, M., Ager, A., Snider, L., Scholte, W.F., Kaiser, R., Olff, M., Rijnen, B., Gotway Crawford, C., Zhu, J., & Simon, W. (2013). Pre-deployment mental health and trauma exposure of expatriate humanitarian aid workers: risk and resilience factors. *Traumatology, 19*(1), 41–48. https://doi.org/10.1177/1534765612441978

Feinstein, A., Pavisian, B., & Storm, H. (2018). Journalists covering the refugee and migration crisis are affected by moral injury not PTSD. *JRSM Open, 9*(3), 2054270418759010. https://doi.org/10.1177/2054270418759010

Fenton, J., & Kelly, T.B. (2017). "Risk is king and needs to take a backseat!" Can social workers' experiences of moral injury strengthen practice? *Journal of Social Work Practice, Psychotherapeutic Approaches in Health, Welfare and the Community, 31*(4) 461–475. https://doi.org/10.1080/02650533.2017.1394827

Freudenberger, H.J. (1975). The staff burn-out syndrome in alternative institutions. *Psychotherapy: Theory, Research and Practice, 12*(1), 73–82.

Han, S.C., Castro, F., Lee, L.O., Charney, M.E., Marx, B.P., Brailey, K., Proctor, S.P., & Vasterling, J.J. (2014). Military unit support, post-deployment social support, and PTSD symptoms among active duty and National Guard soldiers deployed to Iraq. *Journal of Anxiety Disorders, 28*(5), 446–453. https://psycnet.apa.org/doi/10.1016/j.janxdis.2014.04.004

Houldey, G. (2021). *The vulnerable humanitarian: Ending burnout culture in the aid sector*. Abingdon, Oxon: Routledge.

Hughes, G., Burck, C., & Roncin, L. (2019). Therapeutic activism: Supporting emotional resilience of volunteers working in a refugee camp. *Psychotherapy and Politics International, 18*(1). https://doi.org/10.1002/ppi.1517

Hunt, M.R. (2008). Ethics beyond borders: How health professionals experience ethics in humanitarian assistance and development work. *Developing World Bioethics, 8*(2), 59–69. https://doi.org/10.1111/j.1471-8847.2006.00153.x

Jachens, L. (2018). *Job stress among humanitarian aid workers*. [Unpublished doctoral thesis]. University of Nottingham, United Kingdom. http://eprints.nottingham.ac.uk/52237/2/Jachens July 2018.pdf

Jachens, L., Houdmont, J., & Thomas, R. (2018). Work-related stress in a humanitarian context: A qualitative investigation. *Disasters, 42*(4), 619–634. https://doi.org/10.1111/disa.12278

Jameton, A. (1993). Dilemmas of moral distress: Moral responsibility and nursing practice. *AWHONN's clinical issues in perinatal and women's health nursing, 4*(4), 542–551.

Janoff-Bulman, R. (1992). *Shattered assumptions: Towards a new psychology of trauma.* New York: Free Press.

Jennings, P.L., Mitchell, M.S., & Hannah, S.T. (2015). The moral self: A review and integration of the literature. *Journal of Organizational Behavior, 36*(Suppl 1), S104–S168. https://doi.org/10.1002/job.1919

Jones, L. (1998). The question of political neutrality when doing psychosocial work with survivors of political violence. *International Review of Psychiatry, 10*, 239–247. https://doi.org/10.1080/09540269874835

Koenig, H.G., Youssef, N.A., & Pearce, M. (2019). Assessment of moral injury in veterans and active-duty military personnel with PTSD: A review. *Frontiers in Psychiatry, 10*. https://doi.org/10.3389/fpsyt.2019.00443

Lamiani, G., Borghi, L., & Argentero, P. (2017). When healthcare professionals cannot do the right thing: A systematic review of moral distress and its correlates. *Journal of Health Psychology, 22*(1), 51–67. https://doi.org/10.1177/1359105315595120

Litz, B.T., Stein, N., Delaney, E., Lebowitz, L., Nash, W.P., Silva, C., & Maguen, S. (2009). Moral injury and moral repair in war veterans: A preliminary model and intervention strategy. *Clinical Psychology Review, 29*(8), 695–706. https://doi.org/10.1016/j.cpr.2009.07.003

Lopes Cardozo, B., Gotway Crawford, C., Eriksson, C., Zhu, J., Sabin, M., Ager, A., Foy, D., Snider, L., Scholte, W., Kaiser, R., Olff, M., Rijnen, B., & Simon, W. (2012). Psychological distress, depression, anxiety, and burnout among international humanitarian aid workers: A longitudinal study. *PLoS One, 7*(9): e44948. https://doi.org/10.1371/journal.pone.0044948

Maguen, S., Griffin, B.J., Copeland, L.A., Perkins, D.F., Richardson, C.B., Finley, E.P., & Vogt, D. (2020). Trajectories of functioning in a population-based sample of veterans: Contributions of moral injury, PTSD, and depression. *Psychological Medicine*, 1–10. Advance online publication. https://doi.org/10.1017/S0033291720004249

Maslach, C., & Jackson, S.E. (1981). The measurement of experienced burnout. *Journal of Organisational Behaviour, 2* (2), 99–113. https://doi.org/10.1002/job.4030020205

McCormack, L., Douglas, H., & Joseph, S. (2021) Isolation, self-blame and perceived invalidation in aid personnel: Identifying humanitarian-specific distress using the PostAID/Q. *Journal of International Humanitarian Action* 6(8). https://doi.org/10.1186/s41018-021-00094-8

Oh, Y., & Gastmans, C. (2015). Moral distress experienced by nurses: A quantitative literature review. *Nursing Ethics, 22*(1), 15–31. https://doi.org/10.1177/0969733013502803

Papadopoulos, R.K. (2020). The traumatising discourse of trauma and moral injury: Distress and renewal. In R. Papadopoulos (Ed.), *Moral injury and beyond: Understanding human anguish and healing traumatic wounds* (pp. 1–21). Abingdon, Oxon: Routledge

Papanikolaou, A. (2020). What is moral about moral injury? A virtue approach. In R. Papadopoulos (Ed.), *Moral injury and beyond: Understanding human anguish and healing traumatic wounds* (pp. 93–103). Abingdon, Oxon: Routledge

Pigni, A. (2016). *The idealist's survival kit: 75 simple ways to avoid burnout.* Berkeley, CA: Parallax Press.

Rodney, P.A. (2017). What we know about moral distress. *American Journal of Nursing, 117*(2 Suppl 1), S7–S10. https://doi.org/10.1097/01.NAJ.0000512204. 85973.04

Schwartz, L., Sinding, C., Hunt, M., Elit, M., Redwood-Campbell, L., Adelson, N., Luther, L., Ranford, J., & DeLaat, S. (2010). Ethics in humanitarian aid work: Learning from the narratives of humanitarian health workers. *AJOB Primary Research, 1*(3), 45–54, https://doi.org/10.1080/21507716.2010.505898

Shay, J. (1991). Learning about combat stress from Homer's Iliad. *Journal of Traumatic Stress, 4*(4), 561–579. https://doi.org/10.1002/jts.2490040409

Siegrist, J. (1996). Adverse health effects of high-effort/low-reward conditions. *Journal of Occupational Health Psychology, 1*(1), 27–41. https://doi.org/10.1037/ 1076-8998.1.1.27

Sugrue, E.P. (2020). Moral injury among professionals in K–12 education. *American Educational Research Journal, 57*(1), 43–68. https://doi.org/10.3102%2F000283121 9848690

Talbot, S.G., & Dean, W. (2018). Physicians aren't "burning out". They're suffering from moral injury. *Stat News.* www.statnews.com/2018/07/26/physicians-not-burn ing-out-they-are-suffering-moral-injury/

Tapson, K., Doyle, M., Karagiannopoulos, V., & Lee, P. (2021) Understanding moral injury and belief change in the experiences of police online child sex crime investigators: An interpretative phenomenological analysis. *Journal of Police and Criminal Psychology, 30*, 1–13. https://doi.org/10.1007/s11896-021-09463-w

Truman, J., & Berdondini, L. (in press). Potentially Morally Injurious Experiences (PMIEs) in the humanitarian sector: The role of moral expectations [Special issue]. *Displaced Voices: A Journal of Archives, Migration and Cultural Heritage.* www.livin grefugeearchive.org/researchpublications/displaced_voices/displaced-voices-about- the-journal/

Turner, S.W., & Gorst-Unsworth, C. (1993) Psychological sequelae of torture. In J.P. Wilson & B. Raphael (Eds.), *International handbook of traumatic stress syndromes* (pp. 703–713). New York: Plenum Press.

UNHCR. (2001). *Managing the Stress of Humanitarian Emergencies.* Geneva: United Nations High Commissioner for Refugees. www.refworld.org/pdfid/ 4905f1752.pdf

UNHCR. (2016). *Staff Wellbeing and Mental Health in UNHCR.* Geneva: United Nations High Commissioner for Refugees. www.unhcr.org/56e2dfa09.pdf

Williamson, V., Greenberg, N., & Murphy, D. (2021). Predictors of moral injury in UK treatment seeking veterans. *Child Abuse and Neglect, 112*, 104889. https://doi. org/10.1016/j.chiabu.2020.104889

Williamson, V., Murphy, D., & Greenberg, N. (2020). COVID-19 and experiences of moral injury in front-line key workers. *Occupational Medicine, 70*, 317–319 Advance Access publication on 2 April https://doi.org/10.1093/occmed/kqaa052

Williamson, V., Stevelink, S., & Greenberg, N. (2018). Occupational moral injury and mental health: systematic review and meta-analysis. *British Journal of*

Psychiatry: The Journal of Mental Science, 212(6), 339–346. https://doi.org/10.1192/bjp.2018.55

Young, H. (2015, 23 November). Guardian research suggests mental health crisis among aid workers. *The Guardian.* www.theguardian.com/global-development-professionals-network/2015/nov/23/guardian-research-suggests-mental-health-crisis-among-aid-workers

ZDOGGMD. (2019, March 8). It's not burnout, it's moral injury (video file). https://zdoggmd.com/moral-injury/

Chapter 5

Sharing family dilemmas for those working internationally

Beth Hill and David Hawker

Home When Away

Do you have a place that you go to between assignments that you call home? Every reader of this chapter will have a different response to that question. We want to open this chapter reflecting on "family dilemmas" for humanitarian workers by asking you to think about how you might answer that. Would the answer change at different life stages? Is it an easy question to answer, or does it cause you to wonder where is home? Is home related to people, to family, to a partner, to a place that you used to live, to somewhere you retreat to now? If you are reading this chapter to help you support others, how do you imagine the person you are trying to support would answer?

Such a question can be worth considering in psychological assessments, reviews or therapeutic work with humanitarian workers, to assess whether they have a "safe place" to be or a "safe person" to be with. The underlying questions from the therapist are: We know that you are here to talk about your work, but do you have somewhere to go or someone to be with when you are not working? Before we start to have difficult conversations, is there someone or somewhere you can you go to have a "safe place to stand" when feelings are overwhelming, as they are for all of us at times? What happens between assignments? How do you, or can you, do life outside of work? Having a safe place or identity beyond work is important. The challenge is that for many humanitarian workers, the nature of work can make it hard to define or maintain the place between assignments that you call "home".

Why is a sense of safety or home important? Home is about both place and relationships. As psychologists, we sometimes look at relationships in a similar way to the bond or attachment that develops between a newborn child and their caregiver. Infants are happier when they develop a sense that their carer will supply what they need, providing a secure base from which they can explore the world (Bowlby, 1988). Older children and adults too, thrive more easily if they have a sense of security in both a place and a network of relationships. Often that means a home and a family, and security becomes shaky when it is hard to define what those are. Stress is harder to overcome

DOI: 10.4324/9781003261971-6

without a secure base. In drawing on this concept, we want to emphasise that we see attachment as a quality of close relationships rather than located in the individual (Meins, 2017). Our previous and current relational and living contexts affect how safe we feel in the world. In this chapter we explore the impact of networks of relationships on those who work away from home countries.

Anyone who travels may be conscious of home as not just a dwelling but also a town, a region or a country where they are surrounded by familiar cultural cues – the language, sights, sounds, smells and other stimuli that make them feel at home. Workers who frequently travel between two locations may find cultural cues which help them feel at home in either place. They are the administrative factors which define home: country of birth; the state issuing a passport (passport country); the state where the individual is living and working, perhaps with legal status recognised by a visa (host country); the state(s) where an individual owns property, has a mortgage, pays tax, was educated or is entitled to state benefits. All these may affect a sense of home.

Both authors can recall clients tearing up as they are faced with the question of where home is. Some share that they do not have anywhere; some that home no longer feels as comfortable as being on the field or being with current or past colleagues; and some that neither their passport country nor their current host country feels like home, but a country they previously lived in does. Some talk of the place they have left as home, even if they are not expecting to go back. Young adults have mourned the loss of home when their parents have sold the family home and gone to work overseas. On the other hand, agencies sometimes more readily provide homes in the field for families whilst expecting single workers to share with each other as flatmates, failing to account for any preference they might have for their own space.

Whilst we are all part of families, it feels that for some humanitarian workers, their network (biological family, partner or friendship group) might be more substantially shaped by their working context, due to times spent on international assignments. For others, their humanitarian work means that family is clearly defined as the group you travel between assignments with. Children of humanitarian workers often report that home is wherever all the nuclear family are gathered, and so it is more about people than place. Others may identify home as a place that they always went in the summer.

So, we start with thinking about home as a way of thinking about important relationships that shape identity, and we use the term "family" to denote that. For the purposes of this chapter, we are thinking of families as the network of significant relationships that individuals call their "family". While we do not have space to reflect on the diversity of relationships which impact and are impacted by humanitarian work, we want to highlight some of the dilemmas shared by those that we have had the privilege of learning from. Any general description misses individual complexity and these reflections are by no means exhaustive. We stress again the diversity of experiences of humanitarian work, both enriching and depleting. We do this with the aim of reminding those supporting humanitarian workers that we are all part of multiple relationship networks, and that attention to these can sustain vocations and enhance relationships, reducing tension and breakdown. We have deliberately spent a larger proportion of this chapter writing about children and young people as a voice often not privileged.

We are sharing what those we have worked with wished those supporting them had understood better, including observations which are not specific to working overseas as well as those that are.

Partners

Moving Together Overseas

For many couples, relocating together internationally can be a time of shared vocation, experiences and adventure. Many couples talk of the need to rely on each other more and a growth in appreciation for the other's skills. For some, spending time with their partner away from previous networks of support deepens the relationships. The same context can place strains on relationships in terms of competing priorities: not being able to have any time for each other (due to overwhelming demands or extensive travel as part of role) or lack of privacy due to living in shared accommodation or in a team compound. Some couples must juggle constant social demands. Others, in isolated contexts, may face the lack of wider social relationships. This can feel suffocating or put strain on relationships, as the context drives pressure to provide for all a partner's needs. Partners may feel differently about their context, with one partner feeling connected to those around them, and the other disconnected.

And all that can happen whether or not each partner has a defined role. Sometimes partners work together, or in complementary activities. More often, one partner will relocate because of another's position, or find themselves expected to fill a role not of their choosing. This can bring its own problems and challenges.

Working Apart Internationally

Many humanitarian workers live and work away from their partners for extended periods of time. There are couples who manage this well and talk of a shared understanding of ways of communicating, for example: breakfast by remote video with the other partner having dinner; routines of work and time off that enable blocks of quality time not always possible when working long hours in the same location; and shared agreements about routines in times of transition between work and home locations. When working apart functions well, it offers an ability for both partners to pursue careers or support family in a way that fulfils values, and there can be pride in the partner's role and achievements or sacrifices. We have heard moving accounts of a deep sense of partnership facilitated by mutually agreed working apart.

We have also heard accounts of deep pain caused by financial, work or family circumstances forcing couples to work apart, and the impact that can have on relationships when it is not a choice, or not a shared choice. Houldey (2021) describes particularly acute strains for some female humanitarians in Kenya, in this case national staff members, working in unaccompanied posts at a distance from their home locations and without options to relocate their children closer to their place of work. Gendered expectations may mean that choices acceptable for male staff members are offered without thought or additional investigation to female workers, who then experience the split demands of work and home life as additionally distressing. Differences in the expatriate experience for those from less wealthy countries may also limit options to establish family in the way that staff members would prefer.

Time apart, combined with the intensity of working in humanitarian contexts, can create intense bonds with colleagues, weaken bonds in existing relationships and lead to jealousy or affairs. Widely read books like *Emergency Sex (and Other Desperate Measures)* (Cain, Thomson, & Postlewait, 2006) capture how disillusionment and trauma can drive attempts to retain humanity through relational choices that individuals might not make in other contexts. Coping mechanisms developed while working on the field (such as increased drinking or drug use, or a change in religious belief or intensity) may also be hard for a partner to understand when they have not had the same experiences or encounters. It is common to hear humanitarian workers say that experiences have changed their perception of a relationship, event or hobby that previously held deep meaning. Whilst this can be navigated, world views may change permanently.

Some LGBTQI+ couples may face discrimination and prejudice in the country where they or their partner are working. These factors can compound the challenge of working apart. They may limit opportunities to visit, to openly build networks of support or to encourage organisations to consider the issues during placement.

Many humanitarian agencies traditionally had better policies for co-locating international workers from Western sending countries with their partners, than for international workers from the majority world. We hope that in this growing international world equal consideration is given to all colleagues.

Recommendations to Consider in Supporting Couple Relationships

We recommend that organisations encourage couples to consider these sorts of interventions routinely.

- Find someone trusted to enquire after their relationship with their partner. Choose someone non-judgemental who will understand that there will be ups and downs, and not try to solve problems or offer solutions, but will just ask about the relationship to help the worker attend to it. We would encourage such a person to ask about emotional, relational and sexual well-being; how the practicalities of daily routines and work feel; and whether both are feeling able to communicate their needs.
- Access couple therapy, not seeing it as a stigma to be in therapy but as a necessary support when living in an unusual and often stressful environment.
- Think about how to manage times of transition between home and field, noting that these might be different for each partner and change with time. For example, one woman talked of how pleased she was whenever her husband returned home safely from a conflict zone. She knew he needed time to adjust, but she found it upsetting to witness his preoccupation with where he had been alongside his pleasure to be home. Her husband began stopping en route for 24 hours to decompress and finish tasks. The couple's initial days together became less fraught. They communicated better, and he reported that he was able to share more about his posting in ensuing weeks when emotions felt less heightened.
- Another couple shared how they had learnt that for a few days after coming back from an assignment, the worker would not want to talk about it. "*She wants to try to pick up life here, while I want desperately to know what she's been doing, but now I know that in time she will want to talk but just not be questioned*".
- Recognise the challenges of being an intercultural couple working across cultures. This advice will resonate more for some couples than others. But we all hail from particular family subcultures, and therefore make assumptions about others' meaning that may not match their intentions. False assumptions can be compounded when you are also trying to understand and participate in another culture. Pay attention to communicating about cultural perceptions of what is important, but also ways that both partners communicate their needs. Working through a book like *In Love But Worlds Apart* (Shelling & Fraser-Smith, 2008) or *A Moveable Marriage* (Pascoe, 2003) may be helpful.

Single Workers and Family

In addressing the dilemmas facing single workers, we recognise the huge diversity in this category of individuals who will also be at a variety of ages and life stages. Some have always been single, some are separated or divorced, and some bereaved. Defining who is your family will be very different for a young adult setting out in humanitarian work, when compared to someone who has served overseas for much of their adult life.

Issues of singleness have been comprehensively addressed elsewhere (Foyle, 2001; Hawker & Herbert, 2013). Here we highlight ways that single workers are part of families and networks and encourage consideration of that by organisations with a duty of care to them.

Single workers may be working in cultures that have expectations about marriage and family. They may frequently face questions about their single-ness (e.g. why their parents have not arranged a match for them), match-making suggestions, marriage proposals or propositioning. All these can be emotionally draining to negotiate whilst trying to build relationships with the host communities.

Single workers also mention experiences of colleagues making assumptions about their sexuality or histories. They describe the challenges of dating or having relationships whilst working in teams in the field, where there may be less privacy than in home countries. Organisations need to create a culture that considers the lived experience of single workers, to be considerate of language used within conversations and to create policies that are inclusive.

One challenge often shared by single workers is being placed in shared accommodation with people that they did not choose. Sometimes living with others is mutually beneficial and supportive, creating a safe place. At other times it can be an intensely challenging and draining, as different lifestyles cause conflicts and misunderstanding. Shared accommodation in humani-tarian settings often includes colleagues from a range of cultures and life stages. This mixture can both enrich experience but also worsen the inevit-able conflicts arising in shared space. Differences in expression or communi-cation style may be causes of conflict in themselves. One of the most common stressors reported by expatriate workers is difficult relationships with man-agers or colleagues (Foyle, 1999; Young, Pakenham, & Norwood, 2018).

Working in demanding contexts heightens the need for ways to unwind during rest time. For instance, whilst some crave privacy, others seek com-munity. Forced-choice shared accommodation can bring such personality or cultural differences to the fore. Couples may differ too, but they have chosen life together.

The first author recalls repeatedly returning to her shared accommoda-tion overseas, hungry after a long day, to find her food being used by her colleague. Her colleague thought this a way of showing they had become such good friends that they could share whatever they had and had been upset by the lack of reciprocation. What was interpreted by one as taking liber-ties was meant by the other as a symbol of appreciation and sisterhood. The colleagues addressed this by initiating both separate and shared fridge spaces.

This experience of shared lives and accommodation illustrates the diffe-rence between living with colleagues and living with family. Colleagues tend to move to new locations or return home permanently or for home assignments.

Couples or families tend to move together. Even colleagues who become close friends in the field and choose to share accommodation may have good reasons to separate when they retire or return to their passport countries. The emotional impact of regular changes of personnel impacts all. But for many singles, the pain of saying goodbye repeatedly is like grieving family, as friends constitute family (Santos, 2013).

For similar reasons, the challenges of being in the field include missing significant events in friends' lives or involvement with them, and not being granted the same permissions to visit as are granted to those visiting family. Drawing from research in New Zealand and Belgium, the UK government introduced the idea of a "support bubble" during the Covid-19 pandemic to address the fact that practical and emotional help from others can be protective for health (SPI-B, 2020). Whilst using this term, we are not advocating restricted or inflexible bubbles, but a process of thinking through support networks with single people. Support bubbles can promote self-care by protecting their health during assignments and their rights to visit or invest in relationships with loved ones.

Recommendations to Consider in Supporting Single Workers

- Consider choice in accommodation as much as possible. Have open conversations about privacy, personal preference and agreements about shared spaces. Where accommodation choices are limited (or there are none), take time to think about how to adapt living spaces to suit the needs of current workers. Openly discuss with individuals what helps them to unwind and what facilitates this.
- Discuss with single workers who are the key people in their lives. To allow participation in key events within support networks, organisations should consider whether to offer the same support and rights (e.g. for compassionate leave, parental leave, carers' leave) as they offer to those with a biological family.
- Create a culture that pays attention to the language used about singleness within the organisation, both informally by employees (avoiding terms like "left on the shelf" to denote single status) and within policies. What does a policy about creating a family-friendly organisation state about those with different relational ties?
- Some single people are tempted to overwork as they do not have family or a partner to return to. Consider identifying someone trusted within the organisation to check in with and encourage them to develop sustainable routines.
- Do not assume that all single workers have similar needs or expectations.

Families Working Internationally and Third Culture Kids

We are living in a world where international migration is an increasing part of many people's lived experience. The World Economic Forum (Edmond, 2020) estimates that there are 272 million international migrants – 3.5% of the world's population. While most people leave their home countries for work, millions are driven away by violence, conflict and/or climate change. The context of migrating for work in the humanitarian/mission sector is complex. Families may be posted to locations to support those affected by humanitarian crises, poverty or civil unrest. This shapes children and young people's lives in particular ways, as decisions about education and friendship networks will be influenced by changing political climates. They may also have fewer resources than some of their peers within international schools whose parents are working for multinational companies; or alternatively, and sometimes at the same time, more resources than those within their host culture living around them in other locations.

Employers and non-governmental organisations (NGOs) vary hugely in how much attention they pay to the children of their staff. Children's needs must not be ignored, because the impact on them of living internationally is usually far greater than on their parents. Typically, parents will come from at least one culture and will take their children to a second culture. The children's experience forms a third culture, which can be a blend of their parents' passport and host cultures, or a different culture entirely, shared with their peer group. Hence, children who have this experience are called "third culture kids" (TCKs).

A third culture can be seen most clearly among children in an international school, who may come from many different passport countries, and may not always be located in the same host country as their parents, but who create a culture among them which matches neither the passport nor any host country.

For instance, the second author recalls a former school in a Himalayan hill station for the children of missionaries. The children there held passports from countries like the UK, Canada, Brazil, the USA, Germany, the Netherlands, Sweden, Australia, New Zealand, South Korea and the Philippines. Generally, they were familiar with the cultures of both the local country and their passport countries. But the culture they lived in was essentially created by their school environment. They tended to speak with American accents. They followed tailored curricula which allowed them to learn together whilst conforming to diverse requirements of International General Certificates of Secondary Education, International Baccalaureates and US high school graduation. They learned how to stop monkeys stealing their food, and how to keep safe walking to the bazaar.

TCKs are not only found in international schools. They may attend local schools with children who are citizens of their host countries. They may be educated at home by their parents because there are no suitable schooling options where they live. They may be living in their passport country, conscious of their history in a different host country and their identity as TCKs, or at least of feeling different from the peers around them. TCKs include the children of missionaries, humanitarian workers, military personnel and the staff of multinational businesses and of diplomatic missions. Whilst some recognise and own their identity as TCKs, others have never heard of the descriptor, and are pleasantly surprised to discover, as children or adults, a phrase to describe the experience they grew up with.

When returning to their passport countries, TCKs often struggle to fit in with peers who use obscenities, show little awareness of world events, seeming more preoccupied with soaps and celebrities and cannot find their host country on a map. When the Himalayan school had to be closed suddenly after a terrorist attack, most of the students chose to be relocated as a whole group to a different country, instead of returning to their passport countries with their parents. They valued the culture they shared among themselves.

Every school creates its own culture, particularly boarding schools. Still, TCKs' sense of belonging is in relationship to others of a similar background (Pollock & Van Reken, 1999; Bushong, 2013). Typically, they relate to others who have had similar experiences of growing up in a mixture of cultures, regardless of the passport or host country, or their parents' work or faith backgrounds. The authors have observed many TCKs, both as children and adults, feeling acute isolation at times but reacting with joy and a sense of security when they meet other TCKs.

It is important to consider TCKs in the context of children who share some but not all related experiences, including multicultural and multiracial children, children of immigrants and refugees, children of parents from a minority racial or ethnic group, international adoptees and domestic TCKs (who have moved between subcultures within the same country). Collectively, children who grow up in more than one cultural environment may be called cross-cultural kids (CCKs). Van Reken (2021) has outlined similarities and differences between TCKs and other types of CCKs.

Uniquely common to TCKs are experiences such as a cross-cultural lifestyle; high mobility; an expectation of being repatriated; and an identity tied up with their parents' sponsoring mission, NGO, business, or armed or government service. Personal benefits of being a TCK include having an expansive world view and a facility for learning new languages and bridging between cultures. Costly in some contexts and beneficial in others are other common characteristics such as a sense of rootlessness (home being both everywhere and nowhere), restlessness, and of belonging and identity being shared with other TCKs rather than determined by race or ethnicity (Van Reken, 2021).

The PolVan Cultural Identity Model (Table 5.1) shows how CCKs' outward appearance can differ from their thoughts and feelings, depending on where they are. For example, after first leaving their passport culture for a

Table 5.1 The PolVan Cultural Identity Model

Foreigner	Hidden Immigrant
Look *different* Think *differently* Speak *differently*	Look alike Think *differently* Speak alike/*differently*
Adopted Look *different* Think alike Speak alike	Mirror Look alike Think alike Speak alike

new culture, TCKs begin as foreigners. After a while they may adopt the cultural identity of their host country, whilst appearing to outsiders as belonging to their passport country. On return to their passport country, they become hidden immigrants, thinking differently from those who look like them. It may take considerable adaptation time before TCKs are able to mirror the thinking of their peers. This sounds like a smooth process, but circumstances can make it much more complicated to negotiate.

Van Reken (2021) has further noted how TCKs can adapt differently to their circumstances. Some become *chameleons*, trying to find an identity that matches their surroundings. Thus, parents have described to us children who live in the moment, and adapt to whatever culture they find themselves in. Some become *screamers*, asserting a different identity from their surroundings. For example, children returning to a European passport country after spending most of their lives in Cambodia may think of themselves as Cambodian and not understand relatives who ask them how it feels to be "back home". Some become *wallflowers*, avoiding having an identity at all, for instance withdrawing into books or bedrooms and trying to be invisible.

When supporting children and young people, we also need to consider those people who children may see as part of the family but who cannot come back to their passport country or move locations with them, including

- local friends and neighbours, who can become very close in the absence of extended family;
- domestic staff, especially those helping with childcare, whom humanitarian workers may take on in countries where labour is cheap;
- children adopted in the host country who cannot join the family in their passport country, and who then can face difficulties reintegrating into their home culture;
- pets, who may have to be found homes with family friends or be put down. It is easy to overlook the loss of pets unless the value of such relationships is recognised.

Living Separately from Family

Parents working overseas have many educational options to consider for their children, including boarding, homeschooling, local schools, international school, multiple schooling options in the host country or passport country, or boarding in a third country.

Recommendations for Work with TCKs

Please see the detailed recommendations given in chapter 11 (this volume).

Relationship with Parents

One of the dilemmas for international workers is the impact of their life-style on wider family. An example of this we encounter often in our work with humanitarian workers is not being able to care for elderly relatives, and the impact that this has on sibling relationships or on their parents. This is particularly pertinent in cultures where care for elders is highly prized and there can be an element of shame at not being present to care for loved ones. Other workers may end work abroad in order to return home to look after parents, often then facing questions of where they will live, especially when returning without a home of their own or the finance to buy one. We have both worked with individuals feeling utterly overwhelmed and destabilised by multiple changes and losses: of a sense of identity as a humanitarian worker; of their own social network; of reverse culture shock; and the need to navigate changing relationships with their wider family. Research has highlighted the impact of transitioning to a caring role and the demands of being a carer (Henwood, Larkin, & Milne, 2017). Humanitarian workers taking on such a role begin it at a point where multiple challenges already affect their well-being and mental health.

We have supported families where grandparents have been deeply angry with workers for limited access to grandchildren, or critical of or concerned about the impact on their grandchildren of the humanitarian lifestyle or presence in war zones. This places strain on relationships across generations but also can create strain within families to prove that they are happy. Consequently, they may not share challenges or difficult aspects of the posting with their support networks. They may not seek appropriate help to change or move on because they feel trapped by a perceived need to justify the decision to work internationally.

We have also supported many families where generations have been humanitarian workers. In these contexts, grandparents or other relatives can draw on their own wealth of experience to encourage and support families through dilemmas. Strong intergenerational ties and rich family culture can draw strength and unity from different cultural traditions, family rituals or places.

For example, some gather to mark a traditional holiday from a previous host country whilst working in another. Some actively choose a shared language after leaving an area to enable a sense of shared identity (or in one instance, so the teachers at the new school did not know what was being said!). Some share favourite camping sites or cooking techniques that build shared identity and enable family stories to be told and enriched.

Recommendations to Consider in Supporting Relationships with Extended Family

- During placement reviews of well-being, ask about relationships with parents, grandparents and other relatives. Explicitly ask about relatives' health and any other worries about them, and how relatives feel about those who work overseas.
- Sometimes it helps (if handled carefully) to link concerned relatives with current workers who can answer questions about the lived experience of living overseas with or without family.
- Whilst Covid-19 has helped us all learn how to communicate virtually, ensure that relatives have practised using the means that you intend to use to communicate before leaving. Knowing how to maintain contact can help people feel connected.
- Plan how often you will communicate and any associated routines (for example, "we do Thursday dinner together each week when they are having their lunch"; or "the children video call at bedtime every Sunday night for a bedtime story with Grandad"). Planning helps manage expectations and reduce frustrations of repeated missed calls or failed communication.
- Be aware of your culture and don't assume others' expectations match yours, whether they are from the same or a different culture. Ask workers what cultural expectations there are for caring for elders within their community, what they see as their network of responsibilities, and how they are feeling about planning to meet or sidestep expectations.
- Discuss in advance among networks what workers would like to happen if a close family member requires care. Within care networks, it can be hard to make decisions at a moment that things are fraught. Often all parties make assumptions about what the others will or will not do. Encourage workers to consider what circumstances would force them to leave the field, and how they can offer support from there. Whilst we all change our minds and need to stay flexible, discussions and shared understandings can create channels of communication that keep dialogue open when it is most needed but hardest to begin.
- Where the worker has sole caring responsibilities for family members, think through in advance what they understand or want these to be. Advance planning will make decisions easier when they become necessary.

Pandemic Complications

We write during the second year of the Covid-19 pandemic. Covid-19 has complicated family adjustment. Families have been kept apart for longer than expected. Travel options have become limited. People who used to travel much more are home more. Children have become depressed because of what they lost during the pandemic, in terms of relational contact, changed travel plans, lockdowns and other restrictions. Changing international travel rules and lockdown policies have played havoc with family life and stability, sometimes separating families for long periods of time. For some, local conditions meant that the pandemic barely affected them, or lockdown provided welcome respite and eased opportunities for virtual communication. The long-term outcome remains uncertain, and a breeding ground for anxiety.

Summary

In this chapter we considered how families are affected when one person chooses to work in a different culture. We considered a wide definition of "family", including not just nuclear and extended families but also close friends and colleagues who can become surrogate family for expatriate workers. We considered how partners are affected when working together and apart. We considered what family means to single workers without partners. We considered how workers affect and are affected by their extended biological family. We outlined how the children of expatriate workers forge an identity as TCKs. We made recommendations for the first three of these. In chapter 11, we give more detail on TCKs and make extensive recommendations concerning them. We are all part of families at some stage in our life, and organisations ignore the families of their workers at their peril.

References

Bowlby, J. (1988). *A secure base: Parent-child attachment and healthy human development.* Abingdon, Oxon: Routledge.

Bushong, L.J. (2013). *Belonging everywhere and nowhere: Insights into counselling the globally mobile.* Indianapolis: Mango Tree Intercultural Services.

Cain, K., Thomson, A., & Postlewait, H. (2006). *Emergency sex (and other desperate measures): True stories from a war zone.* London: Ebury Publishing.

Edmond, C. (2020, 10 January). Global migration by the numbers: Who migrates, where they go and why. *World Economic Forum.* www.weforum.org/agenda/2020/01/iom-global-migration-report-international-migrants-2020/

Foyle, M.F. (1999). *Expatriate mental health* [Unpublished doctoral dissertation]. University of London.

Foyle, M.F. (2001). *Honorably wounded: Stress among Christian workers* (2nd ed.). Oxford: Monarch.

Hawker, D.M., & Herbert, T. (Eds.) (2013). *Single mission: Thriving as a single Christian in cross-cultural ministry*. Fresno, CA: Condeo Press.

Henwood, M., Larkin, M., & Milne, A. (2017). *Seeing the wood for the trees. Carer related research and knowledge: A scoping review*. http://docs.scie-socialcareonline.org.uk/fulltext/058517.pdf

Houldey, G. (2021). *The vulnerable humanitarian: Ending burnout culture in the aid sector*. Abingdon: Routledge.

Meins, E. (2017). Overrated: The predictive power of attachment. *The Psychologist, 30*, 20–24.

Pascoe, R. (2003). *A moveable marriage: Relocate your relationship without breaking it*. North Vancouver: Expatriate Press.

Pollock, D.C., & Van Reken, R.E. (1999). *The third culture kid experience: Growing up among worlds*. Yarmouth, ME: Intercultural Press.

Pollock, D.C., Van Reken, R.E., & Pollock, M. (2017). *Third culture kids: Growing up among worlds* (3rd ed.). Boston: Nicholas Brealey.

Santos, T. (2013). The pain of saying goodbye. In D. Hawker & T. Herbert (Eds.), *Single mission: Thriving as a single Christian in cross-cultural ministry* (pp. 22–23). Fresno, CA: Condeo Press.

Shelling, G., & Fraser-Smith, J. (2008). *In love but worlds apart: Insights, questions, and tips for the intercultural couple*. Bloomington, IN: Authorhouse.

SPI-B. (2020). *Well-being and household connection: The behavioural considerations of "Bubbles"*. www.gov.uk/government/publications/spi-b-well-being-and-household-connection-the-behavioural-considerations-of-bubbles-14-may-2020

Van Reken, R. (2021). *Cross cultural kids*. www.crossculturalkid.org

Young, T.K.H., Pakenham, K.I., & Norwood, M.F. (2018). Thematic analysis of aid workers' stressors and coping strategies: Work, psychological, lifestyle and social dimensions. *Journal of International Humanitarian Action, 3*(19). https://doi.org/10.1186/s41018-018-0046-3

Chapter 6

Supporting grassroots aid workers and volunteers

Leslie Brownbridge

This chapter explores the impact on grassroots volunteers of working in the refugee camps in France and Greece. In doing this it takes a position of solidarity with the volunteers, as summed up by Watson: "If you have come here to help me, you are wasting your time. If you come because your liberation is bound up with mine, then let us work together" (Watson, as cited in Watkins, 2015).

In the chapter, I will discuss the creative ways these volunteers embrace challenges through sheer trial and error, with commitment, dedication and compassion, often on shoestring budgets and with the challenge of creating security without a reliable organisational grounding. It also describes how a group of community activists, psychologists and grassroots humanitarians working with displaced persons used their collective power to develop and implement a supportive network.

The Context

Mould (2017) describes Calais as a site suffused throughout with material precarity, a *"place that mixed hope and despair, richness and conflict, home-making and un-making"*, a description which poignantly encompasses refugee camps worldwide.

Although the impromptu refugee camps in northern France have been in place for 20 years, numbers increased dramatically from 2015 onwards, as those seeking asylum and attempting to reach the UK were held for processing in France. In response, the French and British governments deployed additional police and reinforced border security teams (Joint Ministerial Declaration, 2015) though these rarely operated in accordance with United Nations High Commissioner for Refugees (UNHCR) guidelines for support and adherence to human rights. As a result of continued displacement and inadequate housing, an increasing number of makeshift camps like the ones in Calais and Dunkirk have grown up, each to be subsequently supported by humanitarian workers (Davies, Isakjee, & Dhesi, 2017).

DOI: 10.4324/9781003261971-7

Such settings are often marked by a high degree of humanitarian need, characterised by a lack of shelter, poor sanitary conditions, low access to potable water and an almost total abdication of responsibility by government authorities for the well-being of the residents. This coupled with violence from French authorities profoundly marked the aid workers working in the camps affecting their ability to process what they witnessed (Agier et al., 2018)

Even prior to the dismantling of the second Calais "Jungle" (officially known as Camp de la Lande, an encampment existing from January 2015 to October 2016), volunteers began reporting concerns with conflict and violence in the camps. As tents and temporary structures were dismantled for clearance in the main communal area, displaced people moved into surrounding fields and forests, and were subsequently found and removed, often violently and under cover of night. These evictions, more targeted and personal, had a stronger impact on all involved: an attack on families huddled together in tents trying to survive the elements without the most basic shelter. The public authorities' goal was to curtail the formation of a new camp, and so evictions took place almost daily (Witter, 2021), creating a sense of anxiety and urgency, which increased because clearances could take place at any time of day and throughout the night. To add to the effects of seeing tents dismantled and ripped from people trying to survive, volunteers struggled to prioritise their well-being in the face of the urgent need to manage evictions and support the refugees, and were often left with profound feelings of guilt and inner conflict as they attempted to stand alongside.

The Role of Grassroots Organisations (GROs) in the Camps

According to Lewis (quoted in Elbers 2016), *"non-governmental organisations (NGOs) are a diverse group of organisations that defy generalisation"*. Some have argued that there is a lack of precision in the term "NGO". This is particularly relevant for grassroots organisations that may start as small efforts among friends and within communities but can evolve into larger-scale teams with their own sets of challenging bureaucracies. On the positive side, GRO initiatives can quickly gain momentum as a rapid response to an emerging crisis (Bettencourt, 2022).

The grassroots humanitarian response is similarly varied worldwide, and therefore impossible to fully catalogue. Researching for this chapter, I was struck by how little qualitative research on grassroots organisations and volunteers exists, and specifically on what constitutes effective pre-/during/post-assignment support outside of large and more formal organisations. This chapter is largely based on interviews and case studies to address this lack, and includes the evaluation of the initiatives of some existing GROs, and their attempts to find creative and compassionate ways to support staff with only limited budgets. As much of the work that I, and peers, have done has been in northern France, including Calais, Grand Synthe and Dunkirk, and some parts of Greece, many of the respondents and facilitators have shared perspectives from working in these locations.

While larger or governmentally funded organisations can offer more rigorous support plans for staff, this is often not the case with GROs, whose team members may be transient and temporary, without fixed terms or organisational structure in place. While bottom-up approaches allow individuals or small groups to define goals and objectives creatively, the lack of structure often means that well-meaning initiatives are undermined. Staff may not receive consistent training, clarity of information or access to support to effectively recognise and cope with field experiences or reactions to leaving their posts to return to countries of origin. Compounding this, volunteers consistently report feelings of despair, anger and helplessness at witnessing atrocities (Bochenek, 2017), such as reported use of pepper spray on people, their tents and food by police in situations where they pose no threat, and oppression and injustices from figures of authority in the camps at Calais and Dunkirk.

Key effective coping strategies for all humanitarians include the need for solid social connections and maintaining well-being activities (Young, Pakenham, & Norwood, 2018), but this can be challenging to coordinate without an organisational structure, whether staff are working independently or are connected to a specific GRO. GROs, on their side, often struggle to provide a rapid response for staff in distress, because of their need to focus on the urgent support of vulnerable populations and beneficiaries (Stoddard, Harmer, Haver, Taylor, & Harvey, 2015).

Supporting GRO Activists and Volunteers

Pre-training for grassroots volunteers is important as it is for all other humanitarians. Otherwise, there can be a well-intentioned idealism without sufficient preparation for the realities and difficulties of the work:

> I think there is often a very hopeful feeling when people start out – here are some severe problems that I can help with – followed by a gradual realisation that there is not much you can do to tackle the systemic inequalities and injustices of the way that migrants are treated. This is really distressing, but people mobilise all their resources to work ever harder (getting more and more tired) and gradually realise that no matter how hard they work and how much they give, things don't improve very much. This can be very demoralising, particularly if you have the sense that leaders (either in your organisation or world leaders) are not committed to doing their utmost to address difficulties. The real-world conflicts between political drivers and finances really batter our naive belief that we can work to change things for the better. This has a lot of potential

negative impacts, but all the research shows that, held in a supportive social situation (strong team, good leadership, high camaraderie), these can counterweight the impact.

It is not unusual in many of the camps to find GROs working alongside larger, more established organisations (McGee & Pelham, 2017). For example, Doctors of the World UK (DOTWUK) has more than 400 programmes in over 80 countries offering a wide range of support to "meet the health needs of people globally". In June of 2016, DOTWUK launched an emergency response in which volunteer doctors and nurses, including many from the UK, staffed an emergency clinic in Calais and surrounding areas, seeing on average 130 people per day. They also provided psychosocial therapy, hygiene kits and mobile clinics to smaller groups of refugees dispersed outside camps across the region, with mental health a major focus of their work. Their reports showed that almost two-thirds of the health problems seen were related to the conditions of the camp. Notably, health concerns among the volunteers and aid workers were similar to those of the refugees.

When I volunteered as a clinic worker with DOTWUK, there was a pre-employment two-day training programme to ensure all workers understood the work with vulnerable beneficiaries.[1] A comprehensive training was offered on barriers faced by refugees and vulnerable migrants when accessing UK National Health Service (NHS) care. In addition, prior to starting work, all volunteers were required to sign the European Charter of Humanitarian Aid and a volunteer charter outlining codes of conduct, intention and commitment to safeguarding (adults and children) as well as adherence to the principles of the organisation. Training sessions on self-care and stress management using mindfulness-based approaches were offered as additional support, though not mandatory. As stated, however, although such support may be in place in larger NGOs, it is often limited or non-existent in smaller, more independent organisations.

In some cases, managers and coordinators are very aware of the impact on volunteers of what they are witnessing and experiencing, even as the volunteers themselves are not (Gloster, Zacharia, & Karekla, 2020). In other cases, awareness of the need for support arises from aid workers themselves, as they witness the impact on their teams of attempting to support refugees and asylum seekers. Like many witnessing the expansion of refugee camps in the media and feeling a strong pull to be of service, Juliet Kilpin began visiting the camps in northern France independently. From her weekly visits to the Calais "Jungle" in 2015, in 2016 Juliet co-founded Peaceful Borders,[2] which "seeks to accompany and equip people responding to forced migration" with support both in the field and after relocation. The organisation helps new arrivals navigate life in the UK by signposting and physically accompanying them to appointments, giving appropriate reassurance to combat feelings of isolation and loneliness.

At the start of visiting Calais and Dunkirk, Juliet saw that many like-minded individuals, who were self-funding and loading up their vehicles with donations of clothes, food and tents, felt unable to cope with what they were witnessing: "They were completely shocked. And there was no support structure, nowhere for them to effectively turn to, to process what they were seeing".

Seeking Solutions in Supporting GRO's – Support and Solidarity Network (Ssun)

Juliet reacted to what she was seeing by contacting the staff teams at the Helen Bamber Foundation (HBF),[3] seeking ways for volunteers to access support. Though the HBF worked mainly with refugees, asylum seekers and survivors of trafficking, a group of psychologists worked with Juliet to determine how best to support camp volunteers. Among them was Francesca Brady, then a clinical psychologist and Co-Head of Therapies with HBF. Fran partnered with Sally Zlotowitz, a community psychologist, to set up a virtual response system: "I think it was mostly that sense that something really needed to be done to respond to the humanitarian crisis, and the one thing we could do is support the volunteers who were helping on the ground".

They started by "brainstorming amongst a group of psychologists working with refugees/trauma/aid work, but many didn't have the capacity to remain involved once the idea had formed", so Fran and Sally carried it forward themselves. It was collectively decided not to offer formal "therapy" for two reasons; firstly, governance and regulation would require formal structures that could not be ensured, and secondly, they wanted to avoid pathologising the normal responses of camp volunteers to witnessing atrocities and human rights abuses. There were two predominant goals: to use principles of psychosocial accompaniment (Watkins, 2015) by "standing in solidarity" alongside camp volunteers and offering peer support; and to share in bearing witness to social injustices, repression and non-transparency. The idea was that facilitating mutually agreed-upon meetings between camp volunteers and support volunteers would help the former foster resilience and self-care.

> It was decided to offer a buddying system, whereby camp volunteers either on the ground or returning home could access services for support. They asked qualified mental health professionals (again to avoid concerns about safeguarding) to be paired with camp volunteers for an initial three-month series of conversations to be agreed upon, and potentially extended according to an agreement from both parties.

The conversation was to be led by the camp volunteer with the buddy's role to listen, reflect and show support or offer everyday ideas for self- and collective care. Although not "therapy", this type of buddying is strictly confidential. "Advertising" to camp volunteers was largely word of mouth, though social media and email accounts were generated for contact. Welfare coordinators and organisational leads were asked to put up posters in various areas throughout the camps about the network. The greatest challenge was getting information to people about support, due to the transient nature of the volunteers, and the high turnover of managers/coordinators.

> Lots of volunteers wanted help, but whilst posted felt too busy with other tasks to slow down and access support, but once back in their countries of origin, mainly the UK at that time, they also seemed too busy getting back to "normal" life and wanting to avoid talking about difficult experiences in the camp.

When I came on board with Support and Solidarity Network (Ssun), Juliet and I travelled to Dunkirk and Calais to visit the camps shortly after the dismantling in 2016. There were still a significant number of tents in place, dispersed in a small field outside of Calais, with some families and small groups in more heavily wooded areas seeking protection from the elements, and the authorities. Our aim during the visit was to determine what challenges were being faced from the perspective of those actively working in the field, and to brainstorm ways we could offer psychological support. We met with a variety of GROs based in the camps and surroundings, mainly beneath a large structure called "The Warehouse", an area on the outskirts of the camp housing multiple organisations, as well as donations for basic shelter and other needs. One person we met with was the well-being coordinator from Help Refugees, a GRO which had grown exponentially following new funding and who had recently developed an induction programme for volunteers in their partitioned area within The Warehouse.

Seated on bales of hay and rickety chairs in a small, tented area off the main warehouse in Calais, were a dozen or so "newbies", new volunteers, many of whom had never visited a refugee camp before nor volunteered in similar capacity. It was a diverse group ranging from retirees to groups of friends and a mother and son team, all eager to begin, but most with no formal training. There was one lone heater that we took turns placing in front of where we sat, with a persistent awareness of how much more difficult it must be for those individuals and families battling the elements beyond our drafty enclosure. The coordinator conducting the session had been volunteering in northern France for several years and later explained that this volunteer induction session arose partly from trial and error, from making mistakes and learning more efficient systems. "We learned quickly, and harshly, that some measures had to be put into place, and that the key was adaptability to the ever-changing environmental and political challenges". Several years of supporting and organising volunteers had shown the importance of pre-assignment information, including core messages about volunteer support with regards to boundaries, coping with moral injury (see chapter 4, this volume), and recognising signs of burnout and stress responses.

The coverage of potential challenges in the induction was impressively thorough, from how to manage police brutality towards refugees and hostilities to volunteers, to drawing appropriate boundaries with those with whom they bore witness and with each other. Before the dismantling of the "Jungle", the facilitator stated there had been concerns with substance abuse among volunteer staff and that although bonding and support were important, some relationships that had formed might have been unhealthy in any context. This was one of the most challenging circumstances to navigate as volunteers were independent and without structure, governance or policy. Therefore, imposing rules, curfews or consequences on individuals giving their free time and sometimes self-funding, was difficult.

Volunteers tended to blame themselves for not accessing pre-assignment materials or training prior to volunteering, which added to feelings of guilt. We also noticed how difficult it was for any manager or facilitator of a grassroots organisation to determine how individuals would cope in such intense situations. Though effective management processes may be in place, overseers are ultimately reliant on skills of communication, transparency and recognition of stress among team members. Given the transient nature of volunteering part-time, this is difficult to navigate. Many volunteers gain this insight only on reflection after returning to their home society: "I really realised how unprepared I was for what I was about to experience. I thought I could handle what I was seeing but viewing it on paper or on TV was vastly different".

It was also clear that as volunteers returned to their home base, what may have been ignored or dismissed in the immediacy of the field environment, came to the forefront in the quieter, more stable environment at home. The challenge was therefore how to effectively support volunteers after they left the camps. Although they were often processing difficult experiences they had heard about or seen, alongside this they reported missing the sense of belonging, community and understanding they had experienced within the camps (Agier et al., 2018). This could be exacerbated in situations in which there was a negative view of their work in the camps on their return home, and a lack of understanding of its value. Some volunteers reported feeling there was very little support for their work, and this could, in turn, exacerbate feelings of shame, guilt and a questioning of their own morality (Truman & Berdondini, in press). It is interesting to contrast this experience with that of staff and volunteers during the recent conflict in Ukraine in which the societal discourse has been overwhelmingly supportive to both refugees and those supporting them.

To help amend this, one of the options discussed in meetings with the HBF team and Ssun coordinators was to create a safe space for volunteers to connect (Robjant & Fazel, 2010) by offering space for support in the camps or at the London clinic, potentially with a weekly presence in the form of a workshop or group gathering. Although the welfare coordinators were enthusiastic about implementing this, we noted resistance to this suggestion from the volunteers themselves, particularly attached to feelings of guilt that they got to be offered mental health support", while refugees were living in tents and struggling to meet bare necessities of food, clothing and shelter. Despite this, we invited all volunteers who were in our mailing system and beyond to attend our "Returning Home" workshop. The aim was to learn more from the volunteers about how best to support them using a short questionnaire and then brainstorming words or phrases that came to mind about their experience in the camps to determine how Ssun's response could be improved.

In the responses we received, we noted there were differences in how volunteering was experienced in the field, and after returning home. While in the field much frustration and anxiety was reported around the magnitude of the issues, "It's never enough" was a common refrain, along with feelings of guilt at being able to leave the camps and struggles separating from relationships formed in the camps. Themes that arose from the wordplay were centred predominantly around feelings of guilt, particularly around seeking help, with one volunteer writing, "I shouldn't seek help. My life is much better than my friends (the refugees)". Guilt played a part in most aspects from being able to leave the camp, to feeling that other volunteers had been working in camps longer and were therefore "more committed". There was a sense of feeling weak: "If you are not coping, you are weak". Aid workers also reported a struggle to manage emotional responses to witnessing police brutality and the lack of humanity from other authorities (government, police), and even on social media.

We enquired about barriers volunteers faced accessing psychological support whether in the field or back in countries of origin and received a variety of responses:

- Stigma: not wanting others to view them as "weak" or unable to cope
- Shame/guilt: feeling that their lives were very privileged compared to those whom they were supporting
- Lack of prior understanding about the impact of working in humanitarian settings including limited preparedness for coping with the work during and after volunteering and limited recognition of the effects of stress on them (see chapter 1 for more on this)
- Conflicting demands in the camp setting: Having too many jobs that needed doing; often unstructured hours; variable boundaries.
- Inability to communicate the above feelings and experiences within their own home groups of family, friends, peers or colleagues.

Evaluating the effectiveness of Ssun intervention, surveys were returned with wholly positive comments.

It was helpful having an objective outsider to talk to, but also someone who understood the challenges and difficulties of volunteering in Calais. She (my buddy) was keen to learn about my experiences, but also had really valuable insight into the emotional impact it has left.

Another wrote, "It was nice to chat to someone new and neutral and understand that it's more about accepting the limitations that come with helping refugees than feeling guilty for not being able to help more".

Feelings of isolation were another common theme, with respondents sharing a sense of relief at being able to openly discuss what they were feeling in a space where some facilitators had also experienced the same. Shared resilience through quasi-similar experiences can be empowering and comforting (Nuttman-Shwartz, 2014). Another respondent recognised the support system as "a space to reflect and share my thoughts", writing that their buddy had made some really helpful practical suggestions. Many felt the kind of support they received was instrumental in helping them realise limitations and acknowledge feelings of guilt for not doing more and being able to get away from the camps.

Collaborations with Other Projects and Organisations

The Refugee Resilience Collective (RRC) is another organisation that has worked to support camp volunteers and the refugee populations they work with. A UK-based team of psychotherapists and psychologists, RRC has been offering resilience-based support to refugees and NGO volunteers in Calais and Dunkirk since March 2016 (Hughes et al., 2020). After the clearance of the "Jungle" and the burning down of the Dunkirk camp in 2017, they continued to work with key voluntary associations in the area including Refugee Community Kitchen, Refugee Youth Service and L'Auberge des Migrants. RRC recognised the lack of support for the emotional needs of volunteers and expanded their resources to support them. Their team's approach is partially based on providing narrative therapy interventions (White & Epston, 2015) and addressing burnout associated with stress responses to injustice (Reynolds, 2012), a stance that is also in keeping with that of Ssun. The RRC is a valuable reminder of how collective grassroots organisations can work together to create cross-networks of communication, share information and strengthen accessibility.

As stated above, GROs, whether collective or individual, can lack access to conventional avenues of occupational psychological support (Bhattacharyya & Brenner, 2021), but new opportunities and models are beginning to arise, not just driven by psychologists but also from within community groups and field groups themselves. This can begin with as small a thing as a conversation. However, community-based support without governance or policy has its limitations: Supervision of such self-generated initiatives is often non-existent and safeguarding to protect those who are additionally vulnerable may be compromised or overlooked. Interventions like debriefing and support with trauma processing are often not available or accessible.

In his foreword to *History and Hope: The International Humanitarian Reader* (Cahill, 2013), Lord Owen writes,

> The pursuit of the goals of humanitarianism, whether through assistance or intervention, has no single way, follows no preconceived pattern. Almost by definition, each experience is different. This means, more perhaps than in any other human activity, that practitioners have to be ready to learn from experience and adapt to circumstance.

One of the adaptations made by the initiatives discussed here, and not exclusive to Ssun, is to offer support through digital means (telephone, text message etc.) to accommodate the transient lives of camp volunteers, who are continually relocating and often based where there may be limited access to support (see chapter 13, this volume). Valerie Amos (2013) recognised the digital revolution in the humanitarian sector, and its empowerment of people "who receive humanitarian aid". Basic connectivity and access to utilities and information is of significant value for refugees, migrants and asylum seekers (Granryd, 2017) as well as to those people supporting them, including camp volunteers.

Bobby Lloyd, registered art therapist and CEO of Art Refuge, is a visual artist who has worked extensively in community and international contexts of conflict, crisis and the displacement of people. Her commitment has been to use art-based approaches to "empower and improve the health and well-being of under-served and marginalised populations". Art Refuge is based mainly in Calais, Paris, London and Bristol, yet it also operates online across borders with a team supporting people displaced by conflict, persecution and poverty both in the UK and internationally. Staff are informed by specialisms in trauma work, psychosocial approaches and collaborative programmes. Some of their freelance support artists come from refugee backgrounds, providing a special insight into the potential needs and perspectives of displaced persons. Although the charity is largely funded by individual donations and grants, the artists also raise funds through commissions and in offering training to other services in the NHS, various NGOs and with voluntary groups in Calais and throughout the UK. In summer of 2020 they offered training to volunteers across multiple organisations on topics such as coping and resilience; psychological first aid (PFA); working across cultures, faiths and traditions; and developing a psychosocial toolkit (Lahad, Shacham, & Ayalon, 2013).

Recognising a need for joint support, the team developed the framework of a *Community Table*, which grew from the urgent issues at stake for people trying to survive on the France–UK border: "More than ever we need to be gathering around real and imagined tables, talking to each other and seeking creative responses and solutions". This stresses the recognition and importance of inclusivity with people from different cultures, ideologies and political and socio-economic backgrounds, whether volunteers or refugees. They all make art together, and have found it helps support those in crisis to feel more connected in building coping strategies. The team has developed rituals within their work as well, taking walks together, debriefing and having online calls, which has a marked impact on mental health, creating a shared sense of support and belonging.

> The importance of welfare specialists who look after the volunteering team can't be overstated. This normalises the impact of working in an aid context, the potential impact on workers' mental health and encourages people to access support if needed. Also, early establishment of the expectation of a need for support post assignment (e.g. mentor/peer support when returned to home country) and ideally making this mandatory/opt-out so that people do get access to some support after assignment too.

There is strong merit in volunteers collaboratively supporting one another, whether collectively or in pairs. Traumatised by the reports of a migrant boat sinking in the Channel trying to reach the United Kingdom, Juliet remembers frantic requests for information from refugees approaching volunteers and aid workers, "could it be that someone they know, someone they love, might have been on that boat and could volunteers please find out". The heartbreaking requests for information in turn deeply affected the volunteers, none of whom had reliable information, and who were aware of the hostile environment affecting those seeking more news. To manage the effect of this, Juliet states that the simple act of reaching out and meeting for a coffee was incredibly helpful. "We didn't even have to speak about it if we didn't want to. We each knew what the other was thinking, and just being in each other's presence was enough".

The Impact of the Covid-19 Pandemic

During the pandemic and subsequent travel restrictions, the situation on the ground for camp volunteers changed enormously. Understandably, Ssun reported nearly non-existent contact rates, though as restrictions began to lift and people became more confident in travel, this changed. Originally, it had predominantly been individuals who would reach out to enquire about Ssun services and buddying, whether in the field or back at home. Now, newly formed response teams are enquiring about creating pre-assignment sessions to better prepare their volunteers. This suggests that established groups are realising the need to have support in place for their volunteers as they return to the camps post-pandemic. A strategic response by Ssun might therefore be to expand digital access, putting in place a larger pool of potential buddies and moving beyond initial steps in response.

Other changes have been noticed alongside this. As Juliet Kilpin notes:

> There feels a different category of volunteers responding. For one thing, they're even more transient, as stronger measures and lengths of stay are in place because the UK has left the EU (Brexit). Four years ago, the number of volunteers decreased in the face of travelling restrictions, but ground need continued to increase. My sense is there is a new wave of counters heading out there (Calais, Dunkirk), Brexit has had an impact, you can't now stay for a whole year if you're from the UK, ironically, that part of it may not be the worst thing for volunteers who find it difficult to leave.

The Covid-19 pandemic has made it even more challenging for organisations to support the most vulnerable refuges, and the increasing hostilities directed at volunteers by authorities in Calais have exacerbated this. The conditions on the ground have also changed in some key ways, impacting again on the volunteer experience. As noted by Juliet from Peaceful Borders:

> There is a sense of urgency in trying to support refugees, particularly in terms of the most basic needs, like a tent. As little as six years ago, we were replacing tents struck down by authorities maybe every few weeks. Now it's every 48 hrs. It makes it difficult to feel that it's okay to "rest".

In times of restricted resources, collaborations are often vital, particularly for smaller community groups. When Choose Love (formally Help Refugees) withdrew financial support from several volunteer organisations, it had a massive impact on smaller organisations solely reliant on their funding. Volunteers are facing hard choices and less financial assistance than ever before, though this is imperative for them to continue their work. Despite this, the innovative approaches of volunteers continue to create new responses to the ever-changing needs, and those that support the volunteers must match this creativity in finding ways to further their work.

Recommendations

- Collaborations, potentially pairing top-down agencies with GROs, could help spread skills by sharing the basics of well-being support and policy at the point of start-up.
- Funding must be found to support welfare coordinators to deliver pre-assignment training to include safeguarding and awareness of boundary transgressions. Pre-training for GRO workers is particularly important

before posting to mitigate the clash between expectations and the reality of what they may experience in the field (Hearns & Deeny, 2007).

- Ongoing support is needed for welfare coordinators who look after volunteering teams in camps or areas of conflict, with strong encouragement for volunteers to access support post assignment.
- Psychological First Aid training is something managers can use to build skills in initiating supportive conversations. Increasingly used within organisations, PFA enhances staff members' confidence and ability to respond to those affected by critical incidents or mental health issues at work. It also incorporates guidance on when to refer to other professionals, hence minimising the likelihood of "anxious reactivity" (see chapter 1 for more on this).
- Support from mentors or peer supporters on returning home post-assignment should be offered, which could potentially be made mandatory/opt-out and agreed upon before volunteering. For example, Art Refuge set up Bobby Lloyd advocates for peer support using self-care activities such as fortnightly Zoom meetings, online sharing platforms and other individual self-care activities (yoga, meditation, walking, artwork).
- The very process of setting up avenues for support has an impact on how volunteers view their own contributions to mental health and well-being. Research shows that perceived organisational support is key in letting compassionate first responders know that their contribution is important and has not gone unnoticed (Aldamman et al., 2019).
- There is further work to do in helping new volunteers become informed about their own mental health, ensuring they recognise how the work may affect them and that they deserve to access support at all stages of their experience. This is even more pressing given forced migration and the displacement of vulnerable people are increasing all the time.

Notes

1 www.doctorsoftheworld.org.uk/what-we-stand-for/supporting-medics/resources-and-training/
2 https://peacefulborders.org/about-us/
3 www.helenbamber.org

References

Agier, M., Bouagga, Y., Galisson, M., Hanappe, C., Pette, M., & Wannesson, P. (2018). *The jungle*. Oxford: Polity Press.

Aldamman, K., Tamrakar, T., Dinesen, C., Wiedemann, N., Murphy, J., & Hansen, M. Elsheikh Badr, E., Reid, T. & Vallières, F. (2019). Caring for the mental health of humanitarian volunteers in traumatic contexts: the importance of organisational support. *European Journal of Psychotraumatology, 10*(1). https://doi.org/10.1080/20008198.2019.1694811

Amos, V. (2013). Humanitarian response in the era of global mobile information technology. In K.M. Cahill (Ed.), *History and hope: The international humanitarian reader* (pp. 43–52). New York: Fordham University Press.

Bettencourt, A. (2022). *Grassroots organizations are just as important as seed money for innovation.* UNHCR Innovation Service. www.unhcr.org/innovation/grassroots-organizations-are-just-as-important-as-seed-money-for-innovation/.

Bhattacharyya, S., & Brenner, C. (2021). "Mending broken pieces": A group healing arts psychotherapy model. *Group, 45*(1), 31–52.

Bochenek, M. (2017, 26 July). *"Like living in hell": Police abuses against child and adult migrants in Calais.* Human Rights Watch. www.hrw.org/report/2017/07/27/living-hell/police-abuses-against-child-and-adult-migrants-calais

Cahill, K.M. (Ed.). (2013). *History and hope: The international humanitarian reader.* New York: Fordham University Press. https://doi.org/10.2307/j.ctt13x0c1d.3

Davies, T., Isakjee, A., & Dhesi, S. (2017). Violent inaction: The necropolitical experience of refugees in Europe. *Antipode, 49*(5), 1263–1284. https://doi.org/10.1111/anti.12325

Elbers, W. (2016). David Lewis: Non-governmental organizations, management and development (3rd ed). *Voluntas: International Journal of Voluntary and Non-profit Organizations, 28*(5), 2314–2316. https://doi.org/10.1007/s11266-015-9672-1

Gloster, A.T., Zacharia, M., & Karekla, M. (2020). Psychological aid for frontline healthcare workers. *Clinical Neuropsychiatry: Journal of Treatment Evaluation, 17*(4), 253–254. https://doi.org/10.36131%2Fcnfioritieditore20200406

Granryd, M. (2017, 22 August). Five ways mobile technology can help in humanitarian emergencies. *World Economic Forum.* www.weforum.org/agenda/2017/08/mobile-technology-humanitarian-crisis/.

Hearns, A., & Deeny, P. (2007). The value of support for aid workers in complex emergencies: A phenomenological study. *Disaster Management and Response, 5*(2), 28–35. https://doi.org/10.1016/j.dmr.2007.03.003

Hughes, G., Burck, C., & Roncin, L. (2020). Therapeutic activism: Supporting emotional resilience of volunteers working in a refugee camp. *Psychotherapy And Politics International, 18*(1). https://doi.org/10.1002/ppi.1517

Joint Ministerial Declaration. (2015). *Managing migratory flows in Calais: Joint ministerial declaration on UK/French co-operation.* https://assets.publishing.service.gov.uk/government/uploads/system/uploads/attachment_data/file/455162/Joint_declaration_20_August_2015.pdf

Lahad, M., Shacham, M., & Ayalon, O. (2013). *The "BASIC Ph" model of coping and resiliency.* London: Jessica Kingsley.

McGee, D., & Pelham, J. (2017). Politics at play: Locating human rights, refugees and grassroots humanitarianism in the Calais Jungle. *Leisure Studies, 37*(1), 22–35. https://doi.org/10.1080/02614367.2017.1406979

Mould, O. (2018). The not-so-concrete jungle: Material precarity in the Calais refugee camp. *Cultural Geographies, 25*(3), 393–409. https://doi.org/10.1177%2F147447401 7697457

Nuttman-Shwartz, O. (2014). Shared resilience in a traumatic reality. *Trauma, Violence, & Abuse, 16*(4), 466–475. https://doi.org/10.1177/1524838014557287

Reynolds, V. (2012). An ethical stance for justice-doing in community work and therapy. *Journal of Systemic Therapies, 31*(4), 18–33. https://doi.org/10.1521/jsyt.2012.31.4.18

Robjant, K., & Fazel, M. (2010). The emerging evidence for narrative exposure therapy: A review. *Clinical Psychology Review, 30*(8), 1030–1039. https://doi.org/10.1016/j.cpr.2010.07.004

Stoddard, A., Harmer, A., Haver, K., Taylor, G., & Harvey, P. (2015, October). The state of the humanitarian system, 2015 edition. Active Learning Network for Accountability and Performance in Humanitarian Action (ALNAP). www.alnap.org/system/files/content/resource/files/main/alnap-sohs-2015-web.pdf

Truman, J., & Berdondini, L. (in press). Potentially morally injurious experiences (PMIEs) in the humanitarian sector: The role of moral expectations. [Special issue] *Displaced Voices: A Journal of Archives, Migration and Cultural Heritage.*

Watkins, M. (2015). Psychosocial accompaniment. *Journal of Social and Political Psychology*, *3*(1), 324–341. https://doi.org/10.5964/jspp.v3i1.103

White, M., & Epston, D. (2015). *Narrative means to therapeutic ends.* London: W.W. Norton.

Witter, L. (2021, October 28). Five years after the "Calais Jungle", conditions for migrants continue to deteriorate. *Infomigrants.* www.infomigrants.net/en/post/36044/five-years-after-the-calais-jungle-conditions-for-migrants-continue-to-deteriorate.

Young, T., Pakenham, K., & Norwood, M. (2018). Thematic analysis of aid workers' stressors and coping strategies: Work, psychological, lifestyle and social dimensions. *Journal of International Humanitarian Action, 3*(1). https://doi.org/10.1186/s41018-018-0046-3

Chapter 7

Supporting those with religious faith in the humanitarian sector

Cultural and psychotherapeutic considerations

Graham Fawcett

Introduction

As noted by Ager, Abebe and Ager (2014, p. 103), the "emphasis placed by aid organisations on a secular discourse [...] silences and disempowers the voices and diverse traditions of people from the majority world". An estimated 7% of the world population describe themselves as atheistic (people who believe there is no transcendent force in the universe). Put another way, the remaining 93% of the world's population *do* believe that there is some sort of transcendent entity involved in our lives (Pew-Templeton, 2015). Individuals who have faith work in all sectors of society, but there are some occupations in which the religious are more commonly encountered, and these include high-transition occupations like those of humanitarians (working for both faith-based and non-faith-based organisations) and missionaries.

In this chapter I will present evidence that a majority of workers in the humanitarian space identify as religious, explain the way that some organisations can erase or veil this important area of staff experience and explore ways to open up issues of faith in the workplace to allow for better staff support and improved coherence in worker experience.

Spirituality is associated with meaning, and is often expressed through a subjective connection to nature, the surroundings, other people and a sense of God or the Divine. Religion captures the framework of a particular set of spiritual beliefs and practices often concerned with service, ritual, and institutions. Faith, as a concept, overlaps with spirituality, and is concerned more with belief than experience. Thus, a person may attend a religious setting with a clear belief (faith) in the meaning of what they do but subjectively experience (spirituality) little or no connection to God or their surroundings; another may feel subjectively close to God in a place of beauty but have little or no structured belief about this and not see this encounter in the context of an institution (religion).

However construed, faith-related experiences and behaviours are common to most of humankind, and thus exist, albeit incidentally, within any human organisation. In humanitarian settings, most locally recruited staff have a

DOI: 10.4324/9781003261971-8

meaningful faith and follow religious practices which are integral to their lives (and thus are not "switched off" when they join the staff of a humanitarian agency). These belief systems and practices are integral to identity, self-care and expectations of support, so considering staff beliefs and practices when designing staff support is important.

Challenges Accommodating Faith in Humanitarian Organisations

Despite clear evidence that faith-based or spiritual coping mechanisms support mental health, there can be reluctance to draw on this. The need for psychological support amongst humanitarians is often a source of stigma, but the use of faith as a coping mechanism may be particularly discouraged (Ozcan, Hoelterhoff, & Wylie, 2021). Religious lived experience is often discounted, marginalised or simply erased within humanitarian settings (ibid.). Even in faith-based organisations, there can be a tendency to minimise spirituality and religiosity to better fit into the humanitarian space.

This is problematic as it ignores evidence of the benefits of faith and spiritual behaviour, creating an obstacle to good practice in many humanitarian spaces, for beneficiaries as well as staff (Ager et al., 2014).

> "I'm feeling burnt-out", said the client, a staff member of a major humanitarian agency. We covered the standard issues arising from such a problem and then he mentioned his faith. He found it very helpful to reflect on the support he received from his family during their personal prayer time and regular attendance at wider gatherings. He paused at the end – "it's been incredible to think about my faith and my work – my organisation keeps these two parts of me separate and I don't have anywhere to think how they join together".

Humanitarian organisations aim at promoting human welfare because of its intrinsic worth and to ensure respect and dignity for all. Jean Pictet (1979) summed up humanitarianism as "whatsoever ye would that [others] should do to you, do ye even so to them". Intriguingly, Pictet makes the point that this precept is central to all major world religions, a point taken up further below.

Central to humanitarian practice are the triple values of neutrality, impartiality and independence. These values are seen as essential for the even-handed distribution of aid and support in complex situations. Staff help beneficiaries irrespective of their beliefs, circumstances or history, guided by ideas of equal access to services. From a religious standpoint, this stance accords completely with mainstream religious belief.

Despite this, staff in humanitarian organisations can experience their faith being treated as marginal or erased from working life and decision-making, as the organisation seeks to ensure neutrality, impartiality and independence.

For example, some agencies provide prayer rooms or spaces to engage in religious practices, but these are always separate, and rarely allowed to take place within mainstream activity. The wearing of religious symbols may also be discouraged (Ager et al., 2014). Perhaps more alarmingly, agencies may actively forbid staff from attending local religious ceremonies, again in the name of "impartiality" (Houldey, 2021). Religious staff in such settings may feel unable to be authentic and to contribute as fully to their work. They may also feel dismissed, misunderstood or devalued, and can even endure hostility to their identity (Ager et al., 2014). As Horn (2020) further points out, well-being is often only understood within a Western psychology framework with no attention given to power imbalances, issues of injustice or context-specific therapeutic practices. This excludes the voices of the religious from any background.

Organisations may act in this way from fears about proselytising (actions to persuade someone to change from one religion (or none) to another), something that would run contrary to humanitarian values. Although, it is justified to take steps to guard against this, there is a danger that the voices, opinions or observations of religious staff may be silenced, to the detriment of all.

Members of religious organisations (churches, faith-based organisations) face different challenges. These organisations, although not primarily set up to alleviate suffering, may find themselves doing so as a by-product of their beliefs and ethics. The emotional support they offer may be a component of the regular activities of the institution – for example, prayers for strength, endurance or comfort – or may be reflected in a sense of vocation (one's calling to serve humanity as specified by ethics). Another component may involve gathering together for religious services or ceremonies. As discussed below, such gatherings are highly prosocial, having a profound positive impact on mental health and well-being.

The Value of Religious Faith and Spiritual Practice for Staff Well-Being

Houldey (2021) describes how the act of following a faith transcends socio-economic divides and can be central to well-being. As Houldey notes, "Maybe there is something we can all learn from coping mechanisms that don't involve counselling or yoga and fitness classes" (p. 87). There is strong academic evidence for a religious-based benefit to mental health explored through processes like *adaptation* (e.g. Bulkley et al., 2012), and *reframing* (e.g. Greef and Loubster, 2008). It is also increasingly argued that belief in God is therapeutic in situations of crisis or environmental stress (Joint Learning Initiative on Faith and Local communities, 2013).

Ozcan et al. (2021) summarised research on religious coping using the following definition: "The use of religious beliefs or behaviours to facilitate problem-solving to prevent or alleviate the negative emotional consequences of stressful life circumstances" (Koenig, Pargament, & Nielsen, 1998, p. 514). They conclude: "Religious coping methods are reliably correlated with better psychological outcomes, hope, stress related growth, less depression, anxiety and distress" (p. 3). Further, specific religious behaviours were positively correlated with well-being and protective against symptoms of depression including the frequency of prayer, attendance at religious services and presence of the cognitive attribute *high spirituality.*

While, these authors specifically focus on the benefits of religious coping, one could also speculate that other well-researched positive coping mechanisms that overlap with religiosity might play a role including mindfulness, meditation, social support and feelings of connection to a greater whole. Attendance at the regular rituals arranged by the religious is a highly prosocial activity (discussed in the next section) and can be encouraged for those experiencing common mental health problems.

In addition to strengthening coping, religion gives a framework for ethics, values, meaning and purpose. Often religions point to practical charitable actions such as feeding the hungry, giving to the poor and looking after the dispossessed. The religious, broadly speaking, subscribe to the humanitarian values of impartiality, neutrality and independence with respect to beneficiaries and feel compelled to offer help to the poor, oppressed and marginalised irrespective of their background. Pictet was not the first to come up with the form of words quoted at the start of this chapter, which are noted within the Christ stories, the Torah and other religious writings dating back millennia. Many major religions take things further, insisting on the need to give help, even to enemies. For many religious people, poverty is not only a problem to be solved but also an outrage, an affront to how things should be.

Corruption gets a very bad press in religious texts and writings. Those who lie, steal, cheat or deprive others of what is (rightfully) theirs are viewed as "evil", the opposite of Holy. Given that, organisations with an explicitly religious ethos may become known for their high ethical standards:

> I was at the final customs check listening intently as the customs official suggested that, for a small consideration, my progress to the departure lounge could be speeded up. He asked why I had been in the country, and I mentioned a well-known religious agency I was affiliated to at the time. The official immediately stiffened, looked embarrassed, apologised and waved me through. Checking in with colleagues later, they laughed. This is well known, they said. None of the religious agencies in this country have ever paid a bribe for anything in 200 years. Furthermore, we were the first to bring in schools, sanitation and hospitals. No one ever asks for a bribe from us; it's a waste of time and also rude.

There is also good evidence that spirituality is linked positively to post-traumatic growth (PTG) (Tedeschi & Calhoun, 2004). PTG includes five key areas: Appreciation of life; relationships with others; new possibilities in life; personal strength; and spiritual change, each of which can be transformed in a positive way after traumatic experience. Qualitative analysis suggests that these post-traumatic transformations would not have occurred without the intervening traumatic event and represent new changes in belief and behaviour. Those experiencing PTG will tend to "stop and smell the roses", experience more empathetic relationships with others, be transformed in their understanding of opportunities available to them, find new depths of personal resilience, and experience a greater connectedness to the world around them, other people and the transcendent.

Assessing correlates of PTG is challenging due to the complexity of the phenomena. Generally, those who are open and extroverted seem more likely to experience PTG, and as optimism and future orientation are traits generally found in religious people, this suggests that those with an existing spirituality may be likely to experience greater growth. PTG also arises more often alongside a *partially satisfied search for meaning*. The religious are often actively engaged in meaning making in their lives, and this following traumatic experiences may increase the likelihood of PTG in those with faith.

The Prosocial Value of Religious Institutions

All religions gather adherents together on a regular basis as part of their practice or to mark events or seasons. Such gatherings may be for a combination of worship, prayer, meditation and teaching. Other gatherings mark major milestones such as birth, marriage or death and ceremonies to mark religious milestones – becoming a member of the religion, becoming a priest or teacher, becoming old enough to participate fully in ceremonies. Such gatherings have significant prosocial benefits providing informal social support, facilitating meaning making and fostering a sense of connection to a larger group of people or to a shared sense of the Divine. These are all significant components of human flourishing. Of particular note are services of thanksgiving to commemorate major events or milestones in the lives of a nation, district or organisation. Within these rituals there is often space for laity to participate through welcoming participants, helping with refreshments or with maintenance, again adding to the preservation of mental health through social connectedness and meaningful activity.

Such gatherings are often worked into the fabric of society at large; notably annual remembrance services held around the world to mark the end of the First and Second World Wars and to commemorate those who have suffered in all wars. These events bring together sectors of society that might never meet – serving military, veterans, emergency services and the general public as well as members of religious organisations, often at or near religious sites such as churches.

When working in a staff support role, it may be helpful to explore which of these gatherings are being utilised by clients. Many religious institutions are predicated at least in part on helping others, yet an individual may still feel reluctant to attend the events and services offered. This reluctance can be important to understand and formulate psychologically.

> One client came to see me in therapy exploring the guilt around her presumed part in the death of a colleague. She longed to attend the religious ceremony of remembrance but felt too ashamed to go. Guilt and shame are familiar territory for therapy along with understanding the value of ceremony and ritual in bringing closure. Linking attendance at an important and potentially restorative event with the process of resolving shame enabled her to attend and experience the support of others who were of significance to her colleague. An in-depth understanding by me as a therapist of the nature of the ceremony was not required. The key step was to entertain the possibility that such religious ceremonies could have a positive impact. This recognition, and an open exploration with the client of how to benefit from involvement and understand areas of reluctance, helped her enormously.

Sometimes the gatherings are, on the surface, far simpler. They can represent a pilgrimage, a ritual, a memorial. Often, they can be worked into psychological therapy in a way that enriches the process.

> The bombings had killed many and emotionally impacted an entire city. The aftermath of one bomb was especially grim with body parts strewn amongst the trees of a much-loved park. Seven months later my client, a survivor of the park bombing, neared the end of his successful therapy with me. We discussed revisiting the park and I explained the psychological rationale. The client readily agreed and then asked if it would be alright to bring a candle and some flowers to the session.
>
> Metres from the explosion site and somewhere very private I stood silently as this Christian Orthodox gentleman placed a lighted candle and the flowers on the ground and then took moments to pray silently. "Thank you", he said to me, "it is complete".
>
> As we walked away, I noticed the other candles, cards and notes placed on the spot by other survivors and quite separate to the more formal memorial on the street outside the park. This was a place of pilgrimage for many clients and their therapists that year, the therapists invited to bear witness to intolerable grief and their part in its resolution.

In summary, the prosocial and social support factors involved in most religious institutions and practices are a clear support to mental health and recovery.

Despite this, religious gatherings seem largely absent from formal humanitarian spaces, leaving a gap where otherwise organisations might recall their roots and express gratitude (another prosocial support to mental health), gather in solidarity and reflect. This obtains even in the case of extreme personal events such as death on active duty. Uniformed organisations (military, emergency services) incorporate family into ceremonies to honour the sacrifice made. Aid agencies, at best, ensure the body is accompanied and then "handed over" to the family with little further institutional involvement beyond a letter or phone call from a senior executive and a representative in attendance at the funeral. Where the deceased is religious, this distanced stance can seem odd to families and friends who want to know about their loved one's life and work, and its meaning to them.

Aid work involves myriad complex issues, and informal rituals of solidarity can reach across divides of religion, and culture, to common humanism. Sometimes words fail us, and further discussion seems impotent or pointless:

> The smoke rose in the distance over the site of yet another rocket attack in an area disputed by three religions. The religious agency I was with at the time was staffed by individuals of all three religions and atheists. We had met for a time to be together in the different ways we all approached our understanding of God. Silenced, we stood for a moment and then, spontaneously, moved into a circle to hold hands. There were no words, only an understanding that what united us was greater than the sights and sounds outside.

This rich seam of common beliefs, values and behaviours is, as stated above, often largely invisible to humanitarian organisations, despite its value at a psychosocial level. As Ager et al. (2014) note, "MHPSS [Mental Health and Psychosocial Support] programming has little engagement with available religious sources" (p. 76).

Making Psychological Support Responsive to Humanitarian Spiritual Needs

Problems of Credibility and Appropriateness

> "I won't go to see a (UK) National Health Service therapist. I hear stories that they mock religious people, and they think my beliefs are neurotic, a sort of crutch. Why would I trust those people with my mind?"

I hear this story all too frequently. An ex-NHS therapist myself, I know these fears are broadly groundless. Nevertheless, this narrative has taken hold, amplified on occasion by religious elders. In addition, religious groups may discount the benefits of competently delivered psychological therapy.

Research amongst defined subsets of society (for example, firefighters, veterans, specific event survivors) indicates a strong desire to talk to practitioners who have an understanding or appreciation of their specific experiences, preferably people from the same or similar background, who can understand their situation and circumstances without their having to explain themselves in great depth. These are people of "credibility", as first researched amongst military chaplains (Gal & Mengelsdroff, 1991). A frequent complaint among aid workers is the need to patiently explain the location or details of an incident or action to psychological therapists who have little knowledge or understanding in common with the aid workers, something that can be enough to cause them to avoid mental health services. Similarly, for those who are religious, there can be an antipathy towards secular counselling, often perceived as hostile to their world view. Again, there are parallels with the experiences of military personnel and veterans for whom a barrier to accessing services was the idea of meeting a therapist who might view them as a "child killer" or "murderer".

Religious of any faith show a marked reluctance to engage with psychological therapy as they fear being dismissed or misunderstood. They often say that they profoundly distrust a social science they perceive as mocking them at worst, demeaning them at best. Yet they can also feel, often simultaneously, that their religious institution can't help them either. Sometimes the institution is perceived as possibly disapproving of their thoughts, which they therefore dare not express. Others feel that engaging in psychotherapy somehow contradicts or invalidates their beliefs and they should "simply" trust more or "have more faith" or "attend prayers more diligently".

> I sat with a devout young man for session three of trauma therapy after the bombings which had killed many people. In chatting with me, he had figured out I was religious even though I had been careful not to divulge my belief system. "I don't understand how God can have allowed this", said the man, "but I can't talk to my religious elders about that, it would be heresy. But I can talk with you, we don't believe the same way but at least I feel understood".

There is often a fear that belief in the Divine will be "treated like a neurosis or delusion", but if the therapist can maintain a neutral and accepting stance about a client's underlying beliefs (as they might about a political viewpoint) and focus instead on the issues at hand, good therapeutic work often occurs. It can be helpful for therapists to ask clients about their beliefs in a spirit of curiosity and learning, however, therapy sessions are not the place for a complete education or for questions that get in the way of clients gaining insight, making their own connections or understanding possible cognitive distortions.

On the side of the therapist, understanding a client's faith is important given the impact of this on their beliefs and actions throughout life (often internalised during childhood and adolescence). People may bring beliefs or practices to therapy which are central to their sense of meaning and well-being and which it would thus be odd to exclude or silence. Equally, people may bring conflicted beliefs to therapy which they are seeking to resolve.

Again, using UK veterans' services as an example, an emphasis on the fact that services are military respectful and focused on expert intervention helped increase uptake amongst the population. Once through the front door of the clinic, therapeutic approaches were similar to those used with any other clinical group. A similar stance can be taken with religious clients, making it clear that they are welcomed and respected, and that the services they receive will be as good as those offered others, but also expertly informed to reflect their particular needs. My own organisation, Thrive Worldwide, provides services to both religious and non-religious clients offered by colleagues who, themselves, are a combination of religious and non-religious. Satisfaction levels and outcomes are the same whatever combination of client and therapist is used.

> A highly competent senior manager observed that his strict religious upbringing remained an issue for him although he would self-describe as agnostic. With no particular knowledge of the belief system he was raised in, it was possible to help him explore its impact on his current life and to unpick the automatic beliefs and schemas he felt were no longer relevant to him.

> A self-described religious worker reflected on her current anxiety and emergent agoraphobia during the pandemic lockdown. As she spoke, it occurred to her that her memories of growing up during a prolonged religious conflict, when going outside was frequently lethal, had amplified her fear of going outside in the pandemic.

Beliefs can become problematic in the complexity of humanitarian work. Prayers aimed at resolving the situation or developing inner peace falter; the refugees keep coming and sleepless nights ensue. Therapists at this point may find it helpful to remember that the person's belief system may account for less of their distress than the degree of rigidity with which beliefs are held (Southwick & Charney, 2012). For example, a tendency to cognitive rumination, rigid thinking or perfectionism may be the key difficulty, rather than the content of the beliefs held, religious or otherwise. Such phenomena can be explored and managed in therapy providing the client is given space to surface them. The content of the belief system can also be explored with a suitably qualified religious elder without the therapist becoming sucked into areas they neither understand nor are qualified to deal with.

Psychological formulations drawn from some approaches, for example, cognitive behavioural therapy (CBT), are value neutral and tend not to be affected by clients' beliefs, and even those types of formulations that intersect with belief can be used in more neutral ways. It is important for clients to have space to express thoughts, emotions and beliefs related to their faith and to be encouraged to seek expert help if their queries have a theological aspect to them which the therapist cannot address. Clients are usually very happy to translate terms or concepts which the therapist does not understand once a therapeutic relationship has been established. On the other hand, a therapeutic relationship may falter if the therapist is closed to exploring faith and belief issues openly with clients.

A common therapeutic challenge for adherents to religious beliefs that speak of God as "Father" can be their own problematic relationships with their physical fathers. If that father has been abusive, that abuse can be projected onto "God", as can other attributes, both positive and negative. This phenomenon is well recognised in religious circles and is often managed there. It can, however, transfer across into secular therapy settings and may require the use of formulations based in approaches that pay deep attention to relational process (for example, the internal family systems (IFS) model).

Aspects of Religiosity and Spirituality as Vulnerability Factors for Mental Health Difficulties

In some cases, faith has been viewed as making individuals vulnerable to mental health difficulties, although arguments in favour of this are rarely convincing. As already stated, care needs to be taken not to confound the content of belief systems with the impact on mental health which may be due to rigid thinking styles rather than faith.[1]

Moral injury (explored in chapter 4) is poorly researched amongst those of religious faith, but it is reasonable to surmise that a population attuned to deep moral values will experience the impact of potentially morally injurious events more deeply. Both religious and non-religious humanitarian workers tend to be guided by their conscience or morality, and this "moral compass" provides the setting for the sometimes impossible ethical demands of the work. A person whose belief system cannot flex sufficiently to accommodate this is likely to experience distress, and attention to rigid thinking may again be key here.

Support for Missionaries

Missionaries (those sent by sections of all religions to talk about their faith or to help those in need) often have a transcendent sense of duty and vocation, but this can falter in the face of overwhelming challenges. This risk is increased if individuals are particularly idealistic (a feature of missionaries generally) as feelings of shame or guilt at presumed failings in their mission can be more potent. Elements of cognitive dissonance can creep in – they have travelled far and given up much, so what they are doing and believing *must* be right. This can create additional psychological rigidity, especially if they feel the need to be an example to others or to uphold their beliefs in the face of opposition. In some cases, over time, these factors can combine to make their position untenable, and although they may remain in post, they may feel conflicted and miserable or come home disillusioned. Such styles of cognitive rigidity and perfectionism are not unique to missionaries, and often manifest in humanitarian aid workers more broadly (Houldey, 2021).

Getting help for distressed missionaries can be problematic. They may feel they have failed and not wish to engage with their faith community to explore what has happened. Although their distress may be very real, its traits may be insufficient to trigger referral to mental health services. When referred, however, psychological services can be highly supportive to those working as missionaries. Whichever evidence-based psychological approach is employed, the process of formulating difficulties provides options for effective intervention.

> "I am driven", said the senior cleric in a conflict zone, "to speak about injustice. I feel so angry, so misunderstood, and very isolated. And now my religious institution is about to reject me because I can't stop losing my temper". We spoke at length over several sessions until we arrived at the unexpected death of his father when the client was aged four and was taken into the care of relatives whom, he perceived, didn't like him. "I was so angry, so misunderstood, so alone".
>
> Over the next month we spoke about "threat brain", how the body remembers, how the four-year-old inside him needed soothing. Steadily the client spoke with the internalised four-year-old, took him for walks, sat on park benches until the internalised four-year-old felt soothed enough to stop warning the 60-year-old grown-up of impending existential annihilation. One year later, the cleric was still fighting the good fight but in a more measured, less self-destructive way, which had dramatically enhanced his impact.

In some cases, the greatest help that a psychological practitioner can offer is to help reorient their missionary client in the direction of faith conversations:

> The devout missionary of a religious agency sat quietly: "I'm not sure what to do – in the midst of this suffering my faith has evaporated". There is a well-known response to this existential crisis: "Has God moved or has your understanding developed?" Often the sense of the transcendent remains, the challenge is that the theology no longer feels right, and this is not an area that belongs in the purely counselling realm. The missionary sought help from religious elders and, graciously, continued to speak with me in therapy, finding it helpful to consider the catastrophic

impact caused to her faith by the sense of being let down, and its origins in an alcoholic family upbringing and her need for predictability.

Working Respectfully in Therapy with Religious Themes and Concepts

Psychological therapists have a rich array of helpful models to inform psychological support; it is not necessary to change from one approach to another just because a client is religious. For the purposes of this chapter, we need simply note the plurality of religious experience and practice across different faiths, sects and individuals, and assert that psychological approaches can help make sense of distressing experiences.

Religious literacy for psychological therapists must include learning with each client how, if at all, religion and spirituality provide a framework of values and beliefs to live out their life. It also requires understanding an individual's relationship to the transcendent, whatever that transcendent might be. Asking about a person's relationship with their Divine/transcendent being (meaning and purpose of life) is an important starting point for engaging with religious and spiritual people, and crucial for developing a therapist's religious literacy. This means asking yourself "Who is God?" to your client. If asking this directly sounds like too much, providing reassurance to all your clients that they will be treated with dignity, curiosity and acceptance in relation to faith is a good starting point. Noting at this point whether individuals are overconfident or fixed in their beliefs can be important as this is difficult to work with. The selection process for religious organisations takes care to weed out driven or fixated candidates who can find things problematic when their expectations falter in the face of real experience. Flexible thinking is preferred over rigid or inflexible thinking with its risk of insensitive practices or serious problems if traumatic events "shatter" fixed beliefs (Janoff-Bulman, 1992).

Religious people also present with issues which can be practically resolved independent of their belief systems, for example, sleep disorders; or with more complicated issues such as sadness which can be resolved with a simple CBT approach around negative automatic thoughts. None of these require a deep understanding of the nature of the belief system of the client; however, some formulations do incorporate religious thinking, and bring this into sessions without needing to be an expert theologian. A simple question, using an IFS approach, can be as straightforward as "how are you and God getting on?". This key question yields crucial material about a key relationship which can be worked with therapeutically. Most people will answer readily and in straightforward language.

I work with numerous candidates who are exploring their wish to become priests in a range of belief systems, none of which am I expert in. At the stage they see me, however, they generally feel "close to God" and light up when this question is asked. Some, however, look startled and give an equivocal or vague answer. Some gentle discussion tends to bring forth any disquiet or doubt about the path they are on, and sometimes indicates that they are contemplating withdrawing and taking a different career. Always they mention how grateful they were to have been asked the question by someone not looking for the "correct" answer and for the chance to explore, using non-directive questioning, the potential of their life.

Generally, religious people will not approach a therapist with theological conundrums as they are aware of the limits and capabilities of most therapists. Sometimes they will present with an intersecting problem (for example, feeling bullied by a religious elder they are obliged to show respect to), but it is likely that formulations emerging from this scenario are little different to those in other secular, hierarchical organisations. Where they do present with clear theological dilemmas, it is helpful to direct them back to their religious setting, perhaps suggesting that they also consider finding someone independent of the situation who can bring a fresh perspective.

Supervision Issues

There are three key aspects to supervision of therapy with religious clients: The extent to which the content of a client's beliefs intersects with the therapist's beliefs; the extent to which the client is caught up in a perverse or toxic religious context; and the managing of problematic beliefs which, although they may appear consistent with mainstream belief systems, are causing difficulties. A client may bring strongly held beliefs which a therapist finds objectionable (and this occurs with other, non-religious beliefs, e.g. an extreme political view, a particular prejudice), but therapists can make use of supervision to tease out transference and countertransference issues which may augment this.

More problematic is the assessment of a religious environment as psychologically toxic. Religious organisations are not inherently toxic any more than political, charitable or community organisations are so. All, however, may become toxic as a result of bullying, coercive control or lack of consultation, becoming harmful to members. Supervision can be helpful in unpicking the religious content of such challenges from other well-known organisational factors known to be harmful to mental health.

The content of a client's beliefs and their adherence to doctrine is beyond the scope of psychotherapists to address; we are not theologians. Nevertheless, there are warning signs that are helpful to consider in supervision. To what extent does the belief system have an obsessional or fixated quality? Is there a delusional quality to the beliefs, or are they open to doubt? Is there a safeguarding issue with vulnerable clients (e.g. someone with a learning disability giving their earnings to an institution) or evidence of coercive behaviour (e.g. religious adherents being guilt-tripped into attending events)? Is there evidence of behaviours associated with cults? These are all psychological phenomena which therapists are skilled at uncovering and addressing.

In many settings there may be religious leaders able and willing to advise on the veracity of a belief system and the extent to which individuals or groups are at risk from a particular expression of religion.

Recommendations

For Individuals

- Draw on your faith for support in times of difficulty, being aware of the way it can enhance coping and post-traumatic growth and maintain pro-social activities

For Organisations

- Respect the role that spirituality plays in the lives of your staff and draw from its supportive strengths
- Staff care should draw on spirituality and faith to form part of a suite of supportive interventions

For Psychological Therapists

- We neglect a key area in our therapy if we work with staff in distress and overlook or ignore religious, spiritual or religious beliefs or practices
- Seek out specialist support and supervision for your work to consider what aspects of the presentation belong to psychology and what to theology, together with clarifying aspects of the presentation that would be viewed as problematic by fellow adherents. If you work in a setting or community in which you have access to support from religious leaders, draw on this for help

Conclusion

Religion is a way of life for the overwhelming majority of the population of the planet and cannot simply be ignored or wished away by psychological services. There are ways to improve the accessibility of these services to those who are religious. Furthermore, it is possible to help clinicians demystify any behaviours that manifest in a religious context by encouraging them to explore these behaviours respectfully through the lens of standard psychological models and formulations. When delivering services, psychological therapists have much to offer within their competency frameworks. It is possible for them to cultivate awareness of when they are being asked to stray into territory that is theological and beyond their competence, and refer individuals to those with competence in this area.

Religion is not a barrier to receiving psychological services, but often the assumptions of, and about, psychological services can be a barrier to accessibility. Where services can address accessibility without compromising standards, the needs of the religious can be addressed as successfully as those of any other segment of the population. Services should design their provision for the 93% of people on the planet with religious belief, not just the 7% without.[2]

Notes

1   Someone presenting with a delusional belief that they are Napoleon or Jesus does so due to underlying cognitive distortions (e.g. the *jumping to conclusions bias*, Dudley, Taylor, Wickham, & Hutton, 2016)) and a hyper-elevated threat system. Claims that they are a particular character derive from their social context rather than their faith. Similarly, fixated beliefs may focus on the Pope, the local imam or a neighbour, but beliefs did not "cause" the delusional system to occur.
2   Grateful thanks to my wife, Nanci Hogan, for her helpful input to early drafts and to colleagues at Thrive Worldwide for numerous illuminating conversations over several years. Also to Cynthia Eriksson at Fuller Seminary for an insightful introduction to the extensive literature available in this area.

References

Ager, J., Abebe, B., & Ager, A. (2014). Mental health and psychosocial support in humanitarian emergencies in Africa: Challenges and opportunities for engaging with the faith sector. *The Review of Faith & International Affairs, 12*(1), 72–83. https://doi.org/10.1080/15570274.2013.876729

Bulkley, J., McMullen, C., Hornbrook, M., Altschuler, A., Grant, M., Herrinton, L., & Krouse, R. (2012). PS1-10: Spiritual well-being and the challenges of living with an ostomy: Resilience, adaptation and loss among colorectal cancer survivors. *Clinical Medicine & Research, 10*(3), 146. https://doi.org/10.3121/cmr.2012.1100.ps1-10

Dudley, R., Taylor, P., Wickham, S., & Hutton, P. (2016). Psychosis, delusions and the "jumping to conclusions" reasoning bias: A systematic review and meta-analysis. *Schizophrenia Bulletin, 42*(3): 652–665. https://doi.org/10.1093/schbul/sbv150

Gal, R., & Mangelsdorff, A.D. (Eds.). (1991). *Handbook of military psychology.* Hoboken, NJ: John Wiley & Sons.

Greeff, A.P., & Loubser, K. (2008). Spirituality as a resiliency quality in Xhosa-speaking families in South Africa. *Journal of Religious Health, 47,* 288–301. http://dx.doi.org/10.1007/s10943-007-9157-7

Horn, J. (2020). Decolonising emotional well-being and mental health in development: African feminist innovations, *Gender & Development, 28*:1, 85–98. https://doi.org/10.1080/13552074.2020.1717177

Houldey, G. (2021). *The vulnerable humanitarian: ending burnout culture in the aid sector*. Abingdon, Oxon: Routledge.

Janoff-Bulman, R. (1992). *Shattered assumptions: Towards a new psychology of trauma*. New York: Free Press.

Joint Learning Initiative on Faith and Local communities. (2013, February). *Refugee Studies Centre*. www.rsc.ox.ac.uk/files/files-1/wp90-local-faith-communities-resilie nce-2013.pdf

Koenig, H.G., Pargament, K.I., & Nielsen, J. (1998). Religious coping and health status in medically ill hospitalized older adults. *Journal of Nervous and Mental Disease, 186*(9): 513–521. https://doi.org/10.1097/00005053-199809000-00001

Ozcan, O., Hoelterhoff, M., & Wylie, E. (2021). Faith and spirituality as psychological coping mechanism among female aid workers: a qualitative study. *Journal of International Humanitarian Action, 6*, article 15. https://doi.org/10.1186/s41 018-021-00100-z

Pew-Templeton. (2015). Religious composition by country, 2010–2050. Pew-Templeton: Global Religious Futures Project. www.pewresearch.org/religion/2015/ 04/02/religious-projection-table/

Pictet, J. (1979). The fundamental principles of the Red Cross: Commentary. *ICRC*. www.icrc.org/en/doc/resources/documents/misc/fundamental-principles-comment ary-010179.htm

Southwick, S.M., & Charney, D.S. (2012). *Resilience: The science of mastering life's greatest challenges*. Cambridge: Cambridge University Press. https://doi.org/ 10.1017/CBO9781139013857

Tedeschi R.G., & Calhoun, L.G. (2004). Posttraumatic growth: conceptual foundations and empirical evidence. *Psychological Inquiry, 15*(1): 1–18. https://doi. org/10.1207/s15327965pli1501_01

Chapter 8

Seafarers: "They that go down to the sea in ships to do business in great waters"[1]

Pennie Blackburn

The work of seafarers is of global importance. As George writes:

> On ship-tracking websites, the waters are black with dots. Each dot is a ship; each ship is laden with boxes; each box is laden with goods. In post-industrial economies, we no longer produce but buy, and so we must ship. Without shipping there would be no clothes, food, paper, or fuel. Without all those dots, the world would not work. Yet freight shipping is all but invisible. (George, 2014)

According to the Maritime Labour Convention (MLC), "*A seafarer is any person, including a master, who is employed or engaged or works in any capacity on board a ship and whose normal place of work is on a ship*". There are more than 1.6 million "*seafarers serving on internationally trading merchant ships from virtually every nation*" (International Chamber of Shipping (ICS), n.d.), and at least 90% of the goods that we buy are transported by sea. As those on social media who promote awareness of the industry say, "no shipping, no shopping". Seafarers work on a range of "foreign going" vessels from privately owned yachts to cruise ships, oil or gas tankers, dredgers, container ships, bulk carriers and more. Seafarers navigate the vessel (known as the deck department) and keep the vessel operating and in good order (the engineering department), but the term also includes chefs, stewards and other "hotel" staff on "pleasure vessels", contractors, shopkeepers and even hairdressers and dancers. They come from across the globe, as far afield as China, the Philippines, Indonesia, the Russian Federation, Ukraine, India, Africa, Europe, Australasia, Korea and the United States of America.

Mental health in the maritime sector is an emerging field. Traditionally, seafarers are considered, and consider themselves, resourceful professional problem solvers; when on board, any and every problem that arises must be managed by the crew. Not so long ago, Morse code was the normal means of communication between sea and shore, and every vessel had a radio room. As communications technology has developed, support from shore has become more achievable, but reliable internet connections are expensive to provide

DOI: 10.4324/9781003261971-9

(and in some regions almost impossible), which means that many seafarers have limited, slow internet access, if they have any at all. The ship's captain *"carries full responsibility for the safe prosecution of the voyage and the lives of everyone on board"* (Blackburn, 2002). Ships' captains can be held legally and criminally liable for accidents or injuries on board, damage to a vessel or accidental pollution, for example. This means that seafarers must be very adept problem solvers, able to manage everything from day-to-day living requirements to major emergencies; there is no emergency service on hand if a seafarer has a cardiac arrest, or a fire breaks out on board when the vessel is in the middle of the ocean and several days from port.

In relation to mental health, seafarers are resilient. They have developed ways of coping with separation from family and friends and making do with limited access to the things so many of us take for granted on shore, like returning home at the end of a working day, going out with friends at the weekend, accessing social media, going for a run or spending time at the gym. The insights that Covid-19 restrictions gave us shed light on why mental health is relevant for a population who live with similar restrictions as a part of their working lives. As national "lockdowns" became prevalent in the early days of the pandemic, there was recognition of a dramatic effect on mental health as people learnt how to live and work in the same space and were no longer able to pop out to the shops, the gym or to see friends and family. People became worried about loved ones that they could not be there to help, and hugely reliant on technology for everything from work to social interaction and exercise. We went from never having heard of Zoom to Zoom fatigue in short measure (Machemer, 2021). There was a dramatic rise in loneliness and isolation, reports of abuse and domestic violence increased, and access to physical and mental health care was significantly reduced. One seafarer who joined me on a panel discussion from a quarantine hotel joked that it was *"rather like being on board, except the room was a bit nicer and the Wi-Fi was better"*.

Seafarers have always had to find ways to manage exactly these kinds of issues, and for young seafarers, adjusting to this way of living can be challenging.

> One seafarer who went to sea for the first time believing that it would be an effective way to support his family at home, found himself extremely distressed and contemplating suicide. He worked in the engine room where he felt claustrophobic with no natural light and the noise of the heavy machinery. He didn't want to let his family down who had extended themselves financially to enable his training. He couldn't see a way out and felt trapped by his decision to go to sea.

One of the lasting benefits that may come from the lockdown experience for the maritime industry is greater awareness of the impact of living and working in a confined space for extended periods; an understanding of why seafarers consistently ask for affordable Wi-Fi to be made available; and empathy for the way it feels when a loved one is sick or struggling and you can't be there to help. Very often, it is these kinds of concerns that challenge seafarers most.

> An Indian seafarer's family home was destroyed by flooding, two of the members of his close family were also killed. The urge to be there following a sudden event like this is strong for all of us, but for this sea-farer the restrictions on travel and quarantine arrangements in place at the time made that impossible. Understandably, he was acutely distressed, his grief compounded by the distress of his family and the inability to respond as needed.

Until recently, mental health was simply considered irrelevant to the maritime industry. The *Seafarers' Mental Health and Wellbeing Report* (Sampson & Ellis, 2019) found that 55% of the employers interviewed said that they had not introduced *any* practices or policies relating to mental health in the previous 10 years. In the three-quarters of the human resources respondents that said mental health had not been identified as an issue or priority in their company, this figure rose to 90%. The argument was that seafarers are strong, resourceful, resilient; they are simply unlikely to suffer with their mental health.

To join a vessel, all seafarers must attain a valid medical certificate. Health conditions that require daily medication or could pose a risk of emergency health care might preclude a seafarer from sailing. The "healthy worker effect" is nowhere more pronounced than in the maritime sector. Routinely only cruise vessels would have medical professionals on board; most medical needs must be met remotely or wait until the next port of call. The assumption is that the healthy worker effect would also extend to mental health.

Research into mental health in seafarers is sparse. Even the best of the studies is limited either by relatively low numbers of participants or a potentially skewed population of seafarers who are interested enough in mental health to respond. However, one of the most robust independent studies available (Lefkowitz & Slade, 2019) has suggested that 28% of the seafarer respondents, (n = 1572) screened positive for clinical-level disorder using standardised measures of generalised anxiety (General Anxiety Disorder-7 (GAD-7)) and depression (Patient Health Questionnaire-9 (PHQ-9)), and 20% surveyed had reported suicidal ideation on several days or more during the two weeks prior to the survey. A study carried out by Marine Benefits, a crew insurance company, also using the PHQ-9 as self-report measure of depression found that 16% of seafarers (n = 17000) reported mild levels of depression, with 7% scoring in the moderate to severe range (Marine Benefits, 2021) . They report that on average 1.5 seafarers per ship could be considered to suffer with moderate to severe levels of depression.

Whilst many people love life at sea, there are few who would disagree on the challenges inherent in seafaring. In 2019, I wrote guidance called *Mentally Healthy Ships: Policy and Practice to Promote Mental Health on Board* (Blackburn, 2019) aimed at shipping companies, owners and operators, which argued that employers have a duty of care towards seafarers on board vessels. It provided a framework of strategies to promote and protect mental health and ensure effective response mechanisms. In one of the appendices, I set out many of the risks to mental health and well-being that I had found reported in the grey literature and in research studies; there were 70 of them in nine different categories:

- Interpersonal factors (e.g. isolation, separation from family, bereavement at home)
- Contractual issues (e.g. voyage extensions, contract length and voyage-only contracts)
- Interpersonal factors on board (bullying and harassment, language, and communication barriers due to the multinational nature of crewing)
- Management problems (a culture of blame, excessive supervisor demands and discrimination)
- Isolation on board[2] (such as being the only woman or the only person of a particular nationality)
- Work demands (including excessive or unmanageable workloads and deadlines, shift working)
- Occupational exposure (including noise, vibration, excessive heat, and tight working spaces, especially in the engine department, as well as severe weather, risk of piracy)
- Hours of work and rest (lack of shore leave, fatigue,[3] long working hours)
- Living conditions (such as poor food, limited internet access, no access to healthcare, lack of privacy)

Not all these risks apply to all seafarers on every type of vessel. There are many common factors, including separation from loved ones for extended periods, but the risks relevant to a member of a superyacht crew or cruise liner might include the demands of owners and customers (as in an equivalent luxury hotel on shore); whereas, a crew routinely sailing in particular hotspots such as the Gulf of Guinea,[4] might be exposed to the risk of violent piracy attacks. As I write, "Hundreds of seafarers on more than 100 foreign-flagged cargo vessels are stranded in Ukrainian waters in the Black Sea and Sea of Azov 'in the middle of the line of fire'" (McVeigh, 2022). The ships stranded in ports along the coast of Ukraine were on routine operations when the conflict with Russia broke out. One seafarer tragically died when a ship sank following what was believed to be a missile strike; the crew of another vessel had to be rescued from the waters following an explosion nearby; and reports suggest that three other vessels have been similarly hit.

In a recent interview with Safety4Sea, Katie Higginbottom, Head of ITF Seafarers' Trust remarked: "As the research has shown, there are many correlations between poor mental health and operational factors such as fatigue, contract extensions, inadequate manning, and lack of shore leave. These issues could all be addressed – but at a cost" (Higginbottom, 2022). The findings from the ITF Seafarer's Trust and Yale University study (Lefkowitz & Slade, 2019) found that a non-caring company culture was the highest determinant of depression, anxiety and suicidal ideation amongst seafarers; followed by violence at work, low job satisfaction and self-rated health problems. By contrast, seafarers themselves rated isolation from family, supervisor demands, trouble sleeping and contract length as the factors most associated with depression. The challenge here is in raising awareness amongst owners and operators that money invested in creating environments in which people can thrive really does make good business sense, even in an industry which is under intense pressure to drive costs down.

The Crew Change Crisis and the Covid-19 Pandemic

Covid-19 has raised awareness of seafarer mental health. Usually, as seafarers finish their contracts, they return home and others join vessels. However, when the pandemic began, as national borders were shut down, hotels were closed and travel routes overland or air halted, travel became impossible. It was estimated that about 25% of crew changeovers were cancelled. The "crew change crisis", as it quickly became known within the industry, saw more than half a million seafarers stuck on board vessels around the world. Industry regulations stipulate a maximum of 11 months on board; in practice this means that seafarers, particularly lower ranking seafarers (known as *ratings*), often work to a 10-month contract. Each week, hundreds of seafarers were added to the toll of crew stuck on board vessels, more and more of them (about 26% according to the ITF Seafarers' Trust survey) overstaying the legally permitted tenure. Some remained on board for as long as 18 months. Of course, international trade could not stop. People still needed food and fuel and all the essentials of life, so shipping had to continue. Seafarers on board became increasingly exhausted and like the rest of us, acutely worried about their loved ones at home. Tradewinds published a story by the Secret Captain (2020):

> Sixteen members of my crew are over their contract time, and, despite my best efforts, there is nothing I can do to get them relieved by a fresh crew. Worst of all, I cannot even provide them with any idea of when they might be able to get home.
> Seafarers tend to be a tough bunch. We are used to dealing with difficulties and we have all been in situations where things don't go to plan. But this is different because it is not temporary anymore. There is no

hope left and no light at the end of the tunnel. Day in, day out, I am working with an exhausted crew, some of whom are suffering enormous damage to their mental health. I give them as much rest as I am able to and I spend as much time as I can talking to them, but that does only so much, because I cannot give them what they want – their home and their family.

In the weeks I have been back on board, I have lost count of the number of times I have sat in my cabin consoling desperate men, who are in tears. As the master, I need to remain strong and supportive for all of them, but there have been times I have woken up crying because it all seems so hopeless. I did not sign up for this. None of us did. (The Secret Captain, 2020)

A similar number of people were stuck at home unable to embark. Traditionally, of course, seafarers came from coastal countries where fishing, trade and warfare were waged across the seas. Most *"support level ratings are recruited from developing nations where salaries may be significantly higher at sea than that paid for comparative work ashore"* (ICS, 2020). Practice varies globally and across companies, but ratings and some officers are employed on voyage-only contracts, which means they are not paid when they are not on board a ship. Whilst some seafarers were stranded on board, endlessly travelling the high seas, others were at home with no source of income. International Seafarers Welfare and Assistance Network (ISWAN),[5] a charity promoting the welfare of seafarers, received three to four times the number of contacts to its 24/7 global helpline during that period than the same period the year before. The number of contacts from seafarers expressing suicidal ideation more than doubled. The shipping industry does not have a system to collect numbers of people who take their lives at sea; and it is extremely difficult to estimate due to various factors, but there is much anecdotal evidence suggesting that the number of people "missing at sea" following suicide tragically increased during that time.

Despite the scale of the problem, it went largely unreported in mainstream media. Consequently, a Herculean effort took place to campaign for recognition of seafarers as essential key workers and create travel corridors to alleviate the problem. It was many months before any change took place.

Shipping companies in need of crew avoided recruitment in parts of the world where the virus was prevalent, and testing and vaccination was low. At a certain stage the situation in India was particularly acute, contributing to a pre-existing illegal practice of unregistered agents recruiting in exchange for a fee (International Labour Organisation, 2006).

Agents force seafarers to sign a contract that does not comply with the requirements of the MLC [law] and, after flying to the destination, the seafarers are forced to work on some other vessel. In most cases, these vessels are in a bad state without proper supplies and uninhabitable conditions. It has been reported in a number of cases that these seafarers get abandoned on such vessels for months without any payment and it becomes very stressful situation where the agents turn off their phones after the seafarers join a vessel and refuse to take responsibility for the wages and their sign-off. (ISWAN South Asia, 2021)

According to the ITF Seafarers' Trust,

vessel abandonment happens either because the shipowners have financial difficulties or because they can make more money by not paying the wages and the bills they owe. This may be more frequent on older ships at the end of their sea life. In some cases, the ship is worth less than the money owed to crew and other debtors.

The International Labour Organization and International Maritime Organization database reports 74 ships as abandoned in 2021 alone. Seafarers remain on board, their wages unpaid, often without food, potable water or fuel; they can be stuck for months and even years when port authorities refuse to allow them to disembark because of the safe manning regulations. In February 2019, the *Guardian* newspaper reported:

Tourists are more accustomed to seeing kite surfers or kayaks off the idyllic coast of Umm Al Quwain, in the United Arab Emirates. But today they have gathered on sun loungers to sip coffee and gaze at the unusual sight of a 5,000-ton oil tanker grounded on the sand. For the crew inside the Panama-flagged MT Iba, however, being grounded on the beach marks another harrowing chapter in an almost four-year ordeal at sea [...] Abandoned by the vessel's owner, their wages unpaid for 32 months, the five-person crew of the $4m (£2.8 million) Iba are in limbo. If they leave the ship, they will lose their claim to the hundreds of dollars owed to them. [...] The [...] chief engineer from Myanmar [...] says the crew have endured "terrible suffering" and are desperately worried about their families. "I cannot send wages to support my family, my children cannot study, they cannot eat, they have to borrow money." [...] What began as a normal seafaring job turned into a "living hell", the men say, after the tanker's owner, Alco Shipping, once one of the UAE's largest shipping firms, ran into financial difficulty and stopped paying salaries almost three years [previously]. Since then, they were forced to rely on charities for food and water. (McVeigh, 2021)

An ongoing legacy of the pandemic and restrictions on international movement are effects on seafarers' shore leave. Pre-pandemic, most seafarers would take the opportunity, when possible, to spend a few hours of respite off the vessel whilst it was in port, perhaps to access reliable internet at a seafarer centre, visit a doctor or buy toiletries. During the pandemic, however, shore leave was prohibited due to national restrictions; in many countries this has never been lifted. Testing and quarantine requirements are still in force in many places, meaning that contract length is no longer predictable, leaving seafarers and their families in a state of uncertainty and unable to plan family events with any confidence. Despite international efforts to get seafarers consistently recognised as key workers, one seafarer told me recently, "we were in port next to a cruise vessel watching tourists disembark for a day out, whilst we were not allowed". It makes little sense to seafarers confined to their vessel for several months to be denied even a few short hours of respite. There are currently no signs of shore leave returning to become the norm again. Although the shipping industry recognises how important it is to set foot on land, individual countries set their own public health, travel and visa restrictions, and not all have made the move to recognise seafarers as essential workers.

Small, Diverse and Multicultural Crews

In a world where cheap products are demanded, costs of production and transportation are inexorably squeezed. "The typical pre-pandemic price of transporting a 20-foot container from Asia to Europe carrying over 20 tons of cargo was about the same as an economy ticket to fly the same journey" (Nagurney, 2021). In the 1950s, the development of container "boxes" facilitated a massive shift in the economy of trade.

Prior to this, goods were loaded and unloaded by hand in bundles, cartons, bags and barrels. In *Sea Life,* Captain Blackburn describes his first voyage on board in 1948:

> Another cargo we loaded in China was bales of human hair. Quite valuable and used for making wigs. [...] It was long, black and I made the mistake of sitting on a bale while counting bales of silk (another valuable cargo) and suffered with a flea-bitten rear end. (Blackburn, 2002)

Ships at that time would spend days or even weeks in port to complete the complex process of loading and discharging goods, giving many seafarers an opportunity to explore the world, which was an appealing part of the job. Standardised containers can now be loaded at the factory, transported by road or rail, and up to 20,000 of them stacked on board a single ship by gantry crane and delivered to their destinations without any need for repacking. The average time in port has reduced to a few hours. Likewise in 1948, the cargo liner mentioned above had about 100 people on board including a dozen passengers; the crew of a container ship today is typically between 20 and 30 people. "Minimum manning" for safety is required on all vessels, but whilst ships get bigger and technology improves, crew numbers reduce and diversity increases.

Whilst seafarers are often very culturally literate, and English is required as the common means of communication, the multicultural nature of small crews can impact on rest time and time to relax or socialise together. Two of the key issues considered problematic on board are fatigue (driven by long working hours and limited rest hours) and the lack of social interaction (Swift, 2015). Whereas on the TSMV *Soudan*, drinks before dinner, a plunge pool on the deck and a crew mess were the norm, now alcohol tends to be banned and seafarers are more likely to retire to their cabins to watch a movie or play a game on their mobile phone. In a tragic case that colleagues from the Philippines and I responded to after the suicide of a crew member, we were all struck that of the 23 crew members, all reported that they did not really know the person who had died. A recent study called Social Interaction Matters (Pike, 2022), has shown that often crew are too tired to interact during their down time due to the demands of the work, and this has increased during the pandemic. The results of the study are still being collated; however, early indications show "a direct correlation to boosts in mood when the crew have been able to engage with each other recreationally; through a basketball game, party or karaoke for example".[6] For mental health professionals, such news will not be surprising; however, research like this is critical if the industry is to take seriously issues like promoting social interaction, managing fatigue and realising its duty of care towards seafarers.

Promoting Change

I could describe many other day-to-day stresses, like coping with daily time zone changes and the effect of this on sleep and 24-hour shift work schedules as the vessel navigates its course, missing the birth of your baby and for some poor seafarers, even their own wedding. Other less common but more serious factors include piracy, bullying and harassment, sexual violence or the impact of critical incidents, like life-changing or fatal injuries and accidents on board.

Lack of understanding around mental health and the false assumption that the nature of seafarers gives some kind of immunity, has meant that measures to promote well-being, identify risks and respond appropriately have been almost absent across the industry until recently.

When I first met Eva Lianne Veldkamp, she told me, "Seafarers are used to look after themselves, they feel very responsible for their jobs. This is also vital, since the safety of the ship is essential to their own personal safety and vice versa", but she said, "We are all only human. Some experiences can be overwhelming and too big for a human to experience. Mine certainly was". In January 2005, Eva was a deck cadet on board a ship sailing through the Indian Ocean, 11 days after the earthquake that caused one of the largest tsunamis in history. "The warm salt water had affected the countless bodies to such an extent that there was no hope of finding a survivor. Still, my colleagues and I spent hours watching with our binoculars over this floating heap of grief. Hoping to find someone floating on a tree trunk. Some things are worse than you can ever imagine. I felt first-hand how tiny you are as a human in contrast to the big wide ocean". Eva said she had felt hopeless, helpless and overwhelmed. It was such an extreme experience that she and her colleagues could not put it into words, so they didn't. Eva shut it away and moved on.

Some years later, Eva was an officer on board when she received news of a close family member's death. Eva felt the same sense of helplessness, experiencing things from a distance. According to Eva, she "collapsed, physically and mentally" at this time and colleagues supported her and got her repatriated. It was when these feelings returned as the pandemic started to take hold, that Eva refused to be overwhelmed by the helplessness and sought out some therapeutic support. Eva recovered and now, as living proof that this is possible, she campaigns to raise awareness of mental health in the maritime industry.

We have now reached a tipping point; awareness has increased, and companies are starting to appreciate their duty of care and respond by developing policies and procedures. Seafarers are the most valuable asset of any shipping company; without them the shipping industry cannot function, and international trade ceases. As The Secret Captain says, "As the master, I need to remain strong and supportive for all of them [the crew]", but we might ask, at what cost? Who is providing him[7] with support? Has he had any training to support his crew? Is he getting any professional guidance or help to do this? The almost universal idea that seafarers are strong, resilient, professional, problem solvers is fine until problems arise when this same idea may prevent recognition that people are struggling, and worse, stop seafarers from reaching out for help. Stories like Eva's are important, to address the stigma and increase understanding of mental health.

Overall, the trend is an extremely positive one. In 2016, when I was invited to the ITF Seafarers' Trust conference to speak about mental health in the humanitarian sector, the common question was, "how do we identify the people who are likely to have a mental health problem before they join a ship?", with an (sometimes explicitly stated) intention to prevent them from joining a ship at all. These ideas are not yet consigned to history, but increasingly the questions are moving towards prevention, protection and towards identifying signs of difficulty to provide support.

When on board, the fear of disclosing personal problems or difficulties in coping remains one of the greatest challenges to supporting seafarers. Many things contribute to this: stigma and culturally bound misconceptions about mental health alongside the real risk that someone struggling on board may need to be repatriated and put their career in jeopardy. This is a major issue stopping people from speaking out or asking for help, and was described by one officer at a recent training session as "career suicide". When repatriation does occur, it is often in the best interests of all concerned to access familial and professional support at home. Fortunately, some forward-thinking companies are starting to introduce return-to-work policies and include assurance of fair practice in relation to mental health. These companies recognise that many people can suffer with common mental health problems like anxiety, depression or post-traumatic stress disorder *and* recover effectively and resume their duties at sea, perhaps even with better coping mechanisms as a result.

Seafarers on voyage-only contracts often fear that asking for support could mean that another contract will not be offered by the company or the same manning agent. This "blacklisting" of individuals officially should not happen, but is still reported to occur. Seafarers most at risk of this are often in the lowest ranks and are also the most likely to be from community-oriented cultures where they may be the sole income provider for an extended family. Income security is already problematic, and the loss of future income may be enough to make people endure extremely poor conditions, bullying and harassment and even physical or sexual violence. Sadly, some evidence suggests that the most significant factor associated with violence on board ships is seafarer region of origin, with seafarers from the Philippines and the Pacific region (11%), Eastern Europe (9%), and Asia/India (9%) four times more likely than seafarers from Western Europe to report violence or threats of violence (Lefkowitz & Slade, 2019). The voyage-only contract prevents people from speaking out about their concerns, be they safety considerations on board or pressure to falsify their hours of work and rest, rendering them more vulnerable to abuse and preventing them from seeking help and support.

Mental health promotion, well-being initiatives and tools and techniques to support well-being can help seafarers themselves take steps in self-care. The common mental health and well-being advice appropriate on shore is often not applicable at sea. Just as lockdowns during the pandemic required some modification of well-being advice, some thought needs to go into how strategies for good mental health can be modified to fit a population that lives and works on board. The self-help guides I wrote for all seafarers, published and disseminated for free by ISWAN (Blackburn, n.d.), attempt to do just that. The Sailor's Society has also developed a Wellness at Sea app which aims to support seafarers with holistic well-being advice. Another approach is the Well at Sea platform which translates positive psychology principles into short videos, interactive exercises and games that earn seafarers points for completing tasks that support well-being.

Another major challenge is about who is best to provide support. Whereas on shore, we may have friends or family we can approach, in times of trouble at sea there are only your crew mates. If there are only colleagues to turn to, difficulties can arise. On board ship, cultural differences, power and hierarchy all play an important role, while communication with the company tends to go through the master, and poor connectivity can make confidential access to support difficult. The hierarchical nature of a ship's crew means that a cultural and power gap on board can feel insurmountable. The fear of negative reprisals is often given as a reason for not reaching out for help.

ISWAN provides a 24/7 global helpline for seafarers and their families, staffed by helpline officers who speak 12 languages between them and can advise and offer support in any issues seafarers face. The service works by text SMS, phone, ring back, email and messenger apps, such as Facebook/Meta and WhatsApp. In many ports around the world, seafarers' centres run by charities such as Stella Maris, the Sailor's Society and Mission to Seafarers and staffed by chaplains and volunteers provide a friendly face, internet and telephone access, or lifts to the nearest shopping or medical centres. Many of these organisations also do ship visits whilst vessels are in port, bringing pizza or toiletries and a portable Wi-Fi hotspot, or holding prayer services and offering pastoral support, often a vital service for many seafarers. A memorial service and a blessing of the ship and its crew is often deeply appreciated after a death on board a vessel. During the pandemic, some of these charities launched helplines and digital services to supplement their usual work.

Overcoming barriers to accessing support rests largely on building the trust of seafarers in the genuineness of their companies' intentions to promote well-being and provide support, something that takes time. One of the ways we try to address this is through training. Raising awareness around well-being and mental health, addressing stigma and encouraging better understanding that we all have mental health issues and can struggle at times, is important. Title 4 of the Maritime Labour Convention (International Labour Organisation, 2006) requires that seafarers have a safe and healthy work environment and access to medical care. Although this should also apply to mental health care it has been interpreted in the past as relevant only to physical health care. All ships have a designated medical officer on board who is a member of the crew trained in basic medical care and first aid for emergencies. This person has responsibility for medicines carried on board and is supported in delivering care by remote medical service providers on shore. These "telemedical" providers rarely have specialist mental health staff, but there are indicators that this too is starting to change. Some companies are beginning to engage bespoke emotional support lines, counselling or mental health support helplines.

One approach can be to train staff on board as first responders to support their colleagues. As those responsible for the crew and vessels, senior officers often benefit from an understanding of mental health and basic support skills. In some cases, the designated medical officer may benefit from training, while in others, companies might train well-being champions. Several years ago, I developed Maritime Mental Health Awareness training courses, which are offered through ISWAN and delivered by myself and other qualified counsellors or psychologists. This training uses an adapted version of the psychological first aid model (World Health Organization, 2011) to train officers, shoreside staff and crew mates in skills to offer basic support as a first response, and to facilitate access to further support as needed.

It can and does happen on occasion that a seafarer might suffer an acute mental health emergency, such as a first episode of psychosis or acute suicidal ideation. In such a situation, the only way to establish safety is to rely on the master to implement appropriate support until such time as the ship can either be diverted to the nearest port or reach their next port of call and shore-based services can be accessed. In these circumstances, remote support can be provided to the master of the vessel and the shoreside team who are in contact with them. Where the master and key senior staff have had some training in first response and support skills, and the company has pre-established procedures, this is tremendously beneficial. Where they do not, it can prompt the company to consider addressing this.

A member of a shoreside team got in touch to discuss the case of a seafarer who was acting in ways that were out of character. I asked a series of questions about what was happening and who had first noted the problem and, as is often the case, different individuals had portions of information. The seafarer was on the vessel for the first time and had been performing well until this point, when his behaviour became increasingly erratic. It came to light that he had a diagnosis of bipolar depressive disorder not declared in his medical, and his medication had run out. Once this was known, the situation could be resolved. This case illustrates concerns about the need for regular medication to manage a disorder, that might not be readily available when extensions to contracts and unforeseen voyage extensions are a known risk.

In another case, the captain of a private yacht contacted me, explaining his concern that one of the crew members was struggling with suicidal ideation. The crew had been trying to offer support, but it was taking its toll on everyone. They were near to the coast of America and had spoken to a suicide emergency line on shore that suggested an assessment at a walk-in mental health emergency unit. This had been attempted, but due to pandemic restrictions, the seafarer was not seen and had to return to the vessel. An alternative assessment was planned, but the captain was concerned that principles of confidentiality might prevent the crew member providing background information and discussing safety considerations. He felt the crew member needed to be in a place of safety and didn't feel able to continue to support them on the yacht. We were able to talk through the principles of emergency suicide risk assessment and how he might approach the assessment as a supportive employer, as well as some specific questions to ask in relation to establishing safety.

As time goes on, companies are starting to explore how to create environments on board which promote seafarers' well-being, consider how to retain seafarers, how to support them and what kinds of processes need to be in place to enable seafarers to safely return to sea following a leave of absence. This might include conducting well-being assessments, putting psychological support into place during a leave of absence and doing a return-to-work assessment.

Recommendations

For Seafarers:

- Remember, you are human, and we can all struggle sometimes. There are challenges in working at sea and whilst seafarers are resilient and professional, it's important to be mindful of your well-being.
- Look at some of the existing resources for ideas about promoting well-being on board, like ISWAN's series of Good Mental Health guides for seafarers (ISWAN). Download apps and resources that might prove useful before joining the vessel and consider storing shared resources on the ship's drive.
- Build good working relationships with colleagues, cultivate a positive atmosphere on board, seek out opportunities for social interaction and for things you enjoy doing in your off-time.
- Ask your company about their policy for well-being and what they are doing to promote well-being on board. Notice the recurrent stressors and look for ways to communicate them to shoreside so that you can mitigate against them together.

For Shipping Companies, Manning Agents:

- Seafarers are your most valuable asset, and as an employer you have a duty of care towards them. Draft a policy to demonstrate your commitment to seafarer well-being (Blackburn, 2019). Identify key objectives for well-being and involve seafarers across ranks to identify the key pressures on board, to enable you to collaborate on an effective strategy to achieve them.
- The evidence shows that even small changes can make a big difference; it's a great investment in your people and the rewards outweigh any costs (Deloitte, 2020). Consider encouraging good interpersonal relationships on board through support for social interaction and promoting positive

leadership skills; ensure effective internet access to maintain support networks at home and for access to support services; and improve living conditions, communal spaces and facilities for crew to rest and relax during their "off-time", including physical exercise and tasty, nutritious food.

- Be mindful in crewing decisions; consider diversity and wherever possible try to create natural peers on board by ensuring there is more than one woman, cadet or person from a language group. Where this is unavoidable, perhaps allocate a mentor or buddy. Avoid the use of voyage-only contracts wherever possible. Lack of income security prevents people from raising concerns, be they safety considerations, issues such as bullying and harassment, or mental health, creating a barrier to support.
- Consider initiatives to raise awareness about mental health without stigma. Look at what support and response mechanisms are in place and how accessible they are. Consider what processes need to be in place for your seafarers to safely return to sea following a leave of absence. This might include doing well-being assessments, putting psychological support in place during a leave of absence, and performing a return-to-work assessment.
- Remember, in all mental health initiatives seek subject matter expertise from accredited and recognised mental health professionals with experience in or knowledge of maritime issues.

For Psychological Therapists:

- Working in the maritime context is complex and interesting; innovative thinking is required to adapt evidence-based practice and develop effective ways of working for this unique population. To provide effective services, it is essential to understand some of the unique challenges that a life at sea presents and the constraints involved.
- As practitioners, we need to rethink some of the traditional boundaries that surround our work. We may have to work in consultation with shore teams or masters on board to help them provide support. Difficulties with connectivity on board and changing time zones mean that we may not be able to have regular sessions or may have to confine ourselves to online chat platforms. Thus, questions arise as to how we can offer support that meets seafarers' needs despite the unique and challenging contexts in which they work.
- There are only small numbers of mental health professionals working within the maritime industry currently and we need more. We have a fledgling international Community of Practice for accredited mental health professionals, and would be delighted to hear from like-minded colleagues.

Call to Action

Maritime mental health is an emerging field. The shipping industry is complex. The challenges of protecting and promoting mental health and well-being and responding when problems arise are considerable. We have reached a tipping point in the industry where awareness has grown but resources to address concerns have not kept pace. Understanding of mental health in the industry is growing, but there is still some distance to travel before parity with physical health promotion, protection and response mechanisms are in place. High-quality research is urgently needed, both to increase our understanding of the risks to well-being and the scale of the problem, but also to develop the evidence base regarding best practice. At the time of writing, myself and a small handful of other mental health professionals are joining together to establish a community of practice. Our aim is to set standards for practice and policy in the industry; to encourage the maritime industry to utilise technical expertise in mental health; to ensure the principle of "Do No Harm" and to draw on evidence-based practice in other domains to establish practice-based evidence for seafarer mental health and well-being.

Notes

1 Psalm 107:23–31
2 Interestingly, the captain may be one of the most isolated positions on board a vessel, with no readily accessible peer.
3 Fatigue is widely acknowledged in the industry as a major concern, particularly for the impact it has on work-related accidents, injuries and operational incidents. The Maritime Labour Convention (MLC) mandates hours of work and rest, but compliance is known to be imperfect, and falsification of records is talked about not infrequently. Seafarers work hours must not exceed 72 hours in a seven-day period; for reference, the European Union's (EU's Working Time Directive (2003/88/EC) mandates a maximum of 48 hours in a seven-day period.
4 The Gulf of Guinea stretches around 6,000km of coastline from Senegal to Liberia and is reported by the International Maritime Bureau to currently be the world's biggest hotspot for piracy. Others include the Gulf of Aden, Singapore Straits, Indonesia and the Americas.
5 ISWAN International Seafarers Welfare Assistance Network, www.seafarerswelf are.org/
6 Dr Kate Pike, Director of Field-Research, personal correspondence.
7 Of the global seafarer workforce, 1.3% are women (BIMCO/ICS, 2021).

References

BIMCO/ICS. (2021). *BIMCO/ICS Seafarer workforce report, 2021.* www.ics-shipp ing.org/press-release/new-bimco-ics-seafarer-workforce-report-warns-of-serious-potential-officer-shortage/
Blackburn, J.K. (2002). *Sea life.* unpublished manuscript.

Blackburn, P. (2019). *Mentally healthy ships: Policy and practice to promote mental health on board.* ISWAN. www.seafarerswelfare.org/seafarer-health-information-programme/good-mental-health/mentally-healthy-ships

Blackburn, P.J. (n.d.). ISWAN. www.seafarerswelfare.org/seafarer-health-information-programme/good-mental-health/psychological-well-being-at-sea

Deloitte. (2020). *Mental health and employers: Refreshing the case for investment.* www2.deloitte.com/uk/en/pages/consulting/articles/mental-health-and-employers-refreshing-the-case-for-investment.html

George, R. (2014). *Deep sea and foreign going: Inside shipping, the invisible industry that brings you 90% of everything.* New York: Picador.

Higginbottom, K. (2022, 13 January). ITF Seafarers' Trust: Better access to wifi onboard and facilitating shore leave remain key focus areas of crew welfare. (Safety4Sea, Interviewer) Safety4Sea. https://safety4sea.com/cm-itf-seafarers-trust-better-access-to-wifi-onboard-and-facilitating-shore-leave-remain-key-focus-areas-of-crew-welfare/

International Chamber of Shipping (ICS). (n.d.). www.ics-shipping.org/shipping-fact/shipping-and-world-trade-global-supply-and-demand-for-seafarers

International Chamber of Shipping (ICS). (2020). www.ics-shipping.org/current-issue/ilo-minimum-wage-2020/

International Labour Organisation. (2006). *Maritime labour convention, as amended.* www.ilo.org/global/standards/maritime-labour-convention/text/WCMS_554767/lang--en/index.htm

ISWAN South Asia. (2021, 26 February). *Unregistered crewing agencies in India.* www.seafarerswelfare.org/news/2021/unregistered-crewing-agencies-in-india-a-report-by-iswan-south-asia

ITF Seafarers. (n.d.). Abandoned seafarers. www.itfseafarers.org/en/issues/abandoned-seafarers

Lefkowitz, R., & Slade, M. (2019). *Seafarer mental health study.* ITF Seafarers' Trust. www.seafarerstrust.org/sites/default/files/node/publications/files/ST_MentalHealthReport_Final_Digital-1.pdf

Machemer, A. (2021, 20 April). "Zoom fatigue" may be with us for years. Here's how we'll cope. *National Geographic.* www.nationalgeographic.co.uk/science-and-technology/2021/04/zoom-fatigue-may-be-with-us-for-years-heres-how-well-cope

Marine Benefits. (2021). *Refresh wellbeing.* Bergen, Norway: Marine Benefits AS. www.marinebenefitsas.com/refresh/wellbeing

McVeigh, K. (2021, 15 February). Living hell of stranded UAE ship IBA. *The Guardian.* www.theguardian.com/environment/2021/feb/15/living-hell-of-stranded-uae-ship-iba

McVeigh, K. (2022, 16 March). Calls for "blue corridor" to let stranded seafarers leave Ukraine war zone . *The Guardian.* www.theguardian.com/environment/2022/mar/16/ukraine-russia-war-black-sea-azov-blue-corridor-stranded-seafarers

Nagurney, A. (2021, 5 April). *Container ships will keep getting bigger – even after the Ever Given becoming stuck in the Suez Canal. MarketWatch.* www.marketwatch.com/story/container-ships-will-keep-getting-bigger-even-after-the-ever-given-becoming-stuck-in-the-suez-canal-11617637476

Pike, K. (2022). Social interaction matters: Helping shipping and ship management companies to improve social interaction on board. *ISWAN.* www.seafarerswelfare.org/our-work/social-interaction-matters

Sampson, H., & Ellis, N. (2019). *Seafarers' mental health and wellbeing.* Seafarers International Research Centre, Cardiff University. IOSH. https://iosh.com/media/6306/seafarers-mental-health-wellbeing-full-report.pdf

The Secret Captain. (2020, 16 November). The Secret Captain: I have woken up crying because it's all hopeless. *Tradewinds.* www.tradewindsnews.com/opinion/the-secret-captain-i-have-woken-up-crying-because-it-s-all-hopeless/2-1-911603

Swift, O. (2015). *Social isolation of seafarers; What is it? Why does it matter? What can be done.* www.seafarerswelfare.org/assets/documents/resources/Social-Isolation-Article-PDF.pdf

World Health Organization. (2011). *Psychological first aid: guide for field workers.* www.who.int/publications/i/item/9789241548205

Chapter 9

Supporting international contractors working in aid and development contexts

Kate S. Thompson, Mark Snelling and Lynn Keane

Introduction

This chapter starts with a meeting: The first author's encounter with Joe, a non-commissioned officer in the British Army who accessed a psychology service for serving military personnel. Joe had been dogged by health difficulties for some years, and when his relationship ended, this triggered an emotional crisis and he sought help for symptoms of depression, anger and problems negotiating the end of his relationship. As is usual when working with serving personnel, questions of fitness for work need to be considered, and it became clear through our work together that Joe was ready to leave the military. He explained to me that he could make a year's salary in a few months if he took his skills to the private sector and took a contract overseas. He had decided that signing up for a two-year contract would help him manage financial difficulties he had incurred and make all sorts of dreams he had into a reality, including cementing his relationship with his new partner. Although he was disappointed with aspects of his military career, feeling he had not been valued sufficiently once his health started to deteriorate, his sense of a hopeful future in which he would achieve all that had so far eluded him interested me greatly. Would this future as an international staff member really provide all that he hoped for?

In this chapter we explore the experiences of those who decide to work internationally as contractors in conflict settings or fragile states, and the impact of this work on those who choose it. In many ways there are similarities between these individuals and those who take any international role (as described in the introduction), but the backgrounds of those who work in highly stressful settings and their motivations may be somewhat different, as they were for Joe.

In some cases, contractors may have a military background, meaning that they bring their experience of conflict settings, short-term deployments or working with mixed teams to their international consultancy. In other cases,

DOI: 10.4324/9781003261971-10

the consultant may be highly experienced in their field, but has worked mainly in their home country developing specialist skills in construction, engineering, policing, healthcare or indeed any other area before embarking on an international post. In this case, the setting may be quite unfamiliar, and even using familiar skills or existing experience may be challenging.

The motivation to take an international role is usually based on a complex mixture of factors (see introductory chapter) but financial considerations are often key, whether these be in terms of increasing earnings, reducing family-based costs or improving financial prospects (HSBC, 2017). However, this survey also notes other motivating factors. For 38% of the respondents, finding "a new challenge" was a key motivation, while a further 15% reported wanting to discover "a sense of purpose in their career". Franke and von Boemcken (2011), using an online survey, collected data on motivation from 223 civilian police in the USA who had completed at least one assignment in a conflict region. The samples were drawn from a particular organisation whose members work internationally in policing (CivPol Alumni Association), often taking a leave of absence from their usual job to participate in civilian police activities and police development programmes around the world. Only 25% of their respondents listed financial gain as their main motivation, tending rather to report wanting to "face and meet new challenges", "help others", "serve the US" and "make a difference" as their key drivers. The authors note that this should lead us to question the idea of such contractors as mercenaries mainly motivated by money. Interestingly, fewer than one-fifth of the respondents listed adventure and excitement as motivators, although this may be somewhat disingenuous as even the authors note (attributing this quote to Scahill, 2007): "contracting offered a chance for many combat enthusiasts, retired from the service and stuck in the ennui of everyday to return to their glory days" (p. 736).

It is recognised that the transition from military service can be fraught, with individuals who have spent large parts of their lives working in a particular type of context left wondering how best to adjust to the freedoms and limitations of a changed work landscape. In some cases, short-term contracts abroad can offer a way to forestall more permanent decisions about work direction, almost delaying a full transition from military to civilian life. While many home country-based initiatives exist to smooth transition, an international contract can still seem a good way to answer the question of "what to do next". It is also worth remembering the way that such a contract might appear to oneself or to others as a "new adventure", preventing a sense of slump or anti-climax that could otherwise arise at this career point.

For Joe, described earlier in this chapter, there appear to have been a complex mix of motivations driving his interest in working as a consultant overseas. Firstly, and importantly, was his sense of the financial incentive, something that was a powerful part of his desire to take an international job. However, the meaning of the financial reward was not simply one of income.

It appeared clearly linked to areas of reimbursement, in particular the way in which he, as a worker, would be differently valued (as demonstrated by the higher financial reward) for professional experience that seemed hard won, and which had had considerable physical health costs. Further to this, he described a search to validate existing key skills and talents that he felt were being under-prized in his current role. It was as if he was reasoning that the losses incurred through his work in the military might somehow be "made up for" in this imagined future posting.

Although this weighing up might not be realistic, the complex layers of meaning balanced in such career decisions recall the work of Siegrist (1996) on the Effort-Reward-Imbalance model of occupational stress. In this model, stress is seen not simply as due to demands made on an employee (for example, long hours, high workload, urgent tasks) but as resulting from a perceived imbalance between what is expected of an employee (effort) and the reward they receive. This reward may be money, esteem, promotion or, in the case of highly conscientious and vocational workers, rewards such as experiencing fulfilment, being able to meet the needs of service users or being valued by employers. If the effort made is greater than the reward received, the model anticipates that employees will suffer work-related stress. This stress may be increased in situations in which employees have tolerated a feeling of imbalance for a long period (as was the case for Joe) and when they appear over-committed to their occupational role (as may often be the case for those in military service) (van Vegchel, de Jonge, Bosma, & Schaufeli, 2005).

In the case of those transitioning from military service, reports about potential lucrative consultant roles circulate widely, providing a hopeful narrative about the future at a time of some uncertainty or even dread, and when an individual may be measuring whether they will be able to succeed in the civilian world. Despite this, it is the very difference between these contracting roles and the jobs previously done in service that may create difficulties. Far from these jobs being a way to retain something familiar as an individual moves through a period of change, there may be a jarring sense of difference that it would be well to anticipate. The differences in terms of ongoing relationships with colleagues and team members, degrees of camaraderie and the extent of a sense of shared endeavour are all likely to be striking. As one former contractor commented, "it is very different [...] there is no life and death element, and you don't depend on the team in the same way [...] You can easily find yourself wondering, what is it really for?" This change in a sense of common purpose can create profound effects on the staff member including a sense of loneliness and a loss of engagement at work.

Further, the terms and conditions of the contracts undertaken are often very different from those in the public sector and the military, and this leads to a new experience of living from one contract to the next without any degree of certainty about future job security. For those coming from the certainties of military life (where in the words of one former client "your life is mapped out" in a career of potentially two decades or more), this can create great anxiety. The key differences are, of course, not limited to that of job security. Military service often determines healthcare, accommodation, financial arrangements and in some cases family support for serving personnel in a way that is not replicated in the world of international contracting.

These differences are at their most stark where one might consider that the setting had most in common with former service: When military contractors work in security roles and find themselves in the same locations managing the same difficult situations as their military counterparts. The terms and conditions are very different, and Isenberg (2010) quotes one authority as saying that contractors are treated "like disposable trash, used for the job and then thrown away". Concern has been expressed at the high rates of mental health difficulty and suicide amongst contractors who worked for US defence companies in Iraq and Afghanistan, who often have limited access to psychological and psychiatric support, and whose insurance may not cover them in the event of suicide. One widely quoted study in 2007 of contractors training Iraqi police found that 24% had symptoms of post-traumatic stress disorder (PTSD) (Risen, 2007). Similarly, Feinstein and Botes (2009) found that a third of the contractors they studied had PTSD scores in the moderate to severe range, while a fifth exceeded cut-off points for depression and 17% for excessive alcohol use. In discussing this sample, the authors note that only approximately 10% of their participants had access to employer organised psychological help, which for contractors based in the USA might severely limit access to appropriate mental health care.

This is important, as there have been clear links between untreated mental health difficulties and later violence in military contractors. In 2011, Danny Fitzsimmons, working for G4S in Iraq, was found guilty of killing two other contractors during a dispute, only 36 hours into his time in-country. He was sentenced to serve 20 years in jail, but concurrent investigations showed evidence of untreated PTSD in his case, and outstanding criminal convictions which had been overlooked during his screening for work in Iraq. This case followed relatively soon after the 2007 Nisour Square massacre, in which four Blackwater Security Consulting contractors fired on unarmed civilians and were later jailed on manslaughter charges. Blackwater had to cease all operations in Iraq with immediate effect, showing the impact on organisations that such poor recruitment practice can pose (though the risks to colleagues and populations supposedly being supported are of greater importance). Military contractors are individuals not covered by the customary rules of international humanitarian law and cut loose from the disciplines of military structure. Add to this, untreated PTSD and you have a dangerous combination of risk factors.

In summary, the move to become a contractor may appear to be taking an individual who is leaving the military in a familiar direction given its short-term deployment-style assignments and rugged locations. However, this appearance should not be allowed to deceive, and posts require careful evaluation to make sure that key differences in support, benefits, camaraderie and job security can be weighed up with clarity. Organisations should be very careful in screening individuals for military contractor roles given the dangers of triggered reaction to past traumatic experience.

Same Skills But Such a Different Context

Simon had retired after a successful career in the police service in the UK when he took on a position training police officers in an African country. He had been actively recruited because of his skills by a government department concerned with international development. Simon was seen for a pre-deployment screening and reported his interest in using his experience in another context. He stated that he had no major concerns about the role and had developed strong coping resources through his work that he thought would see him through his time as an international contractor. His wife, Lily, and two teenage children were less sanguine about his new job, but he felt that keeping in touch with them remotely, and his visits home every 12 weeks would make the changes manageable. Simon was seen again at the end of his contract when he returned to the UK. He reported having found the work more challenging than he had thought, remarking on how different the setting had been to his expectations. He explained that local corruption had made it impossible to work in the way he had envisaged and that this was a source of great disappointment and frustration to him. He had also found the separation from his family very difficult to manage, despite his frequent visits home, and said that he was not planning a further international contract.

Throughout this volume, the authors have argued in favour of organisational support to prepare staff for their assignments, to support them while working away and to offer support on their return. In the case of Simon, his professional profile may have made him an ideal candidate to train a new professional police force in a post-conflict country, but his expectations of what he might face in the setting were not adequately primed. Had he received a fuller briefing and more effective support in-country, this might have led to a more successful and less personally disappointing assignment. Also important in Simon's case was the mismatch between his values in relation to policing and those common in the context in which he was working. A mismatch of values has been identified as a key driver for burnout (Maslach & Leitner, 2005). When values are more markedly affected, this can lead to moral distress and even moral injury as discussed in chapter 4.

Much work related to the flourishing of expatriates in international roles studies variables like *cross-cultural competence, cultural adjustment* and *emotional intelligence* in individual expatriate workers (see, for example, Liao, Wu,

Dao, & Ngoc Luu, 2021; Jassawalla, Truglia, & Garvey 2004), often finding that strengths in these sometimes loosely defined concepts are predictive of success. While these studies may offer some insights, it has been consistently argued in this volume that the success of any assignment is due to the "fit" between the staff member, the professional role, the organisation and the setting of work (of which one element is the *culture* of the country or region of posting). In Simon's case, we will never know how he might have scored had his cross-cultural competence or emotional intelligence been measured prior to his departure. However, it is safe to speculate that whatever his scores, more information might have helped orient him. This could have included clarification on what might be demanded of him in the role and how it might conflict with core professional and moral values as well as key information about the setting (expectations of policing, attitudes to probity in public life and the negotiation of power relationships within the culture).

Support while working away, preferably from host country nationals with expertise in "interpreting" key expectations of the setting for staff from outside might also have been helpful and is supported by findings that relationships with host country counterparts and mentors have an important role to play in international assignments (Hechanova, Beehr, & Christiansen 2003; Toh & Denisi 2007). This should not, however, blind us to asking whether any given post really requires an international staff member or whether using the right host country national, suitably supported, might not be a more helpful way to manage a specific post, particularly one requiring cultural nuance.

It is also important to attend to the changes that acculturation can bring to the identity of an international worker. As mentioned in the introduction, Adams and van der Vijver (2015) contrast the development of a *cosmopolitan* expatriate identity with that of a *pragmatic* expatriate identity, with the former reflecting a person detached from any specific cultural context and "able to negotiate their social roles [...] with individuals from different contexts and cultural backgrounds within any context" (p. 6). In contrast, those developing a *pragmatic* expatriate identity "only make the minimal adjustments needed to survive in the new cultural context, and maintain their original personal (e.g., values and goals), relational (e.g., work role), and social (e.g., culture) identities as much as possible" (p. 7). The authors note that there are risks inherent in the development of either form of expatriate identity style, with those who develop pragmatic identities perhaps finding it difficult to communicate well while working internationally, and segregating themselves from a fuller international experience, while those with cosmopolitan identities experience greater difficulty when returning to a home country or taking a longer posting, risking a sense of detachment in all cultural contexts.

These reflections on identity are highly relevant to the experience of the international staff considered in this book, particularly international consultants on short-term contracts for whom questions of how far they adjust themselves to the setting of the work and how far they remain detached may be central. Connected with this, individuals can describe changes to their sense of place due to international work. A worker may feel that they exist in two or more places, or compartments, with one associated with their working life and another with relaxation or home life. The R & R (rest and recuperation) and rotation cycles that often govern the work of humanitarians and consultants in fragile states tend to exaggerate the potential pull of this sort of place-compartmentalised life. As one contractor working in the Middle East put it:

> My working life is away, and I tend to work 12–15 hour days and do nothing else. That's fine for me. The place I really live is (home country) and when I get back there after four to six weeks, I can really enjoy it, relax, do whatever I like. My life abroad pays for my good life at home, and this is how it has been for years.

Interestingly, his wife was less happy with this compartmentalisation (and the impact on families of contractor work is discussed below). One of her main concerns about this was the way in which it encouraged him to overwork and make little effort to develop good lifestyle habits of exercise, nutrition and sleep in his work location. This appears understandable: If a person sees themselves as existing in an entirely work-focused stasis for weeks at a time (with "real life" taking place elsewhere and only for short holiday breaks or at the end of contracts), there is little to encourage developing life routines, supportive relationships or any permanent features of life in the country of posting. Interestingly, this sense of a transience developing in connection with place is echoed in a study of academics assigned internationally (Richardson & Zikic, 2007) which notes that participants reported becoming wearied by their transitory connections with others and giving up on building new friendships in international settings.

On the other hand, the work-related compartment may become the setting that is most compelling, encouraging the staff member to invest heavily in relationships with colleagues, and cherish the excitement and energy of the workspace over all other sources of satisfaction. This can lead to a reduced investment at home so that relationships wither and the contractor is obliged to commit and recommit to work without having a secure place to land between postings. In the case of some humanitarian clients, there can be a sense that the person has been working solidly for a decade, moving from post to post and crisis to crisis, almost without lifting their head. It is when they do look up, and perhaps ask questions about next steps in their professional life that they face the dilemma of having lived in such a disconnected way. This can also have a discrepant effect depending on gender, as female contractors may find they are differentially impacted by choices to stay on the move during their reproductive years. As argued by Snelling in chapter 3 (this volume), keeping on the move can represent a choice driven by complex attachment needs. It is the role of good organisational management and reflective psychological support to keep such questions in discussion with individual contractors.

There is, in addition, a darker side that can arise with compartmental-isation. In 2018, revelations emerged about the sexually abusive actions of Oxfam's national director and other senior aid workers in Haiti after the 2010 earthquake, shedding light on the way that some international staff exploit their positions in criminal and immoral ways. Such behaviour has a longer history, perhaps as long as international aid itself. In the Balkans in the 1990s, the presence of peacekeepers was found to have sparked an unprecedented increase in the trafficking of women and girls and helped establish a net-work of brothels and human trafficking that had not existed earlier (Hoang, 2019). As Hoang notes: "*The influx of about 60,000 male staff and soldiers in the region, coupled with their substantial purchasing power, boosted sex work and criminal networks*". In some cases, it was alleged that UN support staff were supporting these criminal networks by illegal activities such as forging documents, facilitating transport across borders and tipping off gangs about impending raids (Barnett & Hughes, 2001).

The fact of being far from home appears to have facilitated a sidestep-ping of usual moral behaviour. As Kathryn Bolkovac, an investigator previ-ously working for the UN, remarks, "many people lose sight of their morals when they are 5,000 miles from home and think they will not get caught. Then they see that even if they are caught nothing of any consequence will happen to them" (quoted in Slankanjic, 2016). Consultants' money impacts impoverished local communities for both good and ill, and in some cases indi-viduals who might never use "sex workers" in their home country are drawn into it in aid, development and conflict contexts. Boredom, peer pressure, a sense of reward for being away from home may be drivers for this behav-iour, but there is also the impact of compartmentalising shown by a failure to equate the exploited in the host country with their equivalents in the home country.

A further possible reaction to frequent transition is that rather than carrying two or more place-compartments, each associated with a different location, an individual may find their sense of place becoming entirely condi-tional, so that every locality feels transitory and as if one might just as well be elsewhere. Eva Hoffman (1989) captures this sense of being disconnected and somehow rootless astutely when she writes,

> The only thing is that in the midst of a conversation [...] I lift off a little too high, to a point from which the room becomes only a place in which I happen to be, where I've found myself by some odd accident [...] Weightlessness is upon me. This is just one arbitrary version of reality [...] Nothing here has to be the way it is. (p. 170)

Hill and Hawker note in chapter 5 (this volume) the importance of the question "where is home for you?", which is of value to consider with all international staff. If the answer is difficult to generate or creates discomfort, there may be something to explore with the sense of place for this person.

In keeping with this, while most of the focus in the literature on international staff explores their adjustment while assigned abroad, there may be significant difficulties with return or repatriation to a home base or country of origin. Chiang, van Esch, & Birtch (2020) describe the range of issues associated with expatriate workers returning to their home bases, noting that 38% of repatriates leave their employing organisation within a year of returning home. The authors note that organisational support can be key in smoothing the return of individuals and families and softening pressures associated with reverse culture shock (see Chapter 5). The authors suggest that employers offer training about repatriation stresses as well as allow pre-return visits to home country and provide time off for settling in at home and possible repatriation counselling. They stress the need for human resources professionals and managers to recognise additional skills gained during international postings and use these for structured career planning once staff return to their home base. These recommendations make sense for expatriates returning to work in their home bases for the same organisations that assigned them internationally. Career planning for those completing successive international postings (for example, humanitarians, mission staff and perhaps some contractors) may also be recognised as valuable by employers. In the case of single assignment contractors, however, there may be no planning for the next steps of the staff member, seen by the employer as a short-term staff member, as independent and expected to return home (or not) by his or her own volition at the end of his or her assignment.

Despite the lack of current planning in relation to contractors, however, we would argue that sending any staff member abroad should entail an organisational duty of care to consider the whole of their international contract period including both expatriation/assignment and repatriation/return/onward posting (Chiang, van Esch, Birtch, & Shaffer, 2018).

Impact on Couple and Family Relationships

Felix sought help after he experienced a panic attack while working as a contractor in a Middle Eastern country. He had previously served in a unit of Special Forces in a military career of over two decades and then transitioned out of the military and began working as a contractor in the oil and gas sector. In the ten years since leaving the military, he had fulfilled both longer and shorter international contracts, often in highly volatile locations, but reported that he enjoyed the variety, and hated above all the idea of boring work. His first marriage, which had lasted through his military career, ended two years after he left the services and he remained in limited contact with his three grown-up children from this marriage. A second marriage, to Audrey, his current wife, was happy, although he tended to see her for rotation breaks every four to six weeks and for short bursts between contracts, and laughingly said that if he was to return home for good, that might be the end of their relationship. Although surprised by the panic attack, he stated that he had served two tours in Iraq and one in Afghanistan and recalled numerous traumatic incidents from these deployments. Felix was aware that he had somewhat avoided a transition to civilian life by remaining on the move as a contractor.

The situation of Felix helps illustrate some additional points for work with contractors. Firstly, echoing the earlier part of this chapter, the way in which an overhang from past military experience may colour the work of the contractor, encouraging the person to pick certain kinds of contract work in certain locations and perhaps continuing a form of place-compartmentalisation first established during military service. In keeping with this, residual reactions to past traumatic events (perhaps not marked enough to have warranted the person's attention or perhaps delayed in onset) may arise and be something that the person concerned has never attended to or has "kept busy" to contain. Many contractors report occasional intrusive recollections or even flashbacks when working in locations that recall past distressing experiences, perhaps triggered by light, smells or sounds with traumatic associations. Because so many contractors have past military experience (in the Franke & von Boemcken (2011) study, two-thirds of the police professionals responding to the online survey had served in the military earlier in their career), it is important to factor in the presence of mental health difficulties associated with service, notably PTSD but also depression and disorders of alcohol misuse.

Felix and his first wife had separated a relatively short time after his end of service, something that is not uncommon (Pollard, Karney, & Loughran 2008). His new relationship with Audrey appeared (to Felix at least) to be built on a compact that included his movement between different posts at a distance from her. In his view, the marriage succeeded at least in part *because* he was away a great deal. Although some contractors may travel with accompanying spouses (and in this case resemble the families of other international staff members discussed in chapter 5, this volume), many leave behind their partners and children. In this sense their experience is in keeping with earlier research on "intermittent husbands" which found that marriages in which one partner worked away could often endure successfully with good levels of marital satisfaction despite these separations. This research explored the experience of wives whose husbands were in a variety of "home-away" occupations including seafarers, oil rig workers and outback pilots, finding in each case that most marriages were able to adjust, although not without some signs of stress (and in a small number of cases driving depressive symptoms in the wives) (Hubinger Parker, & Clavarino, 2002; Ulven, Omdal, Herløv-Nielsen, Irgens, & Dahl, 2007; Morrice, Taylor, Clark, & McCann 1985).

It is important to treat these findings on "seawives" and others carefully, however. The research is now old and reflects gender assumptions no longer widely held and important to question. In all these studies, the intermittent partner was the husband in a heterosexual relationship, and the non-intermittent person (perhaps we should use the word "constant" here) was the wife, usually asked alone about the impact of her marital circumstances. Changes to the world of international work have seen increasing numbers of women working internationally (and thus with the potential to be the *intermittent partner*) as well as LGBTQI⁺ individuals and couples embracing expatriation (McPhail, McNulty, & Hutchings 2014). This said, women remain a minority of expatriates (constituting some 20% according to the Worldwide Survey of International Assignment Policies and Practices, although this is up from 11% in 2015 (Mercer, 2020)) and face different pressures when working internationally linked to their gender and assumptions about them based on traditional models of the family. Evidence from military studies suggests that service and associated deployment is more toxic to marriage when the serving person is a female partner in a heterosexual relationship (Karney, Loughran, & Pollard, 2012; Keeling, Wessley, & Fear, 2016). The strains placed by international assignment vary by gender, and the different juggle between work and home responsibilities faced by women requires acknowledgement and action (Houldey, 2021).

A study by Espino, Sundstrom, Frick, Jacobs, & Peters (2002) on business travellers working for the World Bank adds another layer in considering the impact on family left behind. In this study both World Bank staff and the spouses of staff were asked about the stress of international business travel.[1] Both groups described high levels of stress for workers, spouses and children related to travel for work. Participants were also invited to talk about the impact of this on their children and gave a range of adverse reactions to the travelling spouse's frequent arrivals, absences and departures. Most striking in this study is a list of comments by the children reported as part of the study, including reproaches about long absences, questions about other families the parent might have elsewhere, and the remark of one 13-year-old that "If dad loves us so much, why doesn't he quit his job?" (p. 319). Although taking the family on an international post creates some challenges for the parents, as well as the children (see chapters 5 and 11 by Hawker and Hill, this volume), it is clear that leaving your family behind while you work as a contractor has costs too.

Mathias was an 11-year-old boy seen by one of the authors of this chapter. He was a younger child within a large family. His father worked as an expatriate in a senior position in Somalia, with a rotation pattern of two weeks in Mogadishu and two weeks with family in Nairobi. Dad had served four international missions during Mathias' lifetime and Mathias was thrown by each uprooting. He loved being in Denmark at Christmas, where all siblings and extended family would gather, but his attachment to the idea of "home" was vague and idealised. At the time of his therapy, the older children in the family were at university in locations around the world. Mathias developed acute anxiety within months of arriving in Nairobi. He was distressed and agitated at school and slept poorly. At night he would patrol the house to check locks on windows and doors. On referral for psychological support, it emerged that Mathias hated going to school because he couldn't keep an eye on his mother and younger siblings. He was preoccupied by thoughts of accidents, abductions and plane crashes. His vigilance at night was about literally keeping the family safe as "the man of the house", whilst in his imagination, his "magical thinking" was in service of keeping his father safe while he was away.

Mathias' case illustrates the impact of repeated moves, and the destabilising effect parental choices can have on children in their formative years.

One final observation arising from the study by Espino et al. (2002) relates to a key variable described by the families: The predictability of required business travel. Espino et al.'s respondents often noted the way in which the travelling spouse's movement disrupted family plans, created uncertainty and led to an overall feeling that the family was not a priority for the staff member or their employer. In contrast with this, some assignments have very regular, set periods of leave or rotations in which it is easier to know the home-away patterns of the intermittent partner. As the wife of the contractor discussed on page 150 put it,

> That used to work fine for us as I knew, every four weeks, he would be coming home and then he would be back for about four weeks and then gone again. I used to miss him, but I knew he would be back pretty soon, and then when he was back, just as I started to have enough of him, he would be leaving again. I liked it because I was raising my kids and I was busy, I liked my alone time, but now we're getting older, and I would like more companionship.

Thus, the timing of contracting is also important in the impact it has on families.

Recommendations

For Individual Contractors:

- Be aware of your motivations for taking on an international contract. If you are fleeing something difficult (perhaps a career transition) or trying

to find a sense of value after a difficult end to a primary career, make sure you know this and discuss it if you can. If you may be carrying reactions to past traumatic experience, seek help for this too.
- Consider the impact of your assignment on family and discuss what the contract means with your closest people. If you are in a relationship, do you need to put additional protections in place? Pay particular attention to the needs of your children so they continue to feel your support and love from a distance, and are not driven to take on additional responsibilities because of your absence.

For Organisations:

- You have a duty of care to support contract staff in terms of health and well-being throughout the time that they work for you. Consider a career plan that includes pre-departure training and assessment, in-assignment support and that follows the staff member for a period after their work contract with you ends.
- Be alert to the possibility that staff may be triggered by their time working with you. If they have a military background and are returning to contexts that could recall previous military experience, plan for this.
- A full cultural briefing alongside mentorship or support from host country counterparts may help when there is less of a fit between your contractor and the setting in which they are working.
- Ask about family relationships and, if possible, recognise the importance for the family of predictability and regular routines. Opportunities to involve families will also support your staff member.

For Psychological Therapists Working with Contractors:

- We would recommend taking a full history from anyone you are working with given the complexity of the careers of many contractors. Past military service or difficulties in other work settings may alert you to areas of past occupational disappointment or distress. Do not overlook issues of post-traumatic stress or moral injury (see chapter 4, this volume).
- Consider the relationship of your client with place. Do they use place compartmentalisation to manage assignments abroad? Has their sense of place become conditional after a number of assignments, leaving them rootless, and what impact is this having on them?
- Attend to the pressures of repatriation or return to a home country when contacted by clients at this point of change. Recognise that a contractor who has worked away for a long period may need to renegotiate their relationships with family and mourn the life they have left behind.

There is a limited literature exploring the circumstances and pressures of international contracting and we hope to have offered some ideas that will guide practitioners, organisations and international contractors themselves. It is our hope to see additional research that expands our understanding of organisational fit and best practices in staff support, recognising the differential impact of gender, sexuality, race, country of origin and past occupational experience on this group of global staff.

Note

1 In this study, the vast majority (81%) of spouses were female, while amongst the smaller group of staff only 27.5% of respondents were female, showing again the gender disparity in this group of workers.

References

Adams, B.G., & van der Vijver, F.J.R. (2015). The many faces of expatriate identity. *International Journal of Intercultural Relations, 49*, 322–331. https://doi.org/10.1016/j.ijintrel.2015.05.009

Barnett, A., & Hughes, S. (2001, 29 July). British firm accused in UN "sex scandal". *The Guardian.* www.theguardian.com/world/2001/jul/29/unitednations

Chiang, F.F., van Esch, E., & Birtch, T.A. (2020). Repatriation and career development. In Bonache, J., Brewster, C., & Froese, F. (Eds.), *Global mobility and the management of expatriates* (Cambridge Companions to Management) (pp. 125–150). Cambridge: Cambridge University Press.

Chiang, F.F., van Esch, E., Birtch, T.A., & Shaffer, M.A. (2018). Repatriation: What do we know and where do we go from here? *International Journal of Human Resource Management, 29*(1), 188–226. https://doi.org/10.1080/09585192.2017.1380065

Espino, C.M., Sundstrom, S.M., Frick, H.L., Jacobs, M., & Peters, M. (2002). International business travel: Impact on families and travellers. *Occupational and Environmental Medicine, 59*(5), 309–322. https://doi.org/10.1136/oem.59.5.309

Feinstein, A., & Botes, M. (2009). The psychological health of contractors working in war zones. *Journal of Traumatic Stress, 22*(2), 102–105. https://doi.org/10.1002/jts.20390

Franke, V., & von Boemcken, M. (2011). Guns for hire: Motivations and attitudes of private security contractors. *Armed Forces & Society, 37*(4), 725–742. www.jstor.org/stable/48609031

Hechanova, R., Beehr, T.A., & Christiansen, N.D. (2003). Antecedents and consequences of employees' adjustment to overseas assignment: A meta-analytic review. *Applied Psychology: An International Review, 52*(2), 213–236. https://doi.org/10.1111/1464-0597.00132

Hoang, T. (2019, 26 February). When peacekeepers are part of the problem. *Global Initiative of Transnational Organised Crime.* https://globalinitiative.net/analysis/when-the-peacekeepers-are-part-of-the-problem/

Hoffman, E. (1989). *Lost in translation.* London: Heinemann.

Houldey, G. (2021). *The vulnerable humanitarian: Ending burnout culture in the aid sector*. London: Routledge.

HSBC. (2017). *Expat explorer global report: Broadening perspectives.* HSBC Holding PLC. www.hsbc.com/news-and-media/media-releases/2017/hsbc-expat-explorer-2017.

Hubinger, L., Parker, A.W., & Clavarino, A. (2002). The intermittent husband: Impact of home and away occupations on wives/partners. Queensland Mining Industry Health and Safety Conference 2002, 81–90. www.qmihsconference.org.au/wp-cont ent/uploads/qmihsc-2002-writtenpaper-hubinger.pdf

Isenberg, D. (2010, 26 February). Mental health and private military contractors. *Cato Institute.* www.cato.org/publications/commentary/mental-health-private-milit ary-contractors#

Jassawalla, A., Truglia, C., & Garvey, J. (2004). Cross-cultural conflict and expatriate manager adjustment: An exploratory study. *Management Decision, 42*(7), 837–849. https://doi.org/10.1108/00251740410550916

Karney, B.R., Loughran, D.S., & Pollard, M.S. (2012). Comparing marital status and divorce status in civilian and military populations. *Journal of Family Issues, 33*(12), 1572–1594. https://doi.org/10.1177/0192513X12439690

Keeling, M., Wessley, S., & Fear, N.T. (2016). Marital status distribution of the U.K. military: Does it differ from the general population? *Military Behavioral Health, 5*(1), 26–34, https://doi.org/10.1080/21635781.2016.1213210

Liao, Y.K., Wu, W.Y., Dao, T.C., & Ngoc Luu, T.M., (2021) The influence of emotional intelligence and cultural adaptability on cross-cultural adjustment and performance with the mediating effect of cross-cultural competence: A study of expatriates in Taiwan. *Sustainability, 13*, 3374. https://doi.org/10.3390/su13063374

Maslach, C., & Leiter, M.P. (2005, Winter). Reversing burnout. *Stanford Social Innovation Review, 3*(4), 43–49. https://doi.org/10.48558/E3F1-ZB95

McPhail, R., McNulty, Y., & Hutchings, K. (2014). Lesbian and gay expatri- ation: Opportunities, barriers and challenges for global mobility. *The International Journal of Human Resource Management, 27*(3), 382–406. https://doi.og/10.1080/ 09585192.2014.941903

Mercer. (2020). *Worldwide Survey of International Assignment Policies and Practices.* https://mobilityexchange.mercer.com/international-assignments-survey

Morrice, J., Taylor, R., Clark, D., & McCann, K. (1985). Oil wives and intermittent husbands. *British Journal of Psychiatry, 147*(5), 479–483. https://psycnet.apa.org/rec ord/1987-08922-001

Pollard, M.S., Karney, B.R., & Loughran, D.S. (2008). Comparing rates of marriage and divorce in civilian, military, and veteran populations. Paper presented at the Population Association of America annual meeting, 17–19 April 2008, New Orleans, LA. https://paa2008.princeton.edu/abstracts/81696

Richardson, J., & Zikic, J. (2007). The darker side of an international academic career. *Career Development International, 12*(2), 164–186. https://doi.org/10.1108/136204 30710733640

Risen, J. (2007, 5 July). Contractors back from Iraq suffer trauma from battle. *New York Times.* www.nytimes.com/2007/07/05/us/05contractors.html

Siegrist, J. (1996). Adverse health effects of high-effort/low-reward conditions. *Journal of Occupational Health Psychology, 1*(1), 27–41. https://doi.org/10.1037// 1076-8998.1.1.27

Slanjankic, A. (2016, 29 February). Bolkovac: "UN tries to cover up peacekeeper sex abuse scandal". *DW.Com*. www.dw.com/en/bolkovac-un-tries-to-cover-up-peacekee per-sex-abuse-scandal/a-19082815

Toh, S.M., & DeNisi, A.S. (2007). Host country nationals as socializing agents: A social identity approach. *Journal of Organizational Behaviour, 28*, 281–301. https://doi.org/10.1002/job.421

Ulven, A.J., Omdal, K.A., Herløv-Nielsen, H., Irgens, A., & Dahl, E. (2007). Seafarers' wives and intermittent husbands – social and psychological impact of a subgroup of Norwegian seafarers' work schedule on their families. *International Maritime Health, 58*(1–4), 115–128. https://pubmed.ncbi.nlm.nih.gov/18350981/

van Vegchel, N., de Jonge, J., Bosma, H., & Schaufeli, W. (2005). Reviewing the effort–reward imbalance model: Drawing up the balance of 45 empirical studies. *Social Science & Medicine, 60*(5), 1117–1131. https://doi.org/10.1016/j.socsci med.2004.06.043

Chapter 10

Psychosocial support work with aid and development staff following sexual trauma

Lynn Keane

Introduction

One of the privileges of mental health and psychosocial support (MHPSS) work in the aid and development sector is being alongside people when they are at their lowest. Work with survivors[1] of sexual trauma is one such eventuality. This chapter explores this largely hidden psychological work and offers a personal perspective on the context in which it takes place. I am a self-employed psychotherapist and MHPSS practitioner. I have worked with survivors in the aid sector for a decade. By survivors, I am referring to people who have been subjected to a variety of experiences including sexual assault[2] and/or harassment[3] by colleagues and assaults by strangers – actors in the environment in which they are living and working, including civilians and members of armed state/non-state groups. Some bear agonised witness to the sexual exploitation and abuse of others, often women and children in beneficiary communities, sometimes colleagues. All are survivors and all will be impacted to a greater or lesser degree.

In a departure from most chapters in this book, I will not include direct testimony from survivors of sexual trauma or fictionalised case examples. This is a conscious choice; matters of consent, autonomy and the experience of intrusion lie at the heart of sexual trauma. Unpacking these experiences plays a central role in the therapeutic process for each individual. It is my choice to honour my clients' long-term healing by not including case material. I equally note the loss inherent in not amplifying clients' voices in my work. Clients and I often discuss visibility, or lack of it, alongside the consistent theme of whether they are heard when they speak up. Their words are so rich, so smart, so poignant, so funny, so knowing, so compelling – and yet I cannot feel that it is my place to present them here.

Context

The main aim of this chapter is to shed light on the process of working therapeutically alongside survivors, but first, some thoughts about the complex

DOI: 10.4324/9781003261971-11

context in which psychosocial work takes place, beginning with an important note. Most survivors I have worked with, and all survivors I have worked with over the medium to long term, have been international staff. This usually means that the traumatic incident/s happened far from their permanent or home base. Survivors in a position to access substantive psychosocial support often hail from Europe or North America. In contrast, most survivors of sexual trauma within the aid and development workforce are national, given national staff make up around 90% of fieldworkers globally (Haver, 2007).[4]

There is little firm data exploring sexual harassment and assault against humanitarian and aid workers. The Aid Worker Security Database[5] is a leading data source in the sector and records incidences of "rape and serious sexual assault". However, this database relies on media reports and voluntary reporting. In the latest figures available, for 2020, six cases of rape and serious sexual assault against national staff are recorded. No assaults against international workers have been recorded in the database since 2018. However, as Mazurana and Donnelly (2017) and others point out, sexual harassment, sexual assault and sexual exploitation are catastrophically under-reported and under-researched in the aid and development sectors. Reporting mechanisms are often weak and the responses of agencies problematic. In fact, in a study by the Humanitarian Women's Network (2016), 69% of respondents who experienced sexual assault chose not to report it.

The lack of reliable data in this area is frustrating, leaving a sense of working in the dark, with little ground beneath either your own or a survivor's feet. However, a source of real value is the work of Mazurana and Donnelly (2017) which brings together 78 source materials, using surveys, databases, materials supplied by international non-governmental organisations (INGOs) and NGOs, and interviews with 30 targeted stakeholders (some of whom had left the sector for reasons related to sexual trauma).

Returning to the issue of which survivors have access to psychosocial support, there is a clear hierarchy within employing agencies. UN staff and contractors enjoy the highest level of safety and legal protection against sexual assault, which is true of other employment benefits. More well-resourced agencies will offer, for example, medical evacuation and trained Prevention of Sexual Exploitation and Abuse (PSEA) or internally focused Gender-Based Violence (GBV) Focal Point staff. Employees of smaller, lesser-resourced agencies may have no access to support at all.

Safeguarding has many definitions – some so wide as to include us all being custodians of the planet! Whilst important, this does not help support an employee who is trying to decide whether to report her line manager's suggestive text messages as sexual harassment – or bear with her when she is torn about the impact the process may have on her own and her colleague's career. The UK Foreign, Commonwealth and Development Office broadly defines safeguarding in the international aid and development sector as "an organisation's ability to protect from sexual exploitation and abuse and harassment, children, young people and vulnerable adults they work with as well as their own staff and volunteers" (FCDO, 2018). This definition is broad; there is a marked difference in any setting between a child and a vulnerable or at-risk adult (for example, an adult with physical disabilities or severe mental health challenges), let alone the difference between a humanitarian beneficiary and an international employee. Whilst it is vital that all necessary protections for staff and beneficiary communities are encoded in agencies' policies, defining what duty of care or due diligence should look like in an international context is challenging – local customs, laws and state apparatus all being moving targets to consider.

What is clear is that abuse can involve staff at the highest levels. In one example, the Deputy Executive Director at UNAIDS was cleared of wrongdoing following an internal investigation into sexual harassment claims in 2018. The alleged perpetrator received explicit, public support from the Executive Director of UNAIDs and chose to retire (not pursue the renewal of his contract) a few months later. The principal complainant (there were three in all) was a middle-ranking European staff member. She was dismissed from her role at UNAIDs in 2019 for "sexual and financial misconduct". A further report was commissioned from an independent panel. It was damning. One submission from a staff member referred to UNAIDs as "a predator's prey ground" (UNAIDs, 2018). UNAIDs opened a second investigation which returned its findings in 2021. That report has not been made public, but the current Executive Director of UNAIDs told staff that an unnamed senior official had "failed to observe the standards of conduct required of an international civil servant" and that his "unacceptable [treatment of women was] seemingly tolerated by senior management at UNAIDs at the time, perpetuating an organizational culture which appeared to enable such conduct". A useful source for tracking abuses within the UN is the Code Blue Campaign.[6] This small, passionate team chiefly highlights abuses perpetrated by peacekeepers, but not only.

The UNAIDs case is a rare example of a process that received wide attention and I hope offers a flavour of the divisive and in many respects incredible context in which each survivor must make sense of their experience. It relates to an assault by a colleague who is more senior than the survivor, which according to the available data is the most common type of assault (Mazurana & Donnelly, 2017), but it has other elements which many survivors will relate to: the alleged perpetrator was initially protected, exonerated and lauded for his service. He was allowed to decide his own future. Key individuals and the agency as a whole closed ranks around the perpetrator whilst the survivor's career suffered catastrophically. Given that aid and development is a small world, these injustices resonate deeply with survivors, including those whose struggles do not ever come to the attention of their agency, because they cannot trust available avenues of reporting and redress.

The latest iteration of an UN protocol which seeks to set out "norms and standards" to assist and support victims of sexual exploitation and abuse was published in December 2019 (UN, 2019) but contains no specific guidance for victims who are UN staff and contractors.

Employing Agencies: How They Help and How They Hinder

Aid and development agencies exist within the culture described above. Each agency has a duty of care for its beneficiaries and its staff. How they manage that responsibility, and to what extent they take ownership of it, sets the tone for their employees. I have observed little in the way of state infrastructure or headquarters (HQ) oversight to contain and shape behaviour in the field.

Report the Abuse, a short-lived INGO founded by a survivor, researched relevant policies and procedures in the sector between 2015 and 2016 (Norbert, 2017). The survey found that 30% of the 92 agencies reviewed had a code of conduct. However, by no means did all the codes of conduct address the sexual harassment or sexual assault of employees by internal or, for that matter, external perpetrators. A mere 17% of the agencies indicated that specific training was offered on the prevention of sexual exploitation and abuse (which may not include reporting mechanisms or detail how investigations are conducted). Only 13% of agencies had a specific policy and/or procedure relating to the sexual harassment or sexual assault of staff. Anecdotally, this picture appears to have improved, perhaps due to media reporting of the sexual exploitation of beneficiary communities by Oxfam aid workers in Haiti and similar reports about other agencies including Save the Children, World Vision, UNAIDs and, most recently, the World Health Organization (WHO) (see below). However, the degree to which measures exist on paper as opposed to work in practice, remains a question.

Without appropriate frameworks, training or in-house expertise to respond to complaints, survivors are not incentivised to report internally, as the research bears out. Another factor brought to light by the research is that agencies have the mistaken idea that the greatest threat comes from armed actors. Mazurana and Donnelly's (2017) review of the literature shows that most perpetrators are fellow male aid or security workers, and that the majority of perpetrators are in "supervisory or higher-level positions compared to their victims", as in the UNAIDs case.

Mazurana and Donnelly (2017) describe agency environments which lend themselves to sexual assault and harassment, writing that

> a sexist, homophobic work atmosphere exists (including in housing compounds) and senior management does not stop it; a macho form of masculinity dominates the humanitarian relief space; recreational use of

drugs and alcohol occurs; high levels of conflict- and non-conflict-related violence against local civilian women exist; armed conflict is on-going; and rule of law is weak or non-existent.

In the Report the Abuse survey, 46% of survivors and witnesses did not report incidents to their agencies or law enforcement (Norbert, 2017). Of those who did, only 18% were satisfied with the outcome. In the Humanitarian Women's Network (2016) study of those who reported their experiences, nothing at all happened in 47% of cases. In only 8% of cases, survivors were referred to a therapist or counsellor.

Psychological Interventions

One of the most useful tools available to non-psychological professionals is Psychological First Aid (PFA). PFA is a World Health Organisation–endorsed protocol (World Health Organisation, 2011) which equips individuals to offer humane support and practical assistance to those who have suffered recent exposure to serious, potentially overwhelming, stressors. For a survivor of a critical incident, being attended to safely and respectfully is key to long-term healing, and PFA should be the initial psychological intervention of choice. Safety must be a survivor's first priority (and that of a PFA provider). Once out of danger, challenges may include a lack of home comforts and a lack of privacy. The survivor may stay in a guest house with shared bathrooms, for example, or in a worst-case scenario live in close proximity to their perpetrator.

In addition to the need for effective PFA, and crucially linked with its delivery in the immediate aftermath of an incident, is the task of attending to survivors' medical needs. An established means of providing survivors of sexual assault with emergency contraception and preventative treatments for sexually transmitted infections (STIs) including an HIV post-exposure prophylaxis (PEP) kit should be in place. Mazurana and Donnelly (2017) asked respondents specifically about access to emergency contraception and PEP kits following assault and found that this was unevenly available across organisations and countries. Further, the window for some of the necessary medical interventions and follow-up after attack is as narrow as 72 hours. Travelling to a clinic may present additional risk or may involve an uncomfortable journey with strangers or colleagues whose involvement may be antagonistic to the survivor. Many survivors complain that where medical intervention is provided, the experience has been physically and emotionally intrusive and painful and can amount to victim blaming[7] and retraumatisation. Choices and decisions are questioned. Unsolicited, after-the-fact advice is offered, "I would never have done that … why did you do that?" Survivors' panic, relief, disgust, the agonised reality of self-blame – further experiences of being violated – go unrecognised or are intensified. Retraumatisation, or secondary trauma, can be characterised by the phrase "when the helpers do not help". Survivors frequently present in therapy preoccupied about those who did not help or whose approach to helping was insensitive. This is a source of great pain, and it makes sense that it is harmful. While original perpetrators are often painted in black and white terms, as perhaps faceless, nameless, shadowy figures or as arrogant and unreachable, the faces, words and actions of "rescuers" are crucially important in the immediate aftermath of a terrible, life-threatening experience. Implemented well, PFA is life changing and life affirming. The opposite – a cold, inflexible, bureaucratic and inhumane reporting and debriefing approach – is likely to be damaging.

Client Referrals

I am usually introduced to a survivor by their employing agency or organisation. However, as stated, the data shows that most survivors do not report to their employer. This may well mean that most survivors have no access to a specialist provider of psychosocial support, other than via informal networks like word of mouth, in which case they need to fund the intervention personally (a further potential source of stress, particularly for longer-term therapeutic work).

Whilst formal organisational support puts structure and funding in place for survivors, it adds potentially fraught layers to the therapeutic relationship. The survivor risks their confidentiality by asking for support. They also take a risk around whether they will be treated empathically by colleagues with whom they may have no existing relationship. Survivors who report to their agency risk that their career will be negatively impacted, no matter what early reassurances are offered. Parameters may also be imposed – for example, a requirement to travel to a home base to access support when they do not wish to, or an offer of disappointingly few funded MHPSS sessions. I have found that inflexibility from an employing HQ can have a disproportionately negative impact on a survivor who finds herself in an already distressed state and struggling with secondary trauma.

An additional aspect directly impacting my work is a sense of conflict of interest from employing organisations. Agencies want to manage their reputations, maintain their status in host countries and protect funding streams. When a staff member reports sexual harassment or abuse, the instinct is often to seek to make the problem go away as quickly as possible. One consequence of this is a demand for a quick fix from psychosocial support work. There is also genuine confusion among parties at times as to who I am working for – is it the agency that pays me and employs the survivor, or are the survivor's needs paramount, given my discipline and the fact that they are referred to me in a state of shock and distress?

Some survivors have an existing therapeutic relationship to turn to. This can be ideal, even if the therapist is not familiar with the aid and development sector, because the shared history between practitioner and client is beneficial. In other cases, survivors choose to rely on colleagues, friends and family. Whilst I hope that such survivors are met with empathy and advanced interpersonal skills, there are pitfalls to this approach. Loved ones can become preoccupied with their own responses – distress, anger, vengefulness, anxieties about the future – and the survivor can feel lost or overwhelmed in the mix. Personal relationships lack the helpful boundaries that are built into professional counselling relationships, known as the "working alliance". The working alliance entails that meetings are contracted; they are held at prearranged times, have set durations and focus entirely on the survivor's needs and wishes. These factors are shown by research to underpin the safety of therapeutic work.

When employing agencies fund my work with survivors, I advocate for it to be facilitated long enough to cover the lifespan of any complaint and/or investigation that the survivor wishes to pursue. It is imperative that a survivor is accompanied through the many and complex challenges of a reporting process. Sadly, it is not always agreed as commissioners of MHPSS work can be obliged to adhere to rigid entitlements and budgets. Unfortunately, the withdrawal of funding is often accompanied by pressurising messages which amount to "isn't she over this yet?", further exacerbating survivor distress.

Clinical Realities

At this point, I invite you directly into the counselling room, always a complex place. The sum of a client's life experience is present, be it consciously or unconsciously, and regardless of whether the concerns they are bringing are understood as current, historical or cumulative. Also present are a person's unique thoughts and beliefs about their life experiences and how they perceive the world around them working and "holding" them. For example, a survivor's pre-existing views on authority figures will show up in their therapeutic work.

I see my core task in the consulting room (almost always a remote version of a consulting room) as bearing with the survivor. Bearing with the pain, shock, numbness, disbelief, need to ruminate and so on. Survivors can feel terror, violation, loneliness, rage, vengefulness, confusion or helplessness. They may feel a sense of denial, self-blame, guilt, shame, suicidal ideation or paranoia and this list is not exhaustive. Each feeling is not mutually exclusive from any other, and feelings are often conflicting or contradictory, producing bewildering and destabilised states. I have listened to harrowing accounts of traumatic experiences and of retraumatisation and/or secondary trauma, sometimes with individuals who never disclosed the crimes to anyone and on other occasions with people whose cases made international headlines.

A key focus of my work, then, is on managing trauma reactions. I draw heavily on what is known about the neuroscience of trauma. When working with survivors, I examine their trauma responses in terms of flight, fight but also freeze and fawn/flop responses, because the latter two forms of response can create misperceptions for survivors and those around them. In the animal world, the freeze state is known as "playing dead", when a prey animal senses the presence of a predator and hides, curls up, pulls in its scent or otherwise tries to avert the predator's attention. Survivors of sexual assault who cannot fight or run away may instinctively select the freeze option. I have heard countless times in survivors' narratives that they were reproached for not screaming or escaping or fighting back. The flop or fawn response occurs when the person being assaulted becomes actively cooperative and acquiescent, to the point sometimes – for example, in an abduction – of befriending and assisting the perpetrator/s. Many accounts of survival are predicated on adopting this approach, but it can leave survivors with feelings of guilt or disgust because they aligned themselves with or facilitated the actions of their attacker, however temporarily. Survivors also have to process unhelpful or critical responses from others when they neither fight nor take flight. Awareness of the freeze and fawn/flop response sorely needs to be included in all training packages in the aid and development sector to raise awareness of its instinctual nature and the limited role of conscious control when it is employed by survivors.

I have worked with many survivors who have witnessed the sexual exploitation of beneficiary women and met a lack of organisational will to address it (or worse, have found that it is perpetrated by colleagues). Strong reactions to such situations (known as vicarious traumatisation) require space in therapy to explore feelings of helplessness and impotent fury alongside trauma reactions.

Survivors and I often spend initial sessions sifting through the injuries to self of the early hours and days after an assault or other incident. In many cases, the survivor may have been deprived of the ability to personally select who accompanied and supported them immediately after their traumatic experience. The inability to act on one's own agency (for example, not having a car and needing to use agency drivers and vehicles or being obliged to travel accompanied by security personnel) may have been extremely triggering. Having little choice but to rely on the judgement and decision-making of a local team, or deal remotely with HQ, when in a highly vulnerable state may exacerbate the difficulties. Often, a senior leader, security manager or HR officer has been designated to manage the situation who may be non-empathic, hostile or simply distracted by a heavy workload and range of other responsibilities. The chance to review these aspects of experience is a key way to mitigate reactions of trauma and moral injury (see chapter 4, this volume).

Also important is to explore with survivors how far they have been able to share information with their support network. Some survivors feel that being away from a loved one helps because they can protect them from the horror of their experience. Distance affords survivors an unencumbered space in which to decide whether and when to share the experience of violation with their closest people.

Another core model I draw on in my work with survivors is Kübler-Ross' Stages of Grief (Kúbler-Ross, Wessler, & Avioli, 1972). It comprises five stages of reaction to loss – denial, anger, bargaining, depression and acceptance. The model is relevant to other challenging life circumstances, including recovery from sexual trauma, particularly the stages of bargaining and acceptance. Bargaining is characterised by a survivor's struggles with the "what ifs" of their situation. Most survivors will agonise over questions like "why me?" or ruminations which begin "if only…" Therapists do not seek to reassure or change what the client is thinking and feeling, but to bear with and offer a safe space for the client to move closer to their own sense of integration. Just as in bereavement, a survivor may never fully feel acceptance around their traumatic experience, but they can, in time, relate to it differently, remaining in their personal resilient zone even when in touch with reminders of it.

Conclusion

I encourage the reader to take away the idea that a survivor of sexual trauma will be changed by their experience; sexual trauma is life changing. Among other adjustments, survivors face difficulties in romantic and intimate relationships, difficulties trusting new work colleagues and environments, and struggles with a nervous system that is overly sensitised to threat. Survivors need immediate support and support over the long term. Questioning and bureaucratic processes (however necessary in the longer term) can retraumatise victims, particularly immediately after events and used without sensitivity. The action principles of PFA – to look, listen and link – are important, while choice and the regaining of control are critical to healing and integration.

Recommendations

For Individuals:

Before taking up a role, ask yourself, does the organisation:

- have a **Safeguarding Policy** that is aligned to *and* differentiated from other organisational policies and protocols, such as a code of conduct or staff handbook, anti-harassment and abuse of authority policy, safe recruitment policy and/or grievance and disciplinary procedures?
- have **Security Policies and Protocols** that provide adequate information and assurances about safety relating to staff accommodation, offices (e.g. lone working), and other working environments such as grounds or

whole compounds? Do the policies cover safety and security during all forms of **travel**? *Query gaps when you find them.*

- provide robust and comprehensive safeguarding **training**?
- have a **Code of Conduct** which applies to all staff, volunteers, contractors, partners and visitors.? Are its provisions gender-sensitive? *Query gaps when you find them.*
- have **Reporting Mechanisms** for harassment (complaints that are internal to the organisation), sexual assault and abuse (complaints that may be internal or external), and sexual exploitation (complaints relating to individuals outside of the organisation, typically members of local communities)?
- have policies, protocols, and reporting mechanisms that are **survivor-centred**? *Query gaps when you find them*
- publish **data** on safeguarding incidents, investigations, and outcomes?
- address **Whistleblowing and Protection from Retaliation** in their policies and protocols?
- You may also wish to research the national **legal context** for crimes of sexual harassment and assault in your country of posting if this information is not provided and use **informal networks** to gather information on safeguarding practice on the ground.

During Induction and Initial Period in Role:

- Establish **points of contact** – functions, roles, responsibilities and the current individuals in post
- Continue to query gaps in policy, protocols, procedures and practice
- Enquire as to whether key postholders receive appropriate training including Psychological First Aid (**PFA**) and familiarise yourself with Mental Health and Psycho-Social Support (**MHPSS**) provision from your organisation, and make use of it
- Familiarise yourself with local and national police practice
- Once in role, report differences between policy and practice on the ground

In the Event of an Incident:

- Whether you are victimised personally, you witness wrongdoing, or wrongdoing is reported to you, first attend to matters of immediate safety and security. Activate appropriate sources of support.
- Seek out individuals who feel safe, supportive and soothing to you, in person and remotely. Do not hesitate to set up MHPSS support if you feel it could be helpful. You may wish to retain support throughout the life of an incident. An MHPSS practitioner will aim to assist you in

processing events and feelings over time, making decisions in your own time, retaining autonomy and personalising your recovery.

- Report appropriately. Consider whether you would like support, advocacy and witnessing from a colleague and/or MHPSS practitioner. This is particularly important if you find it difficult to advocate for yourself in the aftermath of a trauma.
- You have the right to confidentiality, with the matter being treated on a "need to know" basis. Ensure that this is explicitly understood.
- You retain choice – remind those dealing with the report and any resulting investigations or related processes to consult you and to offer transparency.
- If your report is blocked, minimised or fails to progress, follow escalation procedures.
- Remember, secondary trauma can be summarised as "when helpers don't help" and continue to seek support to be heard.

For Organisations:

In general:

- Ensure that comprehensive policies and protocols are in place and freely accessible to staff and non-staff. Safeguarding policies and procedures should be integrated with and differentiated from all other policies.
- Provide all stakeholders with a variety of reporting channels and clear reporting and response protocols.
- Update policies, protocols and mechanisms regularly in keeping with best practice.
- Make use of existing resources: Organisations providing safeguarding advice and resources, for example model policy templates, include: Bond www.bond.org.uk/resources-support/safeguarding), the Safeguarding Support Hub (https://safeguardingsupporthub.org), and the Prevention of Sexual Exploitation and Abuse Inter-Agency Standing Committee (https://psea.interagencystandingcommittee.org).
- Adopt and monitor safe recruitment practices. Join the Misconduct Disclosure Scheme (https://misconduct-disclosure-scheme.org).
- Train staff appropriately:
  - Train all staff, including trustees and volunteers, in safeguarding awareness. Ensure that all staff are aware of reporting mechanisms.
  - Train relevant staff in specific knowledge and skills. Ensure that personnel who may deal with a victim-survivor in the first 72 hours after an incident is reported, are fully trained in PFA.
  - Train staff who may have a role in a safeguarding investigation in PFA.
- Appoint Safeguarding Focal Points (or Designated Safeguarding Officers) at all levels of the organisation.

In Response to Concerns, Allegations and Incidents:

- Work towards being an organisation that takes victim-survivors seriously at every step in their journey. Respond quickly, listen carefully, balance safety concerns and organisational needs with victim-survivors' autonomy
- Ensure that all responding staff are open to victim-survivors' accounts and do not judge or coerce
- Allow victim-survivors as much autonomy and choice as possible
- Support all parties: victim-survivors, witnesses and alleged wrongdoers/ perpetrators
- Be aware of the support needs of bystanders and wider impacted teams and communities
- Keep all parties informed and provide as much transparency as possible
- Publish anonymised data

For MHPSS practitioners and psychological therapists, additional factors in dealing with victim-survivors, witnesses, bystanders or other impacted clients include:

- Being trauma-informed in your training and practice
- Being trained in, or at least aware of, PFA
- Aiming to support impacted individuals throughout the life of a concern, allegation, incident and investigation
- Taking more of an advocacy role than is usual, perhaps accompanying clients in dealings with their organisation and in investigation processes
- Developing skills to manage relationships between those responsible for safeguarding responses and investigations in the organisation and your clients
- Seeking appropriate supervision and support for your own well-being

Notes

1   There is ongoing debate about the most appropriate terminology to use when referring to those impacted by sexual harassment, sexual assault and sexual exploitation. The term "survivor" is favoured here for ease of reference, but the alterative term is "victim". Some regard them as interchangeable, some see a distinct difference and, for each victim-survivor it is important that their personal choice is understood and validated. Mazurana and Donnelly (2017) take a stance that deploys both terms, separately and in combination, as follows: "We use the term victim to denote a person who has experienced a violation of domestic or international law or a crime committed by another person under domestic or international law. We use the term survivor to designate the person who was victimised is also someone who shows resistance, action, ingenuity, and inner strength. We combine these two terms victim/survivor to designate that those who experience

violations and abuse are also active agents who challenge the abuse, abusers, and systems that perpetuate violence".

2   I am using the definition of sexual assault cited by Mazurana and Donnelly (2017), which is "any action in which, through coercion (including the use of drugs or alcohol), threat or force, the offender subjects the victim to sexual touch that is unwanted and offensive. Sexual assault can range from unwanted touching and groping, to battery, attempted rape, rape, and sexual torture".

3   I am also following Mazurana and Donnelly's definition of sexual harassment: "Sexual harassment is a form of sex discrimination that includes unwelcome sexual advances, requests for sexual favors, and other verbal or physical conduct of a sexual nature. These acts constitute sexual harassment when this conduct explicitly or implicitly affects an individual's employment, unreasonably interferes with an individual's work performance, or creates an intimidating, hostile, or offensive work environment."

4   Another perspective on this data is that, given the far higher numbers of nationally employed staff, international staff are *proportionally* more likely to be victimised (Mazurana & Donnelly, 2017).

5   https://aidworkersecurity.org/incidents

6   www.codebluecampaign.com/the-problem

7   Victim-blaming is when others explicitly or implicitly hold a victim responsible for their traumatic experience or the crime that they were subjected to. For more information on victim-blaming, see the work of Dr Jessica Taylor, among others www.victimfocus.org.uk

References

Foreign, Commonwealth and Development Office (FCDO). (2018). *Safeguarding against Sexual Exploitation and Abuse and Sexual Harassment (SEAH): Due Diligence Guidance for FCDO implementing partners.* www.gov.uk/government/publications/dfid-enhanced-due-diligence-safeguarding-for-external-partners

Haver, K. (2007, July). Duty of care? Local staff and aid worker security. *Forced Migration Review*, 28. Retrieved from: www.fmreview.org/capacitybuilding/haver

Humanitarian Women's Network. (2016). *Survey data.* www.humanitarianwomens network.org/about

Kübler-Ross, E., Wessler, S., & Avioli L.V. (1972). On death and dying. *JAMA: The Journal of the American Medical Association, 221*(2), 174–179. https://doi.org/10.1001/jama.1972.03200150040010

Mazurana, D., & Donnelly, P. (2017). STOP the sexual assault against humanitarian and development aid workers. Boston: *Feinstein International Centre.* https://fic.tufts.edu/publication-item/stop-sexual-assault-against-aid-workers/

Norbert, M. (2017). Humanitarian experiences with sexual violence: Compilation of two years of report the abuse data collection. *Report the Abuse.* https://reliefweb.int/sites/reliefweb.int/files/resources/RTA%20Humanitarian%20experiences%20with%20Sexual%20Violence%20-%20Compilation%20of%20Two%20Years%20of%20Report%20the%20Abuse%20Data%20Collection.pdf

UNAIDS (2018, 11–13 December). *Report on the work of the independent expert panel on prevention of and response to harassment, including sexual harassment: Bullying and abuse of power at UNAIDS Secretariat.* www.unaids.org/sites/default/files/medi a_asset/report-iep_en.pdf

United Nations (UN). (2019). *UN protocol on the provision of assistance to victims of sexual exploitation and abuse.* www.un.org/en/pdfs/UN%20Victim%20Assista nce%20Protocol_English_Final.pdf

World Health Organization (WHO). (2011). *Psychological first aid: Guide for field* www.who.int/publications/i/item/9789241548205

Chapter 11

Working with children and young people whose families are working away from their home country

David Hawker and Beth Hill

Toxic Family Deployment

The Poisonwood Bible (Kingsolver, 1998) is a novel which illustrates what can go wrong when parents take their children overseas for humanitarian work. A fiery Southern Baptist preacher takes his wife and four daughters to plant a church and win converts in a remote village in the Belgian Congo on the eve of its independence. His wife is less sure of her faith and shared vocation, and three of the girls are teenagers. One of those is very angry about being uprooted, and another is hemiplegic and does not speak. The story is told by the female voices, including the highly articulate thoughts of the latter daughter. During the novel, the family goes against the advice of the mission, and stays after the embassy demands they evacuate. After several disasters, including civil war and murder of the youngest child by the witch doctor, the mother evacuates her children on foot after her husband refuses to leave. This short synopsis may sound like a polemic against missionary work, but a close reading reveals common mistakes which families would be wise to avoid. These include:

1. A first major international move for children in adolescence
2. Partners discordant about the value of their relocation and work
3. Children opposed to relocating
4. Inattention to medical and severe behavioural issues in a child
5. Self-deployment against the advice of an established organisation
6. Refusal to leave when ordered to evacuate by their embassy
7. Lack of safeguarding, for example, putting children at risk from crocodile attack by baptising them in the river
8. Colonial approach – the preacher aiming to "teach" the Congolese how to grow vegetables, which then turn out to be unsuited to local habitat
9. Linguistic blindness (the preacher's translation of "Jesus is Lord" sounds like "Jesus is poisonwood")
10. Cultural blindness – the preacher not appreciating that leading a church is not seen as real work in the village

DOI: 10.4324/9781003261971-12

11. Relational blindness – the preacher making an enemy of the witch doctor, with deadly consequences
12. Social blindness – the preacher not recognising that his converts are mainly the village misfits.

Better Ways to Care for Families

It does not have to be this way. Many children and young people (we use the terms interchangeably in this chapter) thrive in families serving away from their passport country.[1] Many cherish happy memories and global perspectives which enhance future life experience and world view. All young people face unique developmental challenges, whatever their family journeys. Parenting is hard work. Children and young people's needs have often been overlooked to the detriment of their well-being and mental health, and sometimes still are in their passport countries too. However, anyone who has worked in another culture, or read literature like *The Poisonwood Bible*, will be able to see what can go wrong if children's needs are not considered when living and working internationally. It is much easier to spot what others should do better than it is to make those changes within your family or organisation. The advice in this chapter is not a tick list of things to induce guilt among those currently serving or living internationally, but an encouragement to better practice. We begin with some general considerations, before describing what to attend to in the processes of planning entry into a host culture, during assignment and after re-entry to a passport country.

Caring for Families

Notice the Family

It alters the life of every member of a family when just one of them changes culture, region or continent for their work or vocation, and far more so when the family accompanies them. It is, however, quite possible for organisations to consider just the worker, and overlook the impact on partners, children and the wider family. In deployment decisions, spouses' wishes can be subordinated, and children's preferences ignored. Organisations can make a huge difference to families by noticing they are there, taking their needs into account and asking them how they feel about a move.

Christian missionaries who have families are routinely accompanied by them in the field. Though families sometime relocate on their own, they usually move with the support of organisations or churches, who often give at least some attention to the families' needs. Humanitarian organisations, too, by supporting families can make deployments more sustainable. Workers can make a difference through actively considering their family's needs by initiating multiple conversations with their partners, children and extended family, taking age and developmental stage into account, and weighing their perspectives in making a family decision about whether, when and how to relocate. Be warned: if you seek children and young people's views, be prepared to listen, and adapt to what they may say.

Recognise Children's Identity

In chapter 5 (this volume) we described third culture kids (TCKs) as a sub-group of cross-cultural kids (CCKs). Children moving culture with their parents for work will fit into one or both of those categories. Their unique culture does not necessarily match that of their passport or host country. They may also identify as a different nationality from their parents. Organisations that support TCKs well, seek to understand how they see their identity (especially within the identity model: Pollock et al., 2017 – see Chapter 5, "The PolVan Cultural Identity Model"), help them access support from peers who share it, and help them understand its benefits and drawbacks.

Pollock and Van Reken's (1999) work is an excellent starting point for learning about the TCK experience. Living in another culture can be hugely beneficial, helping TCKs learn about race, poverty, language and climate. They may enjoy living in an environment which is always warm, where they can play outside, where neighbours are friendly and helpful, and where wild animals can be seen outside a zoo. On the other hand, TCKs may struggle with environmental factors like heat, food or constant attention from local residents who may be fascinated by their unfamiliar appearance and like to hold them or touch their hair. Risks in the environment like traffic accidents, tropical diseases or violent robbery can cause unforeseen trauma. We discuss further pros and cons below. Parents need to listen to what their children are telling them and consider the benefits and drawbacks of staying or moving internationally.

Member Care

Families need support in the field from their employing organisations. This could include having a contact person or individual responsible for their care. It should be a separate function from line management, which is principally a human resources function. In Christian mission work this is known as *member care*. Member carers can help families by keeping in touch with them, providing support on the ground and by visits to them in the field. However, sometimes well-intended support can be misplaced, and it is important to ask families what support would help them. This may vary culturally – for example, a Latin American worker described her devastation when her family was left alone "to settle in" by British hosts. Later the same worker, when responsible for member care, was surprised when a newly arrived North American worker asked her for less involvement and not to "keep taking her to the supermarket". Needs may also change once families arrive in the field and unexpected events happen.

Organisations can help parents support their children specifically by educating them about what it means to be a TCK, facilitating contact among TCKs, and engaging the support of workers who have experience of, or part of their role dedicated to, working with TCKs. For example, many Christian missions employ member carers specialising in the care of missionary kids (MKs). In the UK, many network with colleagues in the Global Connections TCK Forum, and across Europe, at EuroTCK conferences. We encourage those supporting families to think about collecting resources to share, including books, films, apps and websites. Ask children and young people the language they prefer to use to describe themselves. Do they identify with the term "TCK", "MK", or a particular nationality, or another term? Is that the same or different to others in their family? Then remember to use this term as you talk with and about the child or young person.

Pre-entry

Planning for Entry (and Other Transitions)

Families who consider relocating together need to plan the right time to do it, both initially and subsequently. When does it work to take children to live away from their passport country for the first time? Or to move between different host countries? Or from a host country to a passport country? If parents hold passports for more than one country, which passport country should they to move to?

Transitions before Adolescence

Parents' plans need to take their children's life stages into account. Children's ages have a huge influence on how well they adapt to transitions. Travel with babies depends a lot on parents' confidence. Toddlers and children below school age generally adapt well to international transition. What is most important to them is whether their parents are attentive and able to respond to their needs. Children who move before age five may remember little of their previous home. Aged up to ten or eleven, children need more preparation for a move, are likely to retain earlier memories, and may miss friends and possessions they leave behind. But given time, they can adapt well to international moves too.

Transitions in Adolescence

From the age of 11, and into adolescence, international moves become more challenging. Children at this age are developing their identity. Peers become more important than family, and by mid-adolescence (age 13–16), changing peer group can be devastating. We generally advise against a first significant international move during mid-adolescence. This applies in both directions, to adolescents who have grown up in the developing world and move to their parents' passport country, and adolescents who move from their passport country to a new host country. By their teens, if they do not recall moving before, adolescents are likely to identify with the nationality of the country they have previously known, and with the peer group they have left behind. They may neither want to take on nor shed the identity of a TCK. In clinical practice we have seen times when moving at this time was harmful and had a lasting impact on well-being.

There are, however, exceptions. First, adolescents tend to cope much better with international moves when they remember having made one before, especially if to a similar culture. Parents need to take children's autobiographical memory into account; for example, a 14-year-old who previously moved aged four may not remember it, and probably sees the country they have lived in for ten years as home.

Second, moving is easier when it coincides with educational transition points. For example, a 16-year-old returning to England for sixth form after taking International General Certificate of Secondary Education exams will probably not be the only new starter needing friends in a new peer group. Other countries' educational systems provide natural transition points at 13, 14 or 15, which may therefore make it easier for children to adjust at those ages.

Moving internationally at 18 for further education is a more normative experience and may open up opportunities to meet other overseas students and TCKs. The timing of a move can also be affected by the availability of funding; for instance, three years' residence in England or Wales makes students eligible for lower university fees than those for international students.

Third, a first international move in adolescence can work if the child is excited about it, has visited or experienced the new host culture, and has a rounded understanding of its good and bad points.

Balancing Siblings' Needs

Planning by life stage takes more balancing when children of different ages are involved. Parents planning to raise children away from their passport country need to consider at what stage they will plan to move their family back. Should they come back when the eldest child reaches secondary school age, or university age, or stay until they have seen all their children through secondary education? Should they come back with their children at 16, or 18 (recognising that many university students value a home base they can go to at weekends and vacations), or let them stay with a close relative or friend? What could go wrong with that? How would they know? Which of their children are independent enough to stay without their parents in the same country, and which will need them there? What family home base will children need as young adults?

Transition decisions are not set in stone, and often need revisiting. We shall do so in the sections below on assignment and re-entry.

Making Reasonable Adjustments

Some organisations assess partners and children as part of the selection process. Employment law, at least in the UK, does not allow organisations to refuse international assignment because of a problem in the family. Still, it is wise to know what reasonable adjustments a family may need to help them thrive in a different culture, and to explore practical possibilities with families. For example, if children enjoy walking outdoors and exploring nature, how will that work in a dense humid city? How will a child who enjoys watching trains adjust in a country which has none? What can a family put in place to help these children feel happy? What do they need to budget for holidays suited to their children's needs? Would the family be better deployed elsewhere?

Briefing

Organisations can help parents and their children understand what a host culture will be like. They can brief families with information about the host culture and how to live there; about the normal processes of culture shock, and its emotional roller-coaster effects which will vary among family members; sponsor virtual tours and visits to the host culture; introduce them to other families who live or have lived where they are going; discuss how to help the family settle in; and provide security advice. Briefing information needs to be tailored to each child's developmental stage and emotional milestones in order to prevent it being tokenistic or unhelpful (see Solihull Approach, 2017).

Deployment

Whilst there is no substitute for good preparation, unforeseen circumstances in the field sometimes force families to change plans and abandon recommendations. Regardless of any changes, families need good housing, healthcare, education, safeguarding, rest and recuperation (often known as R & R in the humanitarian sector). In some countries, none of these may be straightforward to provide. Organisations need to ensure families budget for all their needs. For example, one family relocating to the USA was not adequately briefed on the additional expenses needed for everyday items which were free or cheaper in Europe. Both children and parents may need reassurance when they experience different stages of culture shock. There may be questions to consider about timing of home leave, and when it is safe to stay in a country. Above all, parents need to be listened to, and children need their voices heard.

Listening to Children

Workers may routinely receive appraisals or placement reviews to reflect on their assignment. However, all too often children and young people's voices are not heard directly but only through their parents or teachers. Concrete conversations about educational provision are too easily prioritised over the delicacy of checking emotional well-being. Some may be wary of asking children how they are doing as they are concerned about unsettling them. But we far more often hear of children upset not to have been listened to or to have had their opinion sought by adults. We rarely hear children say they wish they had not been asked.

Repeated safeguarding failures teach us that children's genuine and active participation is vital for creating safe organisations (Moore, 2017). Children and adults experience safety differently. The power imbalance between them makes it harder for children to raise concerns. Safe organisations must foster meaningful safe conversations that show they take young people's views seriously.

We recommend that organisations provide member carers, or even TCK specialists, trusted by families and with all appropriate safeguarding measures in place, to ask children how they are finding life in the field. How are they doing? What do they like or find hard about where they live? Who notices when they are missing friends or feeling sad? But be genuine – or young people will see straight through you and just tell you what they think you want to hear. We think that if you really want to know and are prepared to listen, you may just hear truths about TCKs' lives and your organisation that will help shape things for the better.

Safeguarding

Families traveling overseas often find themselves in circumstances where modern Western health and safety law does not apply. For some this can be a worry, for others a welcome relief. But it is important to remember that abuse is most often carried out by individuals known to a child. Opportunities for abuse abound where children play freely in the community; where community cohesion leads them to become familiar with their parents' colleagues, neighbours, faith leaders or domestic staff; or where child protection law is not adequately enforced. On the other hand, such environments may be safer than passport countries, because adults know each other, communities share responsibility, and vigilance for danger is an everyday practice. It is always recommended that allegations of abuse are referred to local statutory services for investigation, and not dealt with by internal investigation. However, we recognise that in some locations, this action may be ineffective or even dangerous.

Organisations need to write and implement safeguarding policies and must remain vigilant about the possibility of abuse. However, the absence of an adequate local social care system does not qualify a mission or development organisation to try and replace it with their own accountability standards, investigation or oversight. Where abuse cannot safely be addressed locally, we recommend organisations consult with experienced safeguarding specialists in a developed country and follow their advice.

Healthcare

Organisations need to ensure that families have adequate health insurance and are funded to access safe healthcare when they need it, either within the host country or in another country. Specialist healthcare, including mental health care, may not be available locally or may be insufficiently resourced in the host country. Families may need to travel or return to their passport country to receive healthcare if remote treatment is not sufficient.

In our experience, many parents who choose to move cross-culturally with their children are nurturing, resourceful and well attuned to their children's needs. Parental support and understanding is a major factor in helping children overcome emotional and behavioural problems, and expatriate families are often ahead of the game. But therapists' frames of reference may not match those of parents or organisations. People naturally judge the severity of problems by comparisons to those around them. Minor problems can seem major in a context where other families seem to function well under extraordinary stress. On occasion, we have found organisations raising extreme concerns about the mental health or safety of children or parents who seem to us to be functioning well within the normal range of behaviour. Organisations and parents often benefit from therapists normalising both TCKs' problems, and parents' uncertainty about how to raise their children.

As they adjust to transitions, it is not usual for children to behave temporarily in ways associated with an earlier developmental stage (see Solihull Approach, 2017, for a guide). A child may resume bed-wetting or temper tantrums or seek comfort from toys they had stopped using. Such behaviours are worth both treating as transitional and paying attention to. They may express feelings children cannot verbalise. Parents can reassure children to lessen their embarrassment, give them time to talk and find other ways to express their feelings, and help them re-establish routines and stabilise what they have lost.

Nevertheless, there are exceptions. Sometimes children get stuck. Sometimes parents or organisations are not attentive enough. Parents who raise their children on a remote rural mission compound may deliberately or inadvertently shelter them from parts of normative development they would learn in the UK, such as how to keep themselves safe, or navigate sex, identity and relationships. Children in need of professional help may be referred for pastoral advice. Or organisations may not know how to respond. As with safeguarding, if parents or organisations are concerned about children's mental health, they should always consult children's mental health specialists.

Finding Specialist Mental Health Support

It is always worth investigating whether suitable mental health specialists (local or expatriate) are available locally or in a nearby country. They may be better qualified, more accessible and less expensive than specialists in a passport country. Whilst many find this support helpful, we have found on occasion that some families are dissatisfied with their contact with local psychiatrists, who may be more ready to prescribe medication than they would like, or unsympathetic to their reason for being in the host country. Parents may then prefer to speak remotely to a mental health specialist in their passport country.

Finding a suitable remote specialist can be the next problem. Few mental health professionals specialise in work with TCKs. Statutory services do not usually provide remote healthcare outside their own borders. It is hard to know where to begin to find a good private provider, and understandable that families want to rely on personal recommendations. However, unregulated psychologists and counsellors can be fraudulent or dangerous. For their own protection, families need to choose a professional who is regulated or accredited with their national professional association. These professionals need to check with their association, insurers and regulator in the family's jurisdiction whether they may legally provide remote therapy, as in some instances they may not (see chapter 13, this volume, for more on this).

Parents who are good at nurturing their children, and are provided with remote mental health support, can potentially safely manage many common children's mental health problems. For instance, depression, anxiety, attention deficit disorder, dyslexia, dyspraxia and autism need not be a barrier to families going overseas with access to support, nor be reasons for them to return home. But serious mental health problems, like anorexia nervosa, psychosis and acute suicide risk, are less safe to manage without adequate local mental health support. Children who are difficult to engage in therapy or who hide their feelings are hard to treat remotely. Children with complex physical health needs or severe and profound learning disabilities are likely to need specialist support available locally to them.

Psychologists, counsellors and therapists working with TCKs need to understand their unique cultural background and the timeline of their life history, which may include multiple transitions between countries. It is important to understand families' reasons for working across cultures too, and especially any faith-based motivation. Many factors are not unique to TCKs and can be understood in the same way as emotional and behavioural problems typically encountered with children. Other factors are more specific, including the various pros and cons of a TCK's identity, and grief for transitions and losses, which can be mistaken for other disorders and need time and understanding to heal (Bushong, 2013).

Changing Transition Plans

Sometimes families need to change their plans because of their children's mental health, which must not be subordinated to parents' work or vocations. Not only acute emergencies but also chronic unhappiness or adjustment difficulties may lead to a decision to relocate to a different part of a host country, or back to a passport country. Decisions are harder when one child is struggling with the environment while their siblings are thriving. This is not unusual. We often work with parents who feel pulled in opposite directions by their children's needs. Often, less drastic changes than moving countries can improve matters – changing school, or even school year, moving to a different part of the country, finding new activities or friendships, or understanding the child better.

Education

Parents face multiple decisions about suitable schooling for their children. Options include homeschooling within the family or in small groups with other children, local schools with national children, international schools (some funded by faith groups such as Christian missions or religious orders, and others by overseas institutions such as the British Council or American universities), boarding schools in the host country or a third country, or even day school in another country, with children living with a host or family member.

Many resources are available to parents and international schools, allowing children to follow curricula compatible with their passport country. As described earlier, education has a great impact on decisions about transition. Many TCKs benefit from small schools, multicultural learning, TCK peer groups or bespoke curricula devised by resourceful parents. Others TCKs struggle with harsh learning environments or a lack of friends their age, or parents may struggle with homeschooling their children when this is not their strength, or with children who respond to education differently from their siblings. It is important to consider what is in the best interests of each child and their mental health, and to keep listening to them.[2]

Re-entry

Contracts and assignments may reach natural end points. Organisations may determine when families re-enter to their passport country, but would be wise to agree timing with families, unless there are defensible reasons not to. Re-entry can be permanent (or for the foreseeable future), or temporary between assignments or for holiday or home leave. Re-entry may be planned or unplanned, for instance because of medical emergencies, military coups or refused visa renewals.

Furlough

From the Dutch *verlof*, "furlough" was a term known to military and mission workers before its use in the Covid-19 pandemic, as a period of leave from the field to spend time in a passport country. For Christian missionaries, furlough is not a holiday but a busy time, involving visiting prayer supporters, giving talks, moving from house to house around a country, raising funds or studying for further qualifications. Children frequently report disliking being taken to a different church every Sunday to fulfil furlough engagements. Families sometimes need permission and assistance to lessen the burden of furlough work, for example by limiting the number of church visits, being provided one temporary home to stay in for an extended period or being encouraged to have a holiday in a third country before or after furlough.

Furlough can be emotional and pressured for families and their networks of extended family, friends and supporters. All families face the challenge of trying to navigate how much time to spend travelling to and being with friends or extended family, and how much time to spend unwinding and relaxing during their time spent on furlough. Each member of a family may want to make the most of doing activities which are not possible in their host country. When time is limited, incompatible activities can cause strong feelings and conflict. We recommend talking through plans, decisions, expectations and emotions in advance, and including rest times. Families have often told us they squeezed in too much and had too little time to rest.

Should I Stay or Should I Go?

Security is a major reason for changing plans about when to leave a country. Generally, a country or region involved in civil war or political unrest is not a safe place for expatriate children. But context is important. During the war in Iraq, Iraqi Kurdistan was largely peaceful for long periods. During the Nepalese Maoist insurgency, expatriate children were generally safe provided they knew where their parents were, and their parents remained vigilant and followed basic security guidance. In times of international terrorism, climate emergency, pandemics, social media risks and youth stabbings or shootings, children are not necessarily safer living in a developed country with a stable government than a developing country in political turmoil.

But security can change quickly and needs constant review and methods of weighing up contradictory assessments. During civil emergencies when quick decisions are needed, it is unfair to place the burden of them on individuals and families. Where security is a concern, organisations need clear security policies, and must be prepared to pull all their expatriates out if the relevant embassy advises it. It is wise to stay in consultation with more than one nation's embassies, and local contacts, as their security information can differ. Expatriates can be reluctant to leave when local contacts do not have that option, but protecting expatriates who have stayed behind may risk increasing danger to their local friends and contacts.

Planning

Particularly because plans can change, planning re-entry begins from the moment of arrival in the host country. Parents can help children maintain key relationships in their passport country (using social media, remote communication and video games if it helps), remain fluent in its language and familiar with its culture, and make use of periods of furlough and holidays. For such purposes, pressured families may need additional time or resources from the organisation.

Parents can prepare more fully as return approaches even in the case of temporary returns. RAFT principles (Pollock & Van Reken, 1999) – *reconcile, affirm, farewell, think destination* – can be a helpful framework for cross-cultural families, and useful to follow for both children and adults. This is how some families have used them:

   Reconcile. One child was so upset about saying goodbye that he fell out with his local friend over a small slight. With his parents' encouragement, he made up with his friend and kept happy memories of the friendship.
   Affirm. Who and what is left behind matters. One family's children left gifts for their neighbours before leaving, to remind them of how special they had been.
   Farewell. One family made sure their children were able to eat at a favourite restaurant, visit favourite places and have final sleepovers with their best friends. Another found friends and neighbours that their children trusted to look after the pets they had to leave behind. Others made albums or videos or took keepsakes with them to remind them of their experiences.
   Think destination. Children need realistic expectations – positive and negative. For instance, some used to visiting their passport country

in the summer can be disappointed by long winter evenings – but excited by the prospect of snow.

Unplanned Returns

When families have to move at short notice, for example because of security, children need a clear narrative about the reason for moving, to know that their parents are keeping them safe, and emergency RAFT building. In an evacuation when each individual was only allowed one item of baggage, one family allowed each child to choose a favourite toy as a way to negotiate this. Age-appropriate discussion helps when there is growing instability (e.g. Why are there soldiers on the streets? When might we have to leave the country?). Children and young people tune into parents' emotional expression even when they try to suppress or hide it (Waters, Karnilowicz, West, & Mendes, 2020). We have worked with children who blame themselves for a move, or who over- or underestimate risks. Being open about what may happen, associated emotions and possible plans will reduce anxiety, misunderstanding and conflicted feelings.

Member Care after Return

Organisations should budget to support families after they return to their passport country, as their duty of care does not end there. Especially if they have spent many years away, families may need help with practical matters, such as a car, a home and briefing about social changes and educational choices for their children. It can take time for adults both to find employment and to be emotionally ready for it. As a rule of thumb, we sometimes advise a month of adjustment for every year of work overseas.

Debriefing

We recommend offering debriefing not just to returned workers but also to their partners and children. This kind of personal debriefing may focus on a critical incident which led to an unexpected return, or on the whole period of living overseas. It should be provided by an independent debriefer who does not report back to the organisation and must be distinguished from operational debriefing with the organisation. It should not be compulsory, but it is less stigmatising to offer it on an opt-out rather than an opt-in basis. Debriefing can be offered to whole families together, or separately to parents and children. For full guidance on debriefing, including how to provide it well and avoid pitfalls which sometimes makes it inadequate or harmful, see Hawker (2018).

Helping TCKs Adjust

TCKs' needs after returning to a passport country are very variable (see chapter 5, this volume). Some may not engage with a debriefer but find that spending time with other TCKs fulfils a similar function. For instance, many TCKs who return to the UK from overseas find Rekonnect summer camps, or church or mission conferences invaluable for making connections with other TCKs they can relate to. Social media presents its own risks but hosts numerous groups for TCKs regardless of their faith background.

It also helps to prepare TCKs before they meet children who do not share their cross-cultural experience. Expatriate adults returning to their home country often report that their friends and families stop listening after two minutes' talk about the host country. This is understandable, as most people allow little time for hearing about experiences they cannot identify with. Children are no exception. TCKs' peers in their passport country may ask silly questions based on stereotypes or partial knowledge – for example, did you live in a pyramid in Egypt or mummify your dead? Parents can suggest or role-play short answers.

TCKs may still talk of the place they have left as home. They may go through a grief process, experiencing shock, denial, anger, bargaining and sadness, before adjusting to their new environment. They may go through the stages of reverse culture shock, with an initial honeymoon period before dipping into unhappiness. There may be triggers for changes – moving to a new school, or physical changes like climate and daylight. Children need time to go through normal adjustment processes.

Professional Help

When TCKs struggle to settle in their passport country, they may need access to child and adolescent mental health services (CAMHS) or other counselling. In the UK such services are free and may be accessed directly or through a family doctor. Therapists are trained to learn from their clients about their culture, which should include the culture of a TCK. We suggest that those seeking help from CAMHS share with their CAMHS worker that identity as a TCK is important to the child or young person, if it is. With the family's consent, the support organisation could be in touch with the CAMHS team to help them understand cultural context or discuss with the children and young people what they want those working with them to understand about their identity, to help them successfully share it with an adult who does not know that context. It can help for organisations to budget for private therapy in the event that suitable CAMHS support is unavailable.

Conclusion

The Poisonwood Bible describes an extreme situation – a family ignoring best practice at a time and place on the cusp of radical changes. The scenario seems fanciful today, when mission is more culturally sensitive, development more self-critical and governance and member care more pervasive. Or is it? Occasionally, we come across accounts from across sectors which remind us of *The Poisonwood Bible*. On further assessment, they usually turn out to be less alarming, but how can families, and the organisations responsible for them, avoid similar mistakes?

We have tried to provide answers in this chapter. Organisations do well to pay attention to the families of personnel they deploy overseas. Children deserve recognition of their identity as TCKs or CCKs, and thoughtful planning around the timing and management of cross-cultural transitions. It is good to prepare and brief families for entry into a new culture and adapt their environment as necessary to help them thrive. During international assignment families benefit from targeted member care, and support with safeguarding, health, and education, among other things. They need support with decisions about future transitions, including furlough, emergency relocation and the ending of assignment. Children need inclusion in and preparation for transitions, as appropriate to their age and the contextual circumstances. Families benefit from extended support after an assignment is complete, and assistance with accessing services they need. Organisations must balance families' autonomy with the need to keep them safe.

In sharing good practice in member care, we note that many Christian missions and churches do it well. However, many do not, or do so in a tokenistic way or not at all. As far as we are aware, fewer secular humanitarian organisations have policies in place to support families. We think families deserve more attention if cross-cultural postings are to be sustainable. As part of organisations' duty of care, we encourage further consideration of the challenges and opportunities for children and young people whose parents work internationally.

Notes

1 Where we mention passport country in this chapter, we recognise that third culture kids may add to their national identities by holding more than one passport or have parents who hold different nationalities from each other.
2 Further advice about education can be found at https://oscar.org.uk/resources/children/childrens-education/christian-education-advice

References

Bushong, L.J. (2013). *Belonging everywhere & nowhere: Insights into counselling the globally mobile.* Indianapolis: Mango Tree Intercultural Services.
Hawker, D.M. (2018). *Debriefing toolkit for humanitarian workers.* www.chsalliance.org/get-support/resource/debriefing-toolkit-for-humanitarian-workers/.
Kingsolver, B. (1998). *The poisonwood bible.* New York: HarperCollins.
Moore, T. (2017). *Protection through participation: Involving children in child-safe organisations.* https://aifs.gov.au/cfca/sites/default/files/publication-documents/protection_through_participation.pdf

O'Donnell, K., & O'Donnell, M.L. (Eds.). (2013). *Global member care* (Vol. 2: *Crossing sectors for serving humanity*). Pasadena, CA: William Carey Library.

Pollock, D.C., & Van Reken, R.E. (1999). *The third culture kid experience: Growing up among worlds*. Yarmouth, ME: Intercultural Press.

Pollock, D.C., Van Reken, R.E., & Pollock, M. (2017). *Third culture kids: Growing up among worlds* (3rd ed.). Boston: Nicholas Brealey.

Solihull Approach (2017). The first five years. https://solihullapproachparenting.com/wp-content/uploads/2021/09/Developmental-and-Emotional-Milestones.pdf

Waters, S.F., Karnilowicz, H.R., West, T.V., & Mendes, W.B. (2020). Keep it to yourself? Parent emotion suppression influences physiological linkage and interaction behavior. *Journal of Family Psychology, 34*, 784–793. https://doi.org/10.1037/fam 0000664

Chapter 12

Who's the client?

Limitations and advantages of therapeutic work as a psychological contractor for aid organisations

Ben Porter

This chapter explores the tripartite relationship between a therapist, a staff person seeking support and their employing aid organisation. Through clinical experience I have found that there are inherent tensions with this dual commitment, though these are outweighed by the advantages this mode of engaging affords. The reality is that both the organisation and the staff person are the "client" for a therapist in this situation, presenting unique strains as well as opportunities. In this chapter I reflect on some of what we can learn from common dilemmas in providing psychosocial support to staff, the impact on both the therapist and the staff person, and end with some recommendations.

Although there are a variety of ways that an aid worker may access counselling, this chapter focuses on the experience of a therapist working for a specialised organisation that contracts with aid organisations.[1] For therapists working in this organisation-to-organisation arrangement, the relationship takes on a unique dynamic. Some of the common questions therapists in this modality ask include:

- How many sessions are offered? How is this communicated to the therapist and staff person, and is there flexibility based on clinical need?
- What are the confidentiality considerations when working as a contractor for aid organisations?
- How am I being utilised by the aid organisation? Is this therapy or a human resources (HR) process?
- How are decisions on risk made? Are there safety concerns; is the timing and environment conducive for therapy; and what is the severity of distress?
- Am I complicit in "patching them up and sending them out" when this may be more in the interest of the aid organisation than the staff person?

In my and colleagues' experience, therapists can feel restricted or disempowered by organisations' inconsistent or inadequate systems of staff care, something that mirrors the unpredictability and reactivity of the humanitarian sector as a whole. For staff in high-risk roles and locations,

DOI: 10.4324/9781003261971-13

insufficient support risks undermining mental well-being. Working in a specialist organisation can provide a framework of support and containment for the therapist allowing dialogue and relationship with the aid organisation to advocate for good psychosocial practice.

An Aid Organisation's Motivations to Provide Psychosocial Support

Due to the security risks in humanitarian and development work, organisations have an ethical and moral responsibility to mitigate the impact on staff. That said, staff work in locations and roles of varying risk, and access to essential services in these locations also varies, making it difficult to discern the extent of an organisation's responsibility. In many places, however, the organisation takes on the mantle of providing key health services that would normally be accessed without occupational involvement in a staff person's home location, blurring the line between work-related issues and personal issues.

Humanitarian roles are not merely the contracted 40 hours, but can be day, night and weekends, particularly in insecure areas where living quarters and offices are in the same compound and junior and senior staff are mixed. In some cases, staff are exposed to the same violence, abuse and suffering as the populations they serve. This leads to an increased and more complex level of responsibility for an employing organisation. As Houldey (2021) reports,

> The experiences we go through in aid work are hard. The situations we're exposed to can remain with us for many years, and without an outlet through which to process them we run the risk that they become lodged in our bodies, creating many serious health problems. (p. 55)

There are clear benefits for organisations to engage in psychosocial support for staff related to improvements in productivity, staff morale, dedication, and lower rates of accidents, sick leave, presenteeism and turnover. Studies show an average return on investment of £5 for every £1 spent on mental health and psychosocial interventions, with early-stage support having an even higher return (Deloitte, 2020). For this reason, many organisations contract with a range of psychological service providers as part of their staff care support plans.

Additionally, more self-interested motivations may include reputational protection and protection from liability, although accountability and redress remain inconsistent across organisations, creating critical gaps. Alongside this, there are difficulties developing standards of care working across national labour laws and jurisdictions for globally based organisations.

Strategic staff care plans are increasingly common in the sector. A study by Porter and Emmens (2009) showed that only one-third of large international non-governmental organisations (INGOs) interviewed had a dedicated staff care plan or policy. Seven years later, however, a Start Network survey (Solanki, 2016) showed that about 60% of the aid organisations interviewed had provisions in place. While there are some useful guidelines for staff care in the sector (see those by the Konterra Group, 2017, Antares Foundation, 2012 and ISO, 2021 for some examples), there is no universal or certifiable standard for provision of psychosocial staff care for this global industry, leaving a loose framework in which each organisation can pick and choose the level of support they offer. Counselling services are similarly variable and can come under particular cost-related pressures. After all, organisations cannot be expected to "write a blank check" for counselling while specialist support organisations need to pay market rates for therapists.

Such pressure points generally remain outside the influence of an individual staff person or therapist, yet directly impact the nature of the therapeutic relationship and treatment options.

Nature of the Tripartite Relationship and Some Associated Dilemmas

Shinde (2016) writes of employee assistance programmes (EAPs): "There is a contractual agreement between the EAP provider and the company [organisation] but the primary client is always the employee. The needs of the client must not be subverted by concerns about profitability" (p. 155). Despite this, therapists are bound by structures established by the staff members' employing organisations. Legally and financially, the therapist contracts with the organisation, and they define the parameters of therapy. This creates tensions, however, when assessed clinical needs go beyond the therapy allocated by the organisation. The British Association for Counselling and Psychotherapy (BACP) lists its first ethical commitment for counsellors as being to: "Put clients first by making clients our primary concern while we are working with them". Finding the right balance between these split priorities is an important task for the therapist working directly with employing organisations.

Additionally, both therapist and staff person are aware of the tripartite relationship, and this can create spoken or unspoken anxieties about the extent of confidentiality and whether information and clinical opinion may be shared with employers, risking the staff person's career and livelihood.

Access to Therapy

Most organisations offer staff only short-term psychological interventions, which can create barriers in client-therapist engagement. While some therapeutic approaches can operate well in as few as four to six sessions, other approaches would consider such limited intervention to be only the very early stages of therapeutic work. Often, decisions around how long an intervention is offered are driven by the norms of the sector and culture of the organisation rather than clinical need. With inflexible policies and no awareness of clinical significance, one aid worker with mild anxiety (potentially treatable with a few targeted sessions) may be given the same allocated support as a colleague with post-traumatic stress disorder (PTSD) (requiring many more sessions).

In the aid–therapist community, we sometimes refer to such short contracts as "extended assessments", supporting the staff person to gain clarity on their issues and determine next steps. However, due to the limited options for onward referral in many of the countries where aid workers live and the lack of organisational funding, it may be impossible for the staff member to access further support following the "assessment" phase. At this point, the therapist has a quandary: Who will support that person, if not them? The inability to make good onward referrals in an international setting adds additional pressure to the work for the therapist working as a contractor.

Similarly, the short-term nature of engagement may inhibit uptake or may be viewed as a token response by employees:

> One client decided not to begin counselling after I explained that her organisation approved only three counselling sessions. I had met her for a one-off debriefing after the death of a colleague. She (and others) blamed this loss on organisational negligence and were exceedingly angry. She also reported being subjected to bullying by her manager for several months, and her distress had accumulated to the point that she was both highly anxious and resentful of her manager and the organisation for extremely poor people management. In her words: "It's not worth opening up when I know we won't have the time to address the important issues, nor do I want to bounce around from counsellor to counsellor telling my story. Plus, I don't see any real commitment to changing this toxic work environment. It's disgraceful to think that the organisation offers three sessions in light of the mess it has created".

On occasion, the extent of provision is not made clear to the therapist or the staff person ahead of time, creating more uncertainty. I have even encountered situations where psychosocial allocation is inconsistent within the same organisation. In one example, a major INGO that allocates four counselling sessions per year for each staff member without further approval, refused a request for additional sessions that might have allowed a piece of key counselling work to be completed. A few months later, a similar situation arose with a different staff person from this organisation, and I prepared the staff person that it was unlikely we would be able to access additional counselling if needed. On this occasion, however, we were granted an additional four sessions. No details of either case were disclosed to the organisation, and both staff were doing similar roles and working at similar levels. This inconsistency is not uncommon. A colleague recently told me that her team knew who to ask (or not ask) in their various client organisations to get additional sessions approved. Such inconsistencies can feed feelings of injustice which create the ground for moral distress (see chapter 4, this volume).

On the other hand, organisations that provide psychosocial support throughout the employment cycle and with flexibility for extenuating circumstances are much more likely to maintain the health and well-being of their people.

> James (not his real name) worked as humanitarian with one organisation for seven years. His organisation offered a psychosocial debriefing at the end of each contract, and we met four times over the span of four years as he transitioned through Central African Republic, South Sudan, Yemen and Syria. In each location he encountered critical incidents, some at close proximity. He had been a diligent employee, often working under extreme pressure for months without a break. Over the years he spoke about witnessing "senseless deaths" in the communities where he worked, rampant corruption, bombings and gunfire, the work-related death of a colleague/friend, as well as experiencing bullying in the workplace himself. Despite the series of critical incidents he encountered, he had established innovative and effective humanitarian interventions, successfully managed multimillion-dollar programmes and consistently reached targets.
>
> When he decided to make a career change and return to his home country, we met for a final debrief. Because of the continuity and positive rapport we had developed, he was open about the current impact of his experiences and reported symptoms including loss of sleep, heart palpitations, difficulty breathing at times and some sensory symptoms linked to traumatic events. Following the debrief, I recommended six sessions (including four with EMDR[2]) to the organisation and this was approved. The six sessions were successful in drastically lowering his symptoms. Processing the painful situations did not remove the reality of the pain, but allowed for a new perspective, a sense of pride in his work and a platform for entering employment and life in his home country with renewed energy. James has maintained a good relationship with, and speaks positively about, the organisation he worked with for seven years.

This demonstrates the importance of walking alongside staff members over time, and the key role of an organisation's recognition of their duty of care.

Confidentiality

As with any client–therapist relationship, confidentiality in an organisation-to-organisation set-up is strictly maintained. A key difference in working with international staff is that the employing organisation often facilitates in-country referrals or manages safety concerns, particularly if the national services in the country of your client are ill-equipped or unknown to the therapist. If the therapist learns of risk to a vulnerable person, the avenue for reporting might not be clear, and it is important to clarify who in the aid organisation may be contacted in situations of concern over a staff member's harm to self or others, and to gain the staff person's consent for communication with their organisation.

The therapist should also be on the lookout for conflict of interest, particularly when working with small to medium-sized organisations. They may be asked to work with people from the same team or location, and there may be line management connections; clients may live in the same house/compound, or have romantic relationships. Whilst maintaining confidentiality, the therapist needs to consider who to inform of these conflicts of interests, and to involve other practitioners quickly when needed. It is advisable for the employing organisation and the specialist provider organisation to have several pre-identified practitioners with relevant skills and cultural backgrounds at hand for referral.

It is also common for aid organisations to request reports about psychological assessments of staff at any point during their international assignment. The therapist needs to carefully consider the type of assessment being requested, whether they have the skill set to complete the assessment, who will be reading and storing the assessment, and what the employment implications are. For example, the therapist will need to know whether it will be read by a medical professional or an HR professional to modify the language and terms used in the report. Informed consent prior to the appointment and consent for the report to be shared must be obtained from the staff person. In this scenario, the organisation is clearly the client, and a frank discussion with the service user about the use of their information and the risk assessment elements of the appointment is important. In some cases organisations may request report for someone the therapist has seen in the past or at the commencement of therapy, and the dual nature of the relationship requires open discussion.

Therapy Used to Manage Other Issues

Sometimes, I have noticed therapy in the organisation-to-organisation format being used to shift responsibility on thorny issues. For example, an organisation may make a referral for counselling when seeking to deal with code of conduct breaches, poor management practices, bullying/harassment, performance-related issues or any other non-clinical issue. Organisations may be anxious or at a loss to know how to manage certain issues, but the therapist needs to be clear on how they are being used, what reporting is expected and whether they have the necessary skill set (for example, the request may be in fact for coaching, conflict negotiation or leadership development skills rather than counselling). Some organisations can have an unrealistic expectation that difficulties can be *outsourced*, with duty of care responsibilities transferred, and may hope that sending a "problem staff member" to counselling will build evidence that they have tried to resolve outstanding issues.

In these situations, the therapist or case manager should liaise with key contacts at the employing organisation to define the parameters of counselling versus other interventions.

In organisation-to-organisation work, the therapist may find themselves dealing with conflicting motivations in the client, for example when they request support around leaving their job or are pursuing legal action against the organisation. Occupationally, the therapist may be asked to provide an opinion to the organisation about extending sick leave or reconfiguring a return-to-work plan, again creating ambiguity in the three-way relationship.

Finally, therapists may feel that they are engaged by organisations for staff to "patch them up to keep them going". Emergency response or surge team members often bounce from assignment to assignment without adequate recovery time. Aid organisations may overlook their policies when capacity is low, and staff may have the implicit or explicit message that their livelihood is at risk if they do not take up the next posting quickly (although some staff members willingly extend contracts and engage in new emergencies, leaving the therapist as the only voice urging caution). When there is excessive flexibility in re-assignment procedures, it opens the possibility for a type of collusion between the organisation and the staff person that can be detrimental to the well-being of the latter (see chapter 3, this volume, for more on this).

> One individual who appeared extremely competent and managed extensive workloads in precarious environments presented to therapy with severe anxiety and multiple symptoms of occupational burnout. She reported undertaking a series of surge postings after which the organisation had promised a period of rest and recuperation (R & R). Yet, at the end of each contract, a new disaster situation arose, and exceptions were made on both sides. Her baseline of well-being appeared to drop after each mission, never returning to previous levels, even after the end of the short breaks she took between missions. During one such short break at home, where the intention had been to develop her relationship with her sister, she found herself caught up in work for 12–14 hours a day and with no time or energy to invest in herself or her relationship with her sister.

In these situations, the therapist may feel that they are being hired to keep their client at work, enabling a system that is exploitative. This is in addition to an inherent friction between the erratic and reactive nature of aid work and core therapeutic aims of creating a containing and consistent space. Emergency meetings, last-minute trips, no internet connection, getting stuck in a location due to Covid-19, new crises/conflicts and so on have the potential to disrupt the therapy process, and the therapist needs to find ways of adapting, remaining flexible and continuing to communicate expectations of therapy with individual clients.

Risk and Safety Issues

Humanitarian aid work is risky, but sometimes coping mechanisms can be risky too. An aid organisation may send a staff person to a therapist because they have concerns and would like to have an objective assessment of risk. On one occasion, I was asked to provide an intervention for alcohol misuse for a staff member working as a driver and still at work. My priority in this case was to stress the danger of using him as a driver before engaging in any work on his drinking. In this example, the need to prioritise risk management for the organisation and other staff even before intervention with the client is clear. However, there are many situations in which this is less clear-cut, where the organisation's motivation may be to safeguard reputation and the therapist has to weigh up their position carefully in judging any intervention (for example, when staff have problematic drug or alcohol use, or are believed to be at risk of inappropriate relationships with the host community).

The therapist may also come across issues directly in therapy and then need to determine whether the aid organisation should be involved. In one example, a staff member allotted four counselling sessions per year contacted me through the confidential booking system. He was working in an extremely remote location where he experienced a critical incident and began to exhibit psychotic symptoms. I was concerned about the potential for self-harm, and we made a plan of action for his safety that involved regular contact but decided not to involve his organisation. When, however, he did not respond to two consecutive check-in emails, I contacted his organisation's HR representative to assist in locating him, expressing my concern for his safety. The HR representative found him, and we worked on a three-way plan that involved getting him to an appropriate location to stabilise. Here, the relationship with the aid organisation was crucial in protecting the staff person's safety and ensuring appropriate follow-up.

A further role for the aid-therapist is to consider the appropriateness and timing of therapeutic work, taking context into account. Some aid workers want to do deep exploratory therapy when there is real threat in their immediate environment, such as ongoing armed conflict or other imminent threat. The therapist should be able to adapt their work to determine the depth and extent of their engagement according to the client's unique environment and capacity to tolerate distress. In some situations, a staff person may want to stop feeling anxious, yet there may be utility to their anxiety. Careful consideration should be made to ensure that the therapist does not "open up" issues that cannot be adequately contained in their context, and ensure that the staff person has not become more vulnerable because of therapy.

Opportunities of Working Organisation-To-Organisation

An organisation-to-organisation format opens the possibility of building relationships with leaders and HR teams in aid organisations. Partnering with these stakeholders creates opportunities to collaborate in designing interventions and cultivating a culture conducive to well-being across the wider organisation. Therapists and aid workers alike understand the significant influence of managers, structures and organisational culture on well-being. One-to-one therapy sessions may be continually undermined if the staff person returns to an environment that is unjust, abusive or threatening. Working in an organisation-to-organisation relationship provides leverage to advocate for good practice and broadens the ability to respond to situations factoring in the context and culture of the workplace.

Some specialist organisations, such as Thrive Worldwide, work as a multidisciplinary team of psychologists, occupational and travel health doctors, and organisational health experts, facilitating a comprehensive pathway for staff health. Within multidisciplinary teams, centralised clinical records are invaluable for cross-discipline collaboration. As therapists, we may encounter problems that seem psychological but that have a medical component, such as adverse reactions to malaria medication or problems with thyroid function. Similarly, our medical team may encounter psychosomatic symptoms related to stress or psychological trauma.

The specialist organisation provides an important layer of protection for the therapist as well. This may be in terms of setting expectations with aid organisations, such as asserting appropriate timelines for delivery of reports, pre-identified pathways of communication with the aid organisation or procedures for managing risk and safeguarding issues. Internally, crucial support comes in the form of clinical supervision, avenues for multidisciplinary referrals, technical advice and a sense of teamwork. This provides a level of clinical safety and predictability that is an important counterbalance to the rapid and ever-changing nature of the industry.

In some cases, the organisation-to-organisation approach means that the therapist team knows the specific resources or systems of support within a given organisation better even than the individuals working for the organisation, and can share this information:

> I worked with a woman who was being sexually harassed in her office. There was only one other woman in the office, and she did not feel that she could turn to her HR officer for help. She decided to speak with a regional HR officer but was put off on three occasions over several

months. When I spoke to her, she was ready to quit her job and worried that she would not be able to get another job in her city or sector due to the influence of her abuser. Knowing the organisation and their good safeguarding policies at the headquarters level, I asked her if she would like to report the harassment to HQ. When she did, her case was taken up immediately and timely action was communicated to her regularly. The safeguarding team was highly professional and was able to manoeuvre within the situation without causing additional risk or exposure to the staff person. The manager who was harassing her was terminated and the staff person resumed work. When we first met, she scarcely left her bedroom and presented with significant clinical symptoms of anxiety and depression because of the harassment. After a couple of weeks back in her office without being harassed, she had no clinical symptoms.

There may be other staff care policies or resources in the organisation such as a buddy system or peer support programme that the therapist can point towards. As a therapist, understanding the organisational culture and knowing their staff care plan is important information in navigating a therapeutic pathway, especially if there is little or no psychosocial support available in the context outside the organisation. Done well, the organisation provides a key holding environment that the worker can rely on as they engage in difficult and sometimes triggering work. Having a strong and healthy relationship between the specialist organisation and the aid organisation creates space for advocacy and negotiation for good practice.

Impact on the Therapist

Being an aid-therapist is an exceedingly niche role. The *Monitor on Psychology* of the American Psychological Association (2018) says,

> Psychologists who want to work with aid workers should have training in humanitarian and trauma therapy. They should have the skills needed to address the issues this population presents with and understand the range of resources to help this vulnerable population. They should also know how to take cross-cultural issues into account and understand what it means to serve out of the country and transition back home. (p. 24)

Shinde (2016) concurs that "the EAP counsellor must be trained not only to be competent in the interventions necessary but also in understanding the work contexts of the clients in counselling" (p. 156).

Despite this, there is no typical pathway or training programme to become a psychological therapist for aid workers, and practitioners will come from all sorts of accredited disciplines. Unlike work in large healthcare systems, there are usually no cohort groups (children, adult, elderly) or known specialisms (as there are often for clinical presentations). The therapist working for a specialist organisation needs to have a robust toolkit to address a variety of needs within a system that changes according to the organisation and the roles/locations of the staff person.

There are also risks to the therapists that can resemble moral injury. When therapists are restricted from supporting clients in the way that they see fit, due to organisational constraints, they may be left with complex feelings of helplessness and guilt (see chapter 4, this volume). Many therapists of aid workers are former aid workers themselves, which introduces a strong personal desire to assist others in the aid context. And while this lived experience is invaluable in understanding and relating to the work, there is an additional emotional toll that therapists may experience when organisational systems inhibit adequate support. In psychotherapy, a "parallel process" refers to a phenomenon between a therapist and their supervisor whereby the therapist re-enacts the client's issues in the relationship with the supervisor. The supervisor can use this in building insight and guidance for therapeutic work. In working with aid workers, we recognise the parallel process that brings feelings of helplessness and moral distress experienced by humanitarian clients (and their beneficiaries), and the sense for the former of never being able "to do enough". The question "have I done enough?" can equally feature between the therapist and the staff person, with in both situations, the aid organisation as an intermediary (and sometimes a receptacle of displaced blame for the difficult situations in which aid workers find themselves).

Many of my clients overwork, take on too much responsibility and sacrifice their well-being as they strive to alleviate the suffering of others. Some arrive in therapy desperate for a solution without the time or energy required to examine root causes. Many are motivated by caring for others in crisis to gain a sense of mastery (which can be reflective of earlier experiences, see chapter 3, this volume), as well as being attracted to a transient lifestyle which can involve lower-risk relationships with less danger of rejection and disappointment. The ideologies of "quick fix" so prevalent in "emergency culture" are pervasive and have a ripple effect, creating a fantasy that quick and lasting change should occur easily in therapy (and leaving the therapist feeling unable or inadequate to fulfil the client's impossible expectations). The relationship with the therapist then mirrors the worker's experience, fluctuating between "saviour" and "disappointer".

As therapists, we should remember that these affective responses are valuable tools in therapy; it is helpful to draw near to them and use them with empathy as well as with distance. Feelings of helplessness and hopelessness are what Gerald Adler (1972) calls "inevitable companions" of the process. Acknowledging this transference, reflecting and holding space for these feelings opens the possibility for an authentic encounter. Yet slowing down and coming to terms with these feelings often proves difficult for the staff person when there is promise of another mission that whisks them away into an emergency response, which has now become habitual and addictive.

Another feeling that I recognise in myself is frustration and anger in the face of injustice. Humanitarians often work in resource-poor locations with dilapidated health services where, not only are mental health issues exacerbated by living in an unjust society, but mental health services may also be scarce or non-existent. The principles of quality and equitable services that the industry strives for externally, are often missing internally when it comes to their staff, particularly national staff members. As Houldey (2021) writes: The sector tends "to collapse mental health and wellbeing within the story of the dominant culture, whereby the experiences of the specific challenges of marginalized groups, including national staff, are often overlooked in efforts by aid agencies to systematize staff care" (p. 18).

I remember attending a staff care workshop in a field location where HQ staff spoke of their workspace assessments, extensive counselling offer, teambuilding and well-being days, chair massages, smoking cessation programme, financial advice, gym memberships and on and on. This in contrast to their national staff's offer of a single workshop, not to mention the disparity in job security, benefits and income. "Justice" is the 6th Principal of the BACP code of ethics. "The therapist must ensure the fair and impartial treatment of all clients and the provision of adequate services". In working with employing organisations, the therapist may feel that they are aligning with or enabling a structure that perpetuates privileged power structures. Awareness of these emotions of frustration and anger on the therapist's part is an important part of building empathy with all aid workers and working effectively.

In parallel with this, however, is the emotional impact of vicarious resilience. Hernandez (2018) defines vicarious resilience "as the positive impact on the personal growth of the therapist of exposure to their client's resilience". A significant counterbalance to feelings of helplessness, anger and cynicism is the awareness of the ways one is growing and being inspired through work. The same diversity of client work that can seem overwhelming, also allows the therapist to feel part of something that is greater than themselves. The therapist engages with a range of professionals from water engineers to human rights defenders, to food and shelter experts, to medical professionals, to programme managers, to environmental activists, all striving to make the world a better place. Sometimes the therapist gets to be part of igniting an individual's resilience despite (or perhaps because of) the various stressors they face. A United Nations High Commissioner for Refugees staff care study (Welton-Mitchell, 2013) indicated that "approximately one-third also indicated some unexpected benefits associated with stress exposure during the course of humanitarian work, including realizing they are stronger than they thought, feeling closer to others, deriving more enjoyment from work, and developing stronger religious faith" (p. 80). This is what Papadopoulos

(2007) calls "adversity-activated development",[3] and therapists may witness this within the communities they support and, equally, within themselves. Supporting staff to transform difficulty, pain and suffering into meaning and growth provides a sense of reward and meaning for the therapist.

Recommendations

For Staff Members:

- Staff should ask about psychosocial support services at the interview stage and learn about the organisation's approach to staff health and well-being. Ask about which psychosocial support services are delivered internally and which externally (and about the extent of experience in the sector any external contractor has). This should help decision-making about a role and allow informed consent and expectations around psychosocial support services.
- Staff may consider developing a Wellness Action Plan with their manager for mutual awareness around staying well. The mental health charity MIND has developed a useful template for this. (See references below)
- It is the staff person's responsibility to make all reasonable efforts to present themselves as fit for work. Be aware of and harness your strategies for well-being. Part of this may be developing a relationship with a therapist before leaving for a difficult assignment.

For Aid Organisations:

- Aid organisations should clearly communicate the extent of psychosocial support available with a specialist organisation, so that the therapist can employ the appropriate pace and depth of work with an individual. This includes the number of sessions and how to request additional sessions if required. These practices should also be communicated during induction processes for staff and applied consistently and transparently. Decisions about further care should be made with consideration of clinical need as well as duty of care based on the role and location of staff member.
- To ensure good usage of psychosocial services, aid organisations should ensure confidentiality, for example, by using codes on invoices and making procedures for requesting additional sessions outside of the staff person's management team. They should avoid requesting feedback about counselling from therapists, whilst also clearly indicating circumstances in which reporting is required (i.e. risk assessments or other mandated sessions which include reports).
- Leaders should model help-seeking behaviour and cultivate psychological safety within their teams. Leaders are encouraged to access

psychosocial support and talk about their experience of accessing services with colleagues.

- While a positive return on investment for mental health and psychosocial support in the global north workforce has been well evidenced, more research is required to understand the type and impact of psychosocial support for staff in the global south. Aid organisations should continue to identify equitable psychosocial practices that support staff as a whole.
- Find ways to confidentially discuss psychosocial trends with any specialist organisation you employ. For example, have "hotspots" or programmes with high counselling uptake been identified? What are the general reasons that staff are accessing counselling: Critical incidents, workplace environment, personal or external environment?

For Therapists and Specialist Organisations:

- With sufficient support from the specialist organisation, therapists can feel confident and safe working with staff of aid organisations. Good clinical governance elements include:
  - Regular clinical supervision (including peer and group supervision)
  - Secure information storage mechanisms that comply with global standards (i.e. HIPAA in the USA and GDPR in the UK)
  - Therapists working within their area of competence and according to their governing bodies' regulations
  - Therapists qualified and accredited in their country of residence with appropriate jurisdictional considerations addressed (see chapter 13, this volume)
  - Therapists carry indemnity insurance
- Specialist organisations should use pre-counselling assessments and clearly define which cases can be accepted, depending on the risk appetite of the specialist organisation. Therapists should be made aware of this definition during their induction.
- There is a growing body of therapists working with staff of aid organisations. Find your community of practice and network to establish effective referrals for clinical specialisms, as well as in relation to language and culture considerations.
- Therapists should invest in relevant continuing professional development and upskill in areas that fit with short-term/solution-focused work and with a cohort of clients that typically experiences trauma.
- Therapists should choose to work within a specialist organisation that adopts a trauma-informed workplace approach. Victim services have long been aware of the vicarious impact of listening to and working with people in psychosocial distress. Any organisation working in the aid industry should have a vicarious trauma workplace plan that mitigates the risk to therapist.[4]

Notes

1 In fact, there are four relationships at play: Therapist, specialist organisation employing the therapist, client/staff member and employing organisation. I am referring to a tripartite relationship in merging the therapist and the specialist organisation into one entity. In some cases, there may be important dynamics to explore in the relationship between the therapist and specialist organisation, but that is not the focus of this chapter.
2 EMDR stands for Eye Movement Desensitisation and Reprocessing therapy.
3 Post-traumatic growth is another term used, and is given attention in Dunkley's (2018) book *Psychosocial Support for Humanitarian Aid Workers*.
4 The Office for Victims of Crime in the USA has a helpful four-step blueprint to follow for create a vicarious trauma-informed workplace. See: https://ovc.ojp.gov/program/vtt/blueprint-for-a-vicarious-trauma-informed-organization.

References

Adler, G. (1972). Helplessness in the helpers. *British Journal of Medical Psychology, 45*(4), 315–326. https://doi.org/10.1111/j.2044-8341.1972.tb02214.x

American Psychological Association. (2018, January). How you can help aid workers. *Monitor on Psychology, 49*(1). www.apa.org/monitor/2018/01/helping-aid-workers

Antares Foundation. (2012). *Managing stress in humanitarian aid workers: Guidelines for good practice.* www.antaresfoundation.org/filestore/si/1164337/1/1167964/managing_stress_in_humanitarian_aid_workers_guidelines_for_good_practice.pdf?etag=4a88e3afb4f73629c068ee24d9bd30d9

BACP. (2018, 1 July) Ethical framework for the counselling professions. www.bacp.co.uk/events-and-resources/ethics-and-standards/ethical-framework-for-the-counselling-professions/

Deloitte. (2020). Mental health and employers: Refreshing the case for investment. www2.deloitte.com/uk/en/pages/consulting/articles/mental-health-and-employers-refreshing-the-case-for-investment.html

Dunkley, F. (2018). *Psychosocial support for humanitarian aid workers: A roadmap of trauma and critical incident care.* Abingdon, Oxon: Routledge.

Hernandez-Wolfe, P. (2018). Vicarious resilience: A comprehensive review. *Revista de Estudios Sociales, 66*: 9–17. https://doi.org/10.7440/res66.2018.02

Houldey, G. (2021). *The vulnerable humanitarian: Ending burnout culture in the aid sector.* Abingdon, Oxon: Routledge.

International Organisation for Standardization. (2021). *ISO 31030: 2021: Travel Risk Management – Guidance for organisations.* www.iso.org/obp/ui/#iso:std:iso:31030:ed-1:v1:en

Konterra Group. (2017). *Essential principles in staff care: Practices to strengthen resilience in international humanitarian and development organisations.* www.konterragroup.net/admin/wp-content/uploads/2017/03/Essential-Principles-of-Staff-Care-FINAL.pdf

MIND. (n.d.). Wellness Action Plan. www.mind.org.uk/workplace/mental-health-at-work/taking-care-of-your-staff/employer-resources/wellness-action-plan-download/

Papadopoulos, R.K. (2007). Refugees, trauma and adversity-activated development. *European Journal of Psychotherapy and Counselling, 9*(3), 301–312. https://doi.org/10.1080/13642530701496930

Porter, B., & Emmens, B. (2009) *Approaches to staff care in international NGOs.* People in Aid and InterHealth. https://gisf.ngo/wp-content/uploads/2020/02/2072-InterHealth-People-in-Aid-Approaches-to-staff-care-in-international-ngos.pdf

Shinde, E.M. (2016). Employee assistance programmes: Emerging ethical issues. In P. Hbola and A. Raguram (Eds.), *Ethical Issues in counselling and psychotherapy practice: Walking the line* (pp. 155–168). New York: Springer.

Solanki, H. (2017). Start Network Humanitarian Wellbeing Survey: Key findings from a 2016 survey of Start Network agencies and personnel. *Start Network.* https://startnetwork.org/learn-change/news-and-blogs/staff-wellbeing-and-duty-care

Welton-Mitchell, C.E. (2013). UNHCR's mental health and psychosocial support for staff. UNHCR. www.unhcr.org/51f67bdc9.pdf.

Chapter 13

Meeting needs remotely

Online support for international staff

Felicity Runchman and Kate S. Thompson

Introduction

Nowadays we could live our lives almost entirely online. The Covid-19 pandemic prompted many people to switch large parts of their work online. However, for international staff working across significant geographical divides, business meetings via video call, or asynchronously contributing to work projects through digital platforms, was probably already the norm. Those drawn to international work due to an interest in world affairs, or commitment to addressing global justice issues, may also have had a long-term, pre-pandemic embeddedness in online culture. Activists, campaigners, journalists and aid workers, for example, tend to use online media to keep abreast of key topics and to publicise their work through blogging, vlogging or other forms of online dissemination. With a younger generation of international workers, typically millennials or "digital natives", this is nothing other than "business as usual". It is therefore unsurprising that employers of international staff, and international staff themselves, look to online mediums as a means of providing and accessing psychological support. This may be ongoing counselling or psychotherapy, which is central to our discussion in this chapter, or stand-alone psychological interventions such as pre-assignment psychological clearances, post-assignment debriefings and initial trauma consultations following critical incidents. In this chapter we will look at the different mediums used for online psychological support, exploring the evidence base that upholds their efficacy, and bringing to light key issues that users and providers of such support should be aware of.

The Evidence Base for the Use of Different Media in Therapeutic Work

The use of different media for psychotherapy has a long history, dating perhaps to Freud himself and his occasional use of letters to patients to supplement his in-person sessions. As our media for communication have developed, continual debate has run alongside about the use of these media

DOI: 10.4324/9781003261971-14

for therapy, usually in terms of supplementing in-person therapy work (now called a "blended" way of working). As telephones became ubiquitous, so too has the use of the telephone as a medium for therapy, although sometimes without much thoughtfulness or guidance (Irvine et al., 2020). Similarly, as video conferencing and text-based media have become ever more present, so too has their use as tools for therapy either alongside or instead of in-person appointments.

Despite these developments, it could be argued that we made less than optimal use of remote methods of psychological therapy until the Covid-19 pandemic in 2020. As argued by Simpson, Richardson, Pietrabissa, Castelnuovo, & Reid (2020), Covid-19's rapid spread necessitated an urgent switch to remote means of offering therapy and the creative use of "a suite of digital mental health modalities or psycho-technologies including text-chat, audio calls, virtual reality, mental health apps and online forums" (p. 410). This expansion of options for therapy can only be of benefit for a globally scattered workforce, allowing greater choice of media and a whole world of therapists to choose from.

Even prior to this Covid-19-driven expansion, research evidence was accumulating on the effectiveness of remote media to offer psychological interventions (see Simpson & Reid (2014) for a very helpful overview). Meta-analyses of many studies indicate similarity of outcomes for video therapy (Backhaus et al., 2012), faster improvements in some client groups (Nelson & Patten, 2016), or enhanced effectiveness (Richardson, Frueh, Grubaugh, Egede, & Elhai, 2009). Simpson et al. (2020) note that video therapy may be particularly effective for clients with mood disorders or interpersonal avoidance who could find in-person sessions overwhelming. In addition, a 24-study review found the therapeutic alliance highly rated in video therapy, both in terms of developing a strong therapy bond and feeling a sense of therapist presence (Simpson & Reid, 2014). Therapeutic rapport has been found to be equivalent or even increased in text-based interventions (Sucala et al., 2012), while using email for therapy is said to improve feelings of pace and safety for some clients (Fletcher-Tomenius & Vossler, 2009). The most consistently reported finding, however, relates to increased client satisfaction, even when there are technological difficulties (Simpson, 2014).

Organisations can move to offering remote therapy for staff, then, knowing that this has a solid evidence base supporting its effectiveness and recognising the diversity of options that it offers for employees to choose their own support. One might ask why online therapy has not been more swiftly embraced by providers of therapy given this evidence base. Research suggests that this is the result of negative therapist attitudes and lower therapist satisfaction with using remote media (Rees & Stone, 2005).[1] This has led to speculation that therapist anxiety about loss of control, difficulties maintaining boundaries or fears of change may play a key role here (Simpson, 2014). There may also be concerns about managing crises effectively or verifying client identities (Rochlen, Zack, & Speyer 2004). Further, writers comment on a widespread belief amongst psychological staff that the "screen" will be a barrier between themselves and clients, impeding the therapeutic relationship despite the evidence to the contrary (Simpson et al., 2020). A key element may also be that therapists have often embarked on working remotely without any additional training and without consulting specific guidance (Pierce, Perrin, & MacDonald, 2020), something widespread during the scramble to skill-up necessitated by lockdown conditions. Pierce and colleagues also found that practitioners were much more likely to embrace using remote media if they worked in settings which had policies to support such work.

Advantages of Online Therapeutic Interventions

There are clear arguments for using online therapy as a means of support for international staff. Staff based in remote locations, or where they do not speak the majority language, are unlikely to find a therapist based nearby with whom they can work with in-person. Even if well integrated in the dominant culture, and speaking the local language, staff may still have a preference – particularly when undertaking a venture as sensitive and nuanced as psychotherapy – to seek out someone culturally similar or with whom they share a common language. Opting for online therapy allows access to the whole world as a source for therapists, and both authors have experience of being specifically sought out by international clients for this reason.

> Erica sought psychological therapy from an online platform after her resignation from a job in finance in the UK, and her return to her home country in Northern Europe. Erica had resigned following ongoing difficulties with her managers and in the context of symptoms she attributed to "burnout" and felt angry about the events which she felt had "forced her out" of her job. Erica was short of money but insisted on paying the top rate for her video-therapy and was reluctant to ask her family for help, either financial or emotional, leaving her isolated at a time of increased need. In a short course of sessions, we explored her experience of being away (she had been working as an expatriate for many years in several settings) and of returning home, as well as her relationships at work, with close others and with the places she had called home. Erica explained that she felt more at ease to work in English and saw the UK as "my second home", but during therapy we also considered whether working with someone in her mother tongue might offer different possibilities. In the end, Erica came to see this as part of her homecoming, choosing to move to a therapist based in her home country and using her home language as one of many steps in moving forward in her life.

Working across cultural difference can bring gains in psychotherapy, prompting the examination of assumptions and encouraging new perspectives (Raval, 1996), but it is also important to give clients choice around who they see. It is always enlightening to ask individuals why they have chosen to approach you for therapy, and how any underlying assumptions about you (perhaps linked to culture, politics or gender) might impact on therapy work. On the other hand, when psychological therapists are working for employing organisations, there may be limits to choice of therapist that need to be reflected upon. Although most organisations aim to employ a range of individuals, they may not be able to collate a team of counsellors to meet the "wish list" of every client, as in this vignette:

Linh was a woman of Vietnamese origin, recently moved to the UK to live with her British husband. She worked remotely for a large international organisation with staff all over the world and was a fluent English speaker. Linh sought support through an employee assistance programme (EAP) and asked for a therapist from a minority ethnic or South-East Asian background. Unfortunately, the EAP was unable to meet this request and Linh was allocated a White British counsellor. The counsellor brought her awareness of Linh's preference into their first session together, explaining the limitations and enquiring how Linh felt about this. She openly acknowledged the contrast in their ethnicity and cultural background, and let Linh know their sessions would be a safe space where she could talk about this and any other differences between them. Linh said she had initially asked for a counsellor from a background like her own because she wanted to discuss issues of racism and marginalisation, and to feel confident of being understood. However, after their conversation, which showed the counsellor's ability to raise and explore such issues frankly, she said she felt comfortable to proceed. A series of sessions followed where Linh was able to explore her experience of racism and other issues of intersectionality (e.g. gender, age, class and educational background) in relation to her identity, her experiences at work and her new home country. After several sessions she commented on feeling well understood by her counsellor, adding that she now found it helpful that they were from different backgrounds. She reflected that, had she worked with a Vietnamese counsellor, she might equally have made unhelpful assumptions about their ability to understand her.

It is also important to acknowledge dual relationships and overlapping responsibilities between employees and the psychological practitioners working with them. Finding ways to reflect on these areas with clients is of real benefit to the development of strong working relationships.

When organisations are involved in sourcing therapists, using online therapy also frees them to look further afield; to choose on the basis of specific skills, experience or competences; and to offer a range of options for support, wider than that available in-person in the local area. In small communities of international staff, and when people live and work in proximity, this flexibility may help in maintaining more privacy than would consulting perhaps the sole practitioner in the area.

Choice of Online Media and Advantages of Text-Based Work

Online therapy allows clients a range of options in how they connect with their therapist. During the Covid-19 pandemic, audio-video sessions using platforms such as Zoom and Signal were the most common form of online support, reflecting perhaps that many therapists had switched from in-person therapy to its closest remote approximation. Working on video enables both therapist and client to see and hear each other on the screen and to talk quite naturally in real time (connectivity permitting). This sort of online therapy suits clients who prefer the immediacy of a synchronous connection with full view of their therapist's face and upper body and the additional cues that this provides.

There is evidence that using adapted forms of video-therapy allows for a wide range of therapeutic approaches addressing many different presenting issues. Studies show the effectiveness of video-based cognitive-behavioural therapy for a range of difficulties (e.g. depression and anxiety (Stubbings, Rees, Roberts, & Kane 2013); agoraphobia and panic (Bouchard et al., 2004); post-traumatic stress disorder (PTSD), eating disorders, anger, physical health including obesity, chronic pain and IBS (Backhaus et al., 2012); and obsessive-compulsive disorder (Stubbings, Rees, & Roberts, 2015)), and this evidence base is continually growing. There is also evidence that other approaches can be successfully adapted to use online including: Schema-Focused Therapy (Simpson & Francesco, 2020); Psychoanalytic Psychotherapy (Agar, 2020); Sensorimotor Psychotherapy (Ogden & Goldstein, 2020), EMDR (McGowan, Fisher, Havens, & Proudlock, 2021) and Narrative Exposure Therapy (known as e-NET: Kaltenbach et al., 2021), to mention but a few. It is important, however, not to be constrained to repeating "practice as usual" when adapting these approaches for online use. Video presents new opportunities too, including the option to experiment with the client and therapist images in a way that can illuminate the relationship by changing the location and size of self–other images on the screen, level of eye contact, and to experiment with sitting closer to, or farther from the camera (Simpson et al., 2020).

When working with online video platforms, the option to turn off the camera is ever present, allowing for some interesting uses of "audio-only" therapy. The use of this medium for therapy is, of course, well established given that the telephone has long been used as an adjunct to in-person therapy (Irvine et al., 2020). Online practitioners may already be aware of situations in which clients request to turn off the video, perhaps when discussing areas of high shame and wishing to limit arousal. In other cases, a client may wish to use audio only throughout their therapy work, perhaps if they find using video triggering (and Francesco mentions this for clients managing physical disabilities who may prefer to engage in therapy without the "barrier" of their disability (Simpson & Francesco, 2020), or when working with those who are highly socially anxious (Simpson et al., 2020). Finally, turning off your video camera significantly reduces the bandwidth required for connection, and clients in areas of low connectivity have long made use of this to improve connection without the loss of therapeutic benefit.

When working across different time zones, or with clients who have poor internet connectivity, this kind of synchronous, bandwidth-dependent support is not always ideal. It may also be unhelpful for clients who struggle to find a private space in which to speak to their therapist. This may be because they live in shared accommodation – as is the case for many international aid workers living alongside colleagues in guesthouses, or international students living in halls of residence. Clients with very sensitive personal issues to discuss, or those who feel at risk due to the nature of their international work – high-profile activists, for example, or those whose jobs involve working on controversial projects or schemes – may feel especially reticent "speaking aloud" to a therapist in a context where they may fear being overheard. This is where text-based online therapy – based on the premise of therapist and client communicating with each other through the written word alone – can be particularly valuable. This communication may take place synchronously as "live chat" on a secure platform such as Zoom or Signal, or asynchronously, with therapist and client agreeing a schedule through which to exchange written correspondence using a secure email platform or by sending password-protected documents. Clients with erratic working lives, or for whom time zone differences make it impractical to connect with their therapist at a set time each week synchronously, may find this asynchronous support well suited to their circumstances. There is now established evidence for the effectiveness of both live chat and email therapy (Reynolds, Hanley, & Wolf, 2012; Rochlen et al., 2004).

There are challenges in text-based work. Stripped of audio-visual indicators such as tone of voice and body language, it can take longer to establish rapport and familiarise with the other person's communication style; however, there can be distinct benefits. Text-based therapy, particularly when carried out over a series of asynchronous scheduled message exchanges, can encourage both therapist and client to slow down and seek deeper layers of meaning in each other's words. Many clients also report the benefits of having a written record of their therapy to look back on – both in between sessions and retrospectively, once therapy is over. Rather like a "transitional object"

(Winnicott, 1953), these transcripts of sessions can bring a sense of ongoing connection to the therapist. Dunn (2014) describes clients "returning to transcripts, sometimes months or years later, and gaining new insights from re-reading the exchanges […] a tangible and permanent link to a relationship that may have occurred at a critical moment in time" (p. 85)). They can also be read and reread to further clients' thinking on personal issues – to help shift perspectives over time and to deepen insights.[2]

> Frank was a British man in his forties who had moved to France three years before to work for an international bank. Ever since his teens, Frank's weight had fluctuated due to a tendency to "binge eat" when he felt isolated or emotionally challenged. Following a recent relationship breakdown, this issue resurfaced and Frank reached out to a British online counsellor for support. He made a specific request for email therapy, saying he felt his busy work schedule would make it difficult to commit to synchronous audio-video sessions. Further into the work, though, Frank acknowledged that the shame he felt about his disordered eating and body image meant talking to a counsellor in person, even through a screen, would have been "too much". Through a series of structured email exchanges, Frank and his counsellor explored Frank's eating habits, making some useful links to his early life and subsequent relational experiences. Frank's counsellor was also able to send Frank links to relevant resources regarding body neutrality, intuitive eating and Health At Every Size (HAES). At the end of their work together, Frank commented on how he had often read and reread his exchanges with his counsellor, and said he believed he would continue to do so, particularly at points in his life where he felt "triggered" to return to unhelpful eating habits.

Even when text-based therapy is not the dominant mode of engagement for therapist and client, online therapy arguably lends itself much more easily to information sharing than in-person work, as the case vignette above illustrates. Whereas in the latter, a therapist seeking to signpost or share information with their client may have to hand them a leaflet or write down a list of resources, in online work this can be done, quite literally, with the "click of a button". This is because the therapist can post links in the chat bar during audio-video consultations or send attachments to their client once the session is over. Whilst training work must be kept distinct from therapy, both authors of this chapter, who work as online trainers as well as therapists, find it useful to bring pertinent slides onto their screens during online therapy sessions for psychoeducation. Similarly, clients can also share resources easily if they wish, in a way that arguably "equalises" the therapeutic process.

There is evidence that clients are more active in the way that they engage in online therapy (Simpson & Francesco, 2020), and the authors have both noted how online clients can be braver about experimenting with new techniques, trying meditation when at ease in their own surroundings, for example. Simpson et al. (2020) argue that this is reflective of a greater "democratisation" in which power is more equally shared between client and practitioner as the client inhabits their own therapeutic space, logging on with their own computer, and is thus less dependent on the practitioner for the therapy environment. Similarly, Reynolds, Stiles, Bailer, & Hughes (2013) note the "online calming effect" demonstrated in reduced arousal for therapists and clients working remotely. This lowered arousal may explain some anecdotal evidence from clinical practice that suggests that online working is well suited to military veterans and others with complex PTSD because it allows for triggers in the environment to be controlled, and that those diagnosed with emotionally unstable personality disorder may be able to stabilise overwhelming feelings more effectively when working remotely, to the benefit of therapeutic work.

Challenges, Contraindications and Confidentiality

For all the advantages online therapy offers there are, of course, some hurdles most online therapists – particularly those working with international clients – encounter on a regular basis. In an increasingly connected world, it's important not to take ease of connectivity as a given, especially when clients are working in remote locations. Giving some thought as to how to manage connectivity issues is important for clients, employing organisations and psychological therapists alike. Both authors have experienced the frustration and discomfort of the connection dropping or faltering at the most crucial point in an audio-video session – typically when a client is sharing something that evokes feelings of vulnerability, or when they are imparting a special piece of information that needs to be understood very clearly. Waiting for the connection to restore or deciding what to do if it does not, can be an uneasy process for practitioners – and one with ethical as well as practical dimensions. If a client cuts out at a moment of crisis, for example, there may be a need to consider whether this is deliberate, and if steps should be taken to speak to their emergency contact – something many practitioners ask for when contracting with a new client. Another response to more concerning clients who "disappear" may be sending them details of local crisis support – again, something most responsible and forward-thinking practitioners research when taking on clients in new geographical areas.

Returning to the practicalities of connectivity issues, whilst maintaining time boundaries is fundamentally important in therapy, there may be times when online practitioners agree to extend disrupted sessions to "make up" time that has been lost on a call due to an unforeseen connectivity problem, or to offer this time free of charge on another occasion once connection has been restored. Such decisions are often made in the spirit of fairness and with the client's best interests at heart. However, it's important that these "contingency plans" and their implications are carefully thought through, agreed by both therapist and client, and discussed within the therapist's supervision to ensure as much containment as possible. When the therapist is working for an organisation, this may also be something to discuss as part of contracting so that there is clarity about what should happen in the case of disruption. Extending and rearranging sessions can impinge upon the schedules of both therapist and client, unsettling the supposedly regulated and contained nature of their relationship. It should therefore be kept to a minimum.

If client sessions are regularly disrupted due to technical or connectivity issues on their end, the question of whether online sessions are a suitable long-term option for them may also need to be raised. Most online therapists will have a clause or two in their contracts about what they will do if connectivity issues disrupt sessions. This aside, occasional glitches in connectivity are perhaps part and parcel of online therapy and may be something to embrace. Having to accept and make do with something suboptimal but outside of one's control can be beneficial for clients with a highly controlled and somewhat perfectionist outlook. Dealing with patchy connection can also be a good starting point for exploration in therapy about how clients cope with things that are frustrating and far from ideal, but largely outside their influence.

It is also important to explore differences in confidentiality in psychological work with international staff. In some cases, the contract the practitioner has may be with the employing organisation (and this is frequently the case with humanitarian employee support). In other cases, the practitioner may be approached privately by the staff member and will develop a contract of service direct with them at the start of therapy. This makes it vital to collect information about emergency contacts as part of contracting, collecting next of kin or preferred emergency contact details, details of a personal doctor or GP, and exploring possible contact points within the employing organisation in case of need. The boundary of confidentiality around privately provided therapy is then more flexible than in same country therapy work, and this can create additional challenges if employing organisations are unclear on the extent to which information can be shared. A careful discussion with staff members at the start of therapy work alongside clear contracting with organisations will help set appropriate boundaries to protect therapy work.

> Gill had been working for eight years for a faith-based organisation when she was referred for help with symptoms of depression. The organisation she worked for had a contract for services with a travel health and well-being organisation and referred many of their staff for medical and occasionally psychological support. Gill attended her online assessment appointment, and a report was written about her difficulties, which she confirmed that she was happy to share with her employing organisation. However, the organisation felt that they did not have enough detail about

her personal circumstances and would struggle to offer her sufficient support. Then followed a series of conversations with the organisation to explain the boundaries of therapeutic confidentiality and some discussion with Gill herself about what she might wish to share with her employers, to allow her to make an informed choice about the degree of personal information she preferred to disclose. Gill made good use of her therapy sessions and was able to resume her work with new coping strategies after a relatively short period.

In all online therapy, whether international or same country, care to maintain confidentiality by using encrypted email, video and telephone platforms alongside secure storage of data is required (see below). The informed consent process at the outset of therapy should provide information on privacy and confidentiality so that clients have a clear idea about how boundaries are maintained (Anthony, Goss, & Nagel 2014) and this information should be shared with employing organisations at the start of any service provision.

An emerging theme here is that online therapy often requires practitioners to work in ways that, at first glance, run contrary to conventional therapeutic norms, basing their decisions on the well-being of their clients and what is practical and reasonable, given their circumstances. International staff living and working in certain situations may find it hard to find an appropriate private space in which to conduct audio-video sessions, and their therapists may have to deal with this in an open-minded and pragmatic way, as this example demonstrates:

> Amina was evacuated at short notice, along with her husband and children, from her home country, due to political instability and the risk her relatively high-profile work created for them there. She was referred for short-term online counselling through a funded scheme to help her manage the transition and ultimately resettle in a new country. During Amina's journey, she and her family stayed in several hotels and other temporary accommodation that meant it was not always possible for her to have counselling sessions in a wholly private space; her husband and children were often somewhere in the room with her. This was also Amina's first experience of counselling, and she came from a culture where talking therapy was not the norm, hence without an established awareness of the importance of privacy.
>
> Knowing Amina's circumstances, her counsellor was reluctant to penalise her by flatly refusing to let her engage in sessions with her family in the room. A more pragmatic and thoughtful response seemed necessary. In an early session the counsellor acknowledged the presence of Amina's husband and children in the background in a warm and curious manner, asking how Amina felt about them being present, and whether she thought this would impede communication. Amina agreed that it

might limit her exploration of emotions. However, she was also keen to stress that she had a strong supportive relationship with her husband and that he and her children were the main point of focus and stability in her life, particularly given all they had been through.

Amina and her counsellor negotiated using headphones during her sessions for privacy and, on some occasions, her husband took the children out during appointments. These were times when Amina's counsellor noticed her speaking more freely. On other occasions, though, this wasn't possible, and Amina would tell her counsellor, "I can't really talk about that today", creating a tacit understanding to leave certain subjects for another time when she was alone. Given her circumstances, there was an advantage to keeping Amina's sessions focused on "stabilisation and resourcing" (helping her to understand stress and trauma symptoms and find the means to manage them). This was opposed to deeper trauma processing work, something that ideally takes place when clients are in more stable settings, and with a greater degree of privacy.

This loosening of rules about where, when and how therapy can take place has been necessary, more generally, for practitioners switching to online work with their clients during the pandemic. Many clients in lockdown, out of necessity, had to undertake their sessions in crowded homes shared with children, partners, parents and housemates. Their therapists, albeit with caution and consideration, had to think of ways of accommodating this. One of the present authors, for example, conducted sessions with a client of hers whilst he was parked in his car, as this was the only place where he felt he could find appropriate privacy.

When working internationally, there are also other factors that therapists (and any organisation employing them) need to consider. Assessing risk (of harm to self or others) and maintaining appropriate measures to ensure safeguarding may be more difficult using online media, even video. Many online practitioners would agree that gauging their clients' state of mind is more complex when working remotely and may require using multiple means of assessment to gain a clear picture. Further, the ease with which clients can intentionally (through clicking a button and exiting a session) or unintentionally (through connectivity issues) vanish often feels precarious. For some clients, this may make online therapy unsuitable, although in all cases the importance of patient choice and the availability of alternatives needs to be weighed against ideas of best practice to guide clinical reasoning. In cases in which clients are in a state of mental health crisis or have a recent history of suicide attempt or self-harm, careful balancing of the options, and the involvement of client healthcare practitioners and, in some cases, the employing organisation may be necessary.

There can also be other risks in working online. The online disinhibition effect (Suler, 2004) has been widely documented and can mean that clients open up more quickly than expected to their therapists, perhaps disclosing information more rapidly than they might have done in in-person settings. This can pose a difficulty if clients are left feeling exposed or experience the therapeutic relationship as moving too quickly and become distressed or dis-engage from therapy. Again, online practitioners should take steps to include this in pre-appointment information and raise it in initial therapy sessions as a known phenomenon that can be managed safely. It is, in effect, the other side of the low arousal and higher comfort found to be associated with remote therapy by many authors (see Simpson & Reid, 2014, Reynolds et al., 2013 and many others) and, as such, represents an opportunity as much as a risk.

Overall, most trained online practitioners are confident to manage risk and engage in remote therapy only with the clients with whom risk can be adequately managed (Smith & Gillon, 2021). However, there is often a great deal of anxiety when discussing risk in the context of remote working. It is perhaps wise to remember the observation of Rochlen et al. (2004) that much of the support work that takes place with individuals at risk happens via emer-gency telephone helplines, thus using a remote medium with populations at perhaps the greatest risk, and managing this by making sure that safeguards are in place.

Practitioners working across international boundaries need to become aware of the different legal requirements this work entails. In some countries, most notably the USA, there is a complex set of state-based legal requirements that prevent offering psychological services in states in which a practitioner is not professionally registered. Clinicians based in any other country (and in any other state) could find themselves liable to legal action if they work with someone resident in that state, even though the appointment is taking place in a liminal space remotely between client and therapist. Although there have to date been no cases raised, this is a grey area of law, and it is as well for practitioners and organisations employing staff in the US to be aware of this.[3] Similarly, practitioners are advised to verify with their insurers that they have appropriate cover to deliver therapy in the countries in which they are operating (see Johnson, 2014 for more on this). Finally, clinicians are encouraged to state the legal jurisdiction under which they work in any contracting documents produced, making it clear to clients and employing organisations that the contract is subject to the jurisdiction of the UK (or any other therapist home country). While this does not prevent legal action being taken in another legal jurisdiction, it will give some grounds to challenge any such action.

Lastly, data protection is subject to different rules depending on the country in which clients reside. However, as Adamson (2018) notes, "there is a common law of confidentiality that applies to counselling whether face to face or online" and this leads necessarily to heightened standards of care for management of personal client data. Operating in European countries, therapists may be familiar with GDPR[4] compliance and may wish to stipulate in contracts that this framework is being used in relation to their international work. Of course, it will then be necessary to maintain these standards for personal data, therapy notes and any other virtual or hard copy material related to clients' care and this may require investing in encrypted hard drives or lockable filing cabinets so that data is always held securely. In the UK, it is considered best ethical practice for all online practitioners to be registered with the Information Commissioners Office as a data controller, something required if you process even one piece of personal information about a client (and even if deleted straight away) (Adamson, 2018).

Recommendations

For All:

- Use an appropriate, high-functioning platform for any remote therapy work with end-to-end encryption. Make sure to master its use and skill up in relation to its functions and the opportunities these provide.

For Individuals Seeking Therapy:

- Do ask about your therapist's experience and training in working online.
- Consider which media you would be prepared to try for therapy work, bearing in mind your preferences and the connectivity in the area in which you are based. If you work long hours and have limited availability, an asynchronous medium of therapy may work better.
- Check on internet connectivity in your posting site and in the place in which you will do your sessions. Do you have an appropriate and private space?
- Remember that with in-person therapy you would have some time before and after your meeting to travel to and from the site of appointment. Consider whether you need some time before and after an online session to reflect and ready yourself for therapy work. Try not to treat this as "just another meeting".

For Organisational Clients/Employing Organisations:

- Make sure you are clear about the degree of connection available in all your bases – are individuals able to access support via video, or is connection too poor? If they are required to use the office-based internet, are there private spaces in the workplace that can be booked and are secure for therapy sessions to take place?
- If you are operational in a number of settings, consider what media will work with your staff – how remotely are they based? Is language an issue?

Are there likely to be critical incidents? What might their expectations be about what support is acceptable?

- Consider funding text-based therapy, given its equivalence of therapeutic outcomes. Email therapy may offer unique benefits for staff who have limited availability and work long hours, so make sure this is offered to staff as an alternative (particularly in areas with lower connectivity).
- Consider carefully how to support staff through distressing situations. Support delivered by "specialists" outside of the organisation can feel tokenistic and uncaring unless accompanied by acknowledgement of the difficulties faced, perhaps with an apology and/or an appropriate expression of concern, from management. Discussions around how best to share duty of care between organisational hierarchies and services providing outside support should take place long before they are needed.
- Once support has been taken up by a staff member, be prepared to step back and allow them to make use of it in a confidential context, unless any kind of feedback or report from the therapist/support provider has been explicitly agreed by all parties.
- Ask questions about the training and experience of anyone you are employing to provide remote therapy (Smith et al., 2020). They should have had specialist training in working online and ideally should be skilled in working with different media. Ask also about their supervision and how they maintain skills and look after themselves. Anyone working online regularly should have specialist supervision for their remote practice.
- Remote therapy may not suit everybody, and organisations may benefit from exploring whether there are local in-person options for support.

For Therapists:

- A key learning point from the literature, and one that we both would reinforce, is that it is important to talk directly with your clients about the differences inherent in having therapy remotely. Invite discussion about the experience of remote therapy. What are clients finding helpful, what not, what adjustments do you both feel could change things?
- Psychological therapists working remotely benefit from specialist training. There are a range of courses at certificate and diploma level and many build skills in working across different media. Practitioners should also consider choosing a supervisor for their online practice who is qualified and experienced in online working.
- It is helpful to provide information about how you work online, the media you use and what to do if there is a connection failure. (Weitz, 2022 suggests the need to have a *Plan B* in case of connection failure, and possibly even a *Plan C*).

- Depending on your practice, you may need to purchase specialist equipment, perhaps including additional cameras or angling devices to allow you to make full use of your space on video, perhaps additional headsets or microphones depending on your space and practice.
- Maintain boundaries dynamically: *"boundaries need to be flexible enough to embrace the benefits that psycho-technologies offer whilst providing a stable base for containment, affective attachment, attunement and safety"* (Simpson et al., 2020, p. 413). If boundaries are too flexible, there is a danger that online appointments become less formal or professional, and more casual, resembling the interactions that clients might have with friends or family. However, this chapter has also highlighted the need for flexibility when working with staff in remote locations or without access to private space.
- If you work with particular techniques or forms of therapy, seek out appropriate support to adapt these to the online medium you are using. Many techniques have found ways to transition effectively (see above in this chapter), and the Covid-19 pandemic has seen a vast expansion of reflection on the changes required.
- In keeping with the point above, do not be constrained in the way that you work. Many creative techniques are enhanced by working remotely, so consider using an online sand tray or building virtual spaces in which avatars may be employed or encouraging clients to take their own steps in using vlogs or blogs.
- In cases of risk, set up safety plans and share these with your clients, bearing in mind the contexts in which they are based and the opportunities for additional support from the networks they can access. Collect relevant information to keep clients safe.
- Be aware that you may find yourself working over an extended period and following your client "on the move" as they transition between different posts and locations. Be prepared to discuss the possibility of working in different time zones or using different online mediums to maintain a therapeutic alliance with your clients as they change locations.
- Take extra care of yourself, recognising the way in which online working brings additional pressures to overwork, skip breaks or even book clients in during your holidays! Zoom fatigue (a specific form of exhaustion related to online video working) has been reported on widely, and practitioners should monitor their working practices, resisting the temptation to book back-to-back appointments.

In summary, online approaches to psychological support for international staff can increase convenience, choice and evidence-based positive therapeutic outcomes. This heightens their appeal to providers, recipients and individual pursuers of such support. Awareness of, and familiarity with, the wide range of mediums and delivery options for online support is vital, as is a willingness to discuss both the evident and perhaps more subtle differences this type of support entails.

Notes

1 There is a longstanding general debate about the value of remote psychotherapy, most particularly with regard to using video, that is beyond the scope of this chapter (for a thorough discussion see, for example, Isaacs-Russell, 2015).
2 With text-based online therapy, key counsellor, and client characteristics such as age, ethnicity and even gender, have the potential to remain hidden – creating increased scope for fantasy and projection that can be usefully explored in therapy (and arguably reducing unhelpful assumptions about these characteristics).
3 In addition to this, practitioners are required by law in the UK (and several other countries) to check client names against an international sanctions list. It is, in practice, highly unlikely that you would be approached to provide a clinical service for someone subject to sanctions, but practitioners who work internationally should be aware of this. For more information see: www.gov.uk/government/publications/financial-sanctions-consolidated-list-of-targets
4 General Data Protection Regulation

References

Adamson, K. (2018). Legal and ethical issues in online supervision. In A. Stokes (Ed.), *Online supervision: A handbook for practitioners* (pp. 215–219). Abingdon, Oxon: Routledge.

Agar, G. (2020). The clinic offers no advantage over the screen, for relationship is everything: Video psychotherapy and its dynamics. In H. Weinberg & A. Rolnick (Eds.), *Theory and practice of online therapy* (pp. 66–78). Abingdon, Oxon: Routledge.

Antony, K., Goss, S., & Nagel, D. (2014). Developing ethical delivery of cross-border services. In P. Weitz (Ed.), *Psychotherapy 2.0: Where psychotherapy and technology meet* (pp. 193–208). London: Karnac Books.

Backhaus, A., Agha, Z., Maglione, M.L., Repp, A., Ross, B., Zuest, D., Rice-Thorp, N.M., Lohr, J., & Thorp, S.R. (2012). Videoconferencing psychotherapy: a systematic review. *Psychological Services, 9*(2), 111–131. https://doi.org/10.1037/a0027924

Bouchard, S., Paquin, B., Payeur, R., Allard, M., Rivard, V., Fournier, T., Renaud, P., & Lapierre, J. (2004). Delivering cognitive-behavior therapy for panic disorder with agoraphobia in videoconference. *Telemedicine Journal and e-health: the official journal of the American Telemedicine Association, 10*(1), 13–25. https://doi.org/10.1089/153056204773644535

Dunn, K. (2014). The therapeutic alliance online. In P. Weitz (Ed.), *Psychotherapy 2.0: Where psychotherapy and technology meet* (pp. 75–88). London: Karnac Books.

Fletcher-Tomenius, L., & Vossler, A. (2009). Trust in online therapeutic relationships: The therapist's experience. *Counselling Psychology Review, 24*(2), 24–34.

Irvine, A., Drew, P., Bower, P., Brooks, H., Gellatly, J., Armitage, C.J., Barkham, M., McMillan, D., & Bee, P. (2020). Are there interactional differences between telephone and face-to-face psychological therapy? A systematic review of comparative studies. *Journal of Affective Disorders, 265*, 120–131. https://doi.org/10.1016/j.jad.2020.01.057

Isaacs-Russell, G. (2015). *Screen relations: The limits of computer mediated psychoanalysis and psychotherapy*. Abingdon, Oxon: Routledge.

Johnson, S. (2014). Comment on chapter 9: Developing ethical delivery of cross-border services. In P. Weitz (Ed.), *Psychotherapy 2.0: Where psychotherapy and technology meet* (pp. 207). London: Karnac Books.

Kaltenbach, E., McGrath, P.J., Schauer, M., Kaiser, E., Crombach, A., & Robjant, K. (2021). Practical guidelines for online Narrative Exposure Therapy (e-NET) – a short-term treatment for posttraumatic stress disorder adapted for remote delivery. *European Journal of Psychotraumatology, 12*(1). https://doi.org/10.1080/20008 198.2021.1881728

McGowan, I.W., Fisher, N., Havens, J., & Proudlock, S. (2021). An evaluation of eye movement desensitization and reprocessing therapy delivered remotely during the Covid–19 pandemic. *BMC Psychiatry, 21*(1), 1–8. An evaluation of eye movement desensitization and reprocessing therapy delivered remotely during the Covid–19 pandemic. *BMC Psychiatry, 21*, 560. https://doi.org/10.1186/s12888-021-03571-x

Nelson, E.L., & Patton, S. (2016). Using videoconferencing to deliver individual therapy and pediatric psychology interventions with children and adolescents. *Journal of Child and Adolescent Psychopharmacology, 26*(3), 212–220. https://doi.org/10.1089/cap.2015.0021

Ogden, P., & Goldstein, B. (2020). Sensorimotor psychotherapy from a distance, engaging the body, creating presence and building relationship in videoconferencing. In H. Weinberg & A. Rolnick (Eds.), *Theory and practice of online therapy* (pp. 47–65). Abingdon, Oxon: Routledge.

Pierce, B.S., Perrin, P.B., & McDonald, S.D. (2020). Demographic, organizational, and clinical practice predictors of US psychologists' use of telepsychology. *Professional Psychology: Research and Practice, 51*(2),184–193. https://doi.org/10.1037/pro 0000267

Raval, H. (1996). A systemic approach on working with interpreters. *Clinical Child Psychology and Psychiatry, 1*(1), 29–43. https://doi.org/10.1177%2F135910459 6011004

Rees, C.S., & Stone, S. (2005). Therapeutic alliance in face-to-face versus videoconferenced psychotherapy. *Professional Psychology: Research and Practice, 36*(6), 649–653. https://doi.org/10.1037/0735-7028.36.6.649

Reynolds, D.J., Hanley, T., & Wolf, M. (2012). Reaching out across the virtual divide: An empirical review of text-based therapeutic online relationships. In B. Popoola & O. Adebowale (Eds.), *Online guidance and counseling: Toward effectively applying technology* (pp. 64–90). Hershey, PA: IGI Global. https://doi.org/10.4018/978-1-61350-204-4.ch006

Reynolds, D.J. Jr., Stiles, W.B., Bailer, A.J., & Hughes, M.R. (2013). Impact of exchanges and client-therapist alliance in online-text psychotherapy. *Cyberpsychology, Behavior and Social Networking, 16*(5), 370–377. https://doi.org/10.1089/cyber.2012.0195

Richardson, L.K., Frueh, B.C., Grubaugh, A.L., Egede, L., & Elhai, J.D. (2009). Current directions in videoconferencing tele-mental health research. *Clinical Psychology, 16*(3), 323–338. https://doi.org/10.1111/j.1468-2850.2009.01170.x

Rochlen, A.B., Zack, J.S., & Speyer, C. (2004). Online therapy: Review of relevant definitions, debates, and current empirical support. *Journal of Clinical Psychology, 60*(3), 269–283. https://doi.org/10.1002/jclp.10263

Simpson, S., & Francesco, V. (2020). Technology as an invitation to intimacy and creativity in the therapy connection. *Schema Therapy Bulletin, 17,* 14–18.

Simpson, S., Richardson, L,. Pietrabissa, G., Castelnuovo, G., & Reid, C. (2020). Videotherapy and therapeutic alliance in the age of COVID-19. *Clinical Psychology and Psychotherapy, 28*, 409–421. https://doi.org/10.1002/cpp.2521

Simpson, S.G. (2014) The online therapeutic relationship. Presentation at the UKCP conference Psychotherapy 2.0. Retrieved from: www.youtube.com/watch?v=00qxxwKJDvU

Simpson, S.G., & Reid, C.L. (2014). Therapeutic alliance in videoconferencing psychotherapy: A review. *The Australian Journal of Rural Health, 22*(6), 280–299. https://doi.org/10.1111/ajr.12149

Smith, A.C., Thomas, E., Snoswell, C.L., Haydon, H., Mehrotra, A., Clemensen, J., & Caffery, L.J. (2020). Telehealth for global emergencies: Implications for coronavirus disease 2019 (COVID-19). *Journal of Telemedicine and Telecare, 26*(5), 309–313. https://doi.org/10.1177/1357633X20916567

Smith, J., & Gillon, E. (2021). Therapists' experiences of providing online counselling: A qualitative study. *Counselling & Psychotherapy Research, 21,* 545– 554. https://doi.org/10.1002/capr.12408

Stubbings, D.R., Rees, C.S, & Roberts, L.D. (2015) New avenues to facilitate engagement in psychotherapy: The use of videoconferencing and text–chat in a severe case of obsessive-compulsive disorder. *Australian Psychologist, 50*(4), 265–270. https://doi.org/10.1111/ap.12111

Stubbings, D.R., Rees, C.S., Roberts, L.D., & Kane, R.T. (2013). Comparing in-person to videoconference-based cognitive behavioural therapy for mood and anxiety disorders: Randomized controlled trial. *Journal of Medical Internet Research, 15*(11), e258. https://doi.org/10.2196/jmir.2564

Sucala, M., Schnur, J.B., Constantino, M.J., Miller, S.J., Brackman, E.H., & Montgomery, G.H. (2012). The therapeutic relationship in e-therapy for mental health: A systematic review. *Journal of Medical Internet Research, 14*(4), e110. https://doi.org/10.2196/jmir.2084

Suler, J. (2004). The online disinhibition effect. *CyberPsychology & Behavior, 7*(3), 321–326. https://doi.org/10.1089/1094931041291295

Weitz, P. (2022). The online therapeutic alliance: the need for digital competence and online relational skill. In H. Wilson (Ed.), *Digital delivery of mental health therapies: A guide to the benefits and challenges, and making it work.* (pp. 21–33). London: Jessica Kingsley.

Winnicott, D.W. (1953). Transitional objects and transitional phenomena: A study of the first not-me possession. *International Journal of Psychoanalysis, 34*, 89–97.

Chapter 14

Concluding remarks

Kate S. Thompson

Working on this book has been a privilege. The chapter authors have brought such richness into their writing across wide areas, drawing on their diverse experience and practice. It has not been without some challenges, however. As I have read through the chapters, I have noted the way in which the work with each group of staff often omits reference to the work with staff in other spheres, as if the differences between groups and settings have trumped areas of similarity. As a result, research on the experience of expatriate workers in international business organisations has not been used to think about humanitarian staff and vice versa, even when the organisations are similar in terms of reach, size and international profile. Again, work in the aid sector rarely considers the experiences of accompanied workers whose partners and children may be alongside them, missing a key opportunity to draw from the learning in member care, which has so much experience supporting mission families. It is as if certain key areas of difference, some of them frankly social or political, are allowed to blind us to the commonalities. Those in the business sector may not want to learn from those in the voluntary sector and vice versa (perhaps as a result of stereotypes about "do-gooders" or evil exploiters); those whose faith directs their work may not wish to see parallels with those who insist that faith is kept out of aid work and contrariwise. However, when workers are on the move in any sector, the best methods to support them should encourage joined up thinking to drive forward best practice.

In one area this does seem to have taken place: in relation to third culture kids. This concept is now used to think about the experiences of children who travel with their parents no matter what the reason, including the children of those on international business assignments, those whose parents serve in a military or diplomatic service, as well as those in the aid and mission sector. There is great benefit in taking an overarching view to the complex lives of these children and exploring shared experience even while retaining focus on specific issues for differing subgroups.

Some groups of workers discussed in this book have traditionally suffered from a kind of neglect in terms of organisational thinking and research. As argued by Pennie Blackburn, seafarers are often overlooked in international

DOI: 10.4324/9781003261971-15

discourse, and this has meant that efforts to support them from a psychological perspective are only recently gaining attention. Drawing from practice with other groups of "workers on the move", and emphasising similarities could strengthen calls to action. In the case of grassroots activists and contractors, the lack of attention to providing support runs alongside limited organisational involvement and some degree of political marginalisation. This should not prevent attention to their needs, however, and a reckoning of how far learning from other groups of staff can be generalised. Finally, this book has also argued for the need to use learning about best practices in psychological support to consider the needs of national staff often working at distance from their home bases, and thus "on the move" in their home country. It is clear that models of psychological support developed mainly for workers from the global North may need to be changed, expanded or even thrown out in order to offer appropriate help for all staff. This requires a truly psychosocial approach, allowing a wider vision of what might be beneficial and considering context as a matter of course.

One theme that has recurred in all the chapters is the key role of employing organisations in attending to staff needs, even when staff are on short-term contracts, or the organisation is little more than a collection of like-minded individuals and is run on a shoestring budget. In all cases, staff are more likely to access support if this is built into their employment terms, and is provided at the right time, in the right place and with the correct emphasis. Many of the chapters argue for a needs assessment approach to establish what staff want in terms of support, and the importance of training is clearly recognised. Similarly, it has been argued that psychological sessions on an opt-out basis, at set points during a worker's period of employment and with a high degree of confidentiality are important in establishing trust. In this sense, the organisational stance that has been argued for in many of the chapters builds on ideas about the importance of psychological safety at work (Edmondson, 2018). Psychological safety at work has been linked with great benefits: Alongside staff feeling able to speak out about difficulties and risk new ideas, research suggests that it creates better staff engagement with employers and stronger team performance. If employers are open to offering staff-driven, non-stigmatising psychological support, this is likely to further enhance the psychological safety of their workplaces, helping them build happy, high-achieving teams, and manage the inevitable problems and critical incidents, while also retaining their workers.

In contrast, organisations that allow low psychological safety in their teams risk creating environments in which vulnerability is denied or sidestepped (with consequent risks of more burnout, bullying and harassment). Houldey's (2021) argument that the humanitarian sector is overshadowed by an archetype, the *perfect humanitarian*, who shows no vulnerability despite the challenges and desperate injustices of aid work illustrates this perfectly. This archetype works against psychological safety, encouraging workers to toil to the point of burnout rather than risk admitting they have needs. It also blinds organisations to the diversity of staff experience, so that people from less privileged backgrounds or those who cannot embrace intensive, relentless work hours and high mobility are effectively barred from the aid sector (clearly disadvantaging female staff and those from the global south (Gritti, 2015)). A pressure to "man up" to meet the demands of the work reveals a problematic narrative of gender and may also be linked to a tendency to use terminology directly drawn from the military ("deployment" rather than "posting/assignment" as one example). While this argument has been advanced in relation to the humanitarian sector, it has some overlaps with the argument that the narrative of the "healthy worker" has blinded employers in the maritime sector to the reality of challenges for seafarers.

The relationship between psychological safety in organisations and attachment security in individuals (as discussed in chapter 3, this volume) is a complex one and would benefit from a more profound exploration. Certainly, the suggestion in Mark Snelling's chapter is that early attachment difficulties may manifest in employees choosing employers who are less psychologically safe or in continuing work contract after contract when highly dissatisfied with a workplace or team. This shows the way in which organisational fit might have a dark side when characteristics of an employer meld in detrimental ways with aspects of the worker themselves. The writers here have highlighted individual factors like personal resilience, coping style, identity across transition and motivation for work, not to mention moral values, when considering psychological well-being amongst workers on the move. However, these need to be considered in context, alongside organisational and other situational characteristics, if we are truly to understand the role of "fit" between employer and employee.

Given the importance of strong leadership, psychological safety and attention to team dynamics discussed in many of the chapters of this book, it could be suggested that employers should consider involving organisational psychologists to look at team functioning, and how best to build and maintain collective resources like resilience, social connection and team reflexiveness (Snelling, 2022, personal communication). In the case of teams, crews or work units that are in difficulty, organisational interventions may deliver change in a way that top-down initiatives or even wider organisational consultation and well-being interventions cannot.

All the authors whose work is included here are psychological therapists and as such have outlined key suggestions for colleagues involved in providing training, assessment and support for staff. We have drawn from our practice-based evidence in doing this, and hope the recommendations made will be helpful to psychological practitioners in a wide range of employment settings. The chapter on the use of remote media for assessment and therapy is a starting point for building models of good practice in remote staff support. There has also been an emphasis on expanding pools of support using skills like psychological first aid to spread options for innovative support more broadly across the workforce. If this creates additional cost implications, there is an argument for expanding the ways in which we assess the impact of such interventions. Evaluation is usually undertaken using subjective self-report measures so that individuals can rate whether they have benefited from counselling or support, or give feedback about training initiatives. This gives a picture of the impact of individual interventions, and staff satisfaction, but it could be argued that what is really needed is to look at the relationship between staff support and work-related outcomes (Snelling, 2022, personal communication). Employers may be more convinced of the need to provide good staff support, particularly in sectors where this provision is patchy, if it can be demonstrated that this improves project outcomes/deliverables and facilitates team objectives. Discovering this would require joint working between monitoring and evaluation staff and staff involved in psychosocial support in ways that are yet to be developed.

This book has argued that international staff were more adversely affected by the Covid-19 pandemic than workers who remained in their home country, even though most people throughout the world were cut off from social networks and coping resources. It will take time to truly understand the impact of the pandemic on us all, and its impact on the world of work particularly. That said, the growth of remote working may lead to key shifts in who travels for work, where and for how long. As the *Economist*'s Bartleby column recently argued, the business case for using expatriate workers, already stretched in recent years, has been shown to be indefensible in many sectors post-pandemic (*Economist* 2021).

Workers on the move will still be needed, however, given that they work in insecure locations where jobs cannot be filled remotely and in sectors that depend on a diverse range of staff skills. Supporting these staff in their complex and highly mobile roles requires active engagement by employers and thoughtful, informed input from psychological practitioners. Learning from the process of this staff support should be shared, and may have relevance to other groups of staff not explicitly considered in this book, who rarely relocate for work. Emergency workers, health workers, workers in the care sector and teachers may all experience similar pressures in their work despite never leaving their home countries. Recommendations offered in some of the chapters are relevant to care for all vocational staff, highlighting the tendency to overwork in the context of high-stress roles, emotional demands, power differentials between groups of staff and pulls towards burnout. The authors hope that this book will act as a stimulus to new ways of thinking for employees, employers and psychological support staff that benefit all workers.

References

Economist. (2021, 18 September). Who needs expats? *The Economist.* www.economist.com/business/2021/09/18/who-needs-expats

Edmonson, A.C. (2018). *The fearless organization: Creating psychological safety in the workplace for learning, innovation, and growth*. Hoboken, NJ: John Wiley & Sons.

Gritti, A. (2015). Building aid workers' resilience: Why a gendered approach is needed. *Gender & Development, 23*(3), 449–462. https://doi.org/10.1080/13552074.2015.1095542

Houldey, G. (2021). *The vulnerable humanitarian: Ending burnout culture in the aid sector*. Abingdon, Oxon: Routledge.

Index

195–196; psychological contractors 195–196, 202; remote therapy 219; resilience, building 36; to seafarers 129, 134, 135, 139; sexual trauma 162, 163; to single workers 86
dyslexia 182
dyspraxia 182

earned security 43, 44, 52–53
eating disorders 182, 210, 212
economic issues *see* financial issues
education 88–89, 91, 178, 183
Effort-Reward Imbalance model of occupational stress 71, 76n6, 146
Eiroa Orosa, F.J. 74
elder care 91
emergency contraception 164
emigration *see* migration
Emmens, B. 191
emotional intelligence 148–149
emotional resilience, building 33–34
emotionally unstable personality disorder 213
empathy: attachment perspective 43–45, 48–51; post-traumatic growth 114; psychological contractors 200; seafarers 128; sexual trauma survivors 165, 166, 167
employee assistance programmes (EAPs) 192, 209
enduring personality change after catastrophic experience (EPCACE) 61–62, 75n2
Eriksson, C.B. 64
Espino, C.M. 154, 155
ethical codes/standards: British Association for Counselling and Psychotherapy 192, 201; and religious faith 112, 113, 119
European Charter of Humanitarian Aid 98
EuroTCK 177
exercise, physical 31–33, 36, 140, 150
expatriates: contractors 144–157; cosmopolitan identity 8, 149; defined 2; financial gains 4; gender issues 154; HSBC survey 4, 12n2; and migrant workers, distinction between 3; non-traditional 6; numbers 3; power 6–7, 44; pragmatic 149; self-initiated 6, 8, 12n3; "sex-patriates" 32; success variables 148–149; traditional 5–6, 7

extended families 91–92, 175; seafarers 136
Eye Movement Desensitisation and Reprocessing (EMDR) 210

faith 110–111, 123–124, 224; attachment perspective 52; challenges of accommodating 111–112; families 183; psychological contractors 201; recommendations 123; respectful working 121; responsiveness of psychological support to 116–121; vulnerability for mental health difficulties 119; well-being 112–116; *see also* missionaries; religion; spirituality
families 93; adjustment process 8; attachment theory 44–45, 46; caring for 175–177; contractors 148, 152–156; Covid-19 pandemic 1, 2, 92, 93; following death in service 116; home 81–83; humanitarian aid workers 19; humanitarian versus business sectors 224; organisational support 8; religious faith 116; resilience, building 36; seafarers 127–131, 133–135, 137; sexual trauma survivors 166; single workers 85–87; toxic deployment 174–175; of traditional expatriates 5; *see also* adolescents; children and young people; couples; extended families; parents; siblings
Feinstein, A. 147
financial issues 75n4; child and adolescent mental health services 187; contractors 144–146; families 179; grassroots organisations 106; higher education 178; humanitarian aid workers and cultural/organisational fit 19; as motivation for migration 4; organisational support 8; professional mental health services 227; psychological contractors 192, 193; psychosocial support for sexual trauma survivors 165, 166; remote therapy 208; seafarers 131, 132, 136, 140
fit, cultural/organisational 8, 15–16, 26–27, 226; anxiety management 22–26; attachment perspective 46; contractors 149, 157; identity 20–22; importance and implications 16–17; motivation 17–20

For Product Safety Concerns and Information please contact our EU
representative GPSR@taylorandfrancis.com
Taylor & Francis Verlag GmbH, Kaufingerstraße 24, 80331 München, Germany

www.ingramcontent.com/pod-product-compliance
Lightning Source LLC
Chambersburg PA
CBHW050638280326
41932CB00015B/2703